ENVISIONING THE FUTURE
OF REFERENCE

ENVISIONING THE FUTURE OF REFERENCE

TRENDS, REFLECTIONS, AND INNOVATIONS

Diane Zabel and Lauren Reiter, Editors

LIBRARIES
UNLIMITED®
An Imprint of ABC-CLIO, LLC
Santa Barbara, California • Denver, Colorado

Library of Congress Cataloging-in-Publication Data
Names: Zabel, Diane, editor. | Reiter, Lauren, editor.
Title: Envisioning the future of reference : trends, reflections, and innovations /
    Diane Zabel and Lauren Reiter, editors.
Description: Santa Barbara, California : Libraries Unlimited, 2020. |
    Includes bibliographical references and index. |
Identifiers: LCCN 2019053920 (print) | LCCN 2019053921 (ebook) |
    ISBN 9781440867378 (paperback) | ISBN 9781440867385 (ebook)
Subjects: LCSH: Reference services (Libraries)—United States. |
    Reference services (Libraries)—Study and teaching—United States. |
    Electronic reference services (Libraries)—United States.
Classification: LCC Z711 .E585 2020 (print) | LCC Z711 (ebook) |
    DDC 025.5/2—dc23
LC record available at https://lccn.loc.gov/2019053920
LC ebook record available at https://lccn.loc.gov/2019053921

ISBN: 978-1-4408-6737-8 (paperback)
        978-1-4408-6738-5 (ebook)

24 23 22 21 20   1   2   3   4   5

This book is also available as an eBook.

Libraries Unlimited
An Imprint of ABC-CLIO, LLC

ABC-CLIO, LLC
147 Castilian Drive
Santa Barbara, California 93117
www.abc-clio.com

This book is printed on acid-free paper ∞

Manufactured in the United States of America

Contents

Acknowledgments   vii

Preface   ix
Linda C. Smith

Introduction   xiii
Diane Zabel and Lauren Reiter

Part I—Education, Skills, and Training   **1**

1   Current Status of Reference Education in the Library and
    Information Science Curriculum   3
    Elizabeth Mahoney, Lauren Reiter, and Diane Zabel

2   New Look, Same Essence: The Enduring Value of Reference Librarianship   7
    Aliqae Geraci and Kelly LaVoice

3   Beyond the Checklist: Effective Onboarding and Training for Reference
    Services Success   19
    Daniel Hickey

4   Continuing Education for Reference/Public Service Librarians   27
    Anne Langley

Part II—Still Evolving Service Models   **35**

5   Save the Time of the Reader: Using S. R. Ranganathan's Fourth Law as the
    Vision for the Future of Library Reference Services   37
    Corey Seeman

6   Reference Next   51
    Marie L. Radford

7   Do-It-Yourself Reference   63
    Naomi Lederer

8   Peer-to-Peer Reference Services in Academic Libraries   73
    Hailley Fargo

9 Public Library Reference Services in the 21st Century 83
Maria K. Burchill and John E. Kenney

Part III—Collections **91**

10 Is the Print Reference Collection Dead? The Future and Value of Print
Reference Collections 93
Melissa Gasparotto and Manuel Ostos

11 Open Access Digital Projects and Their Relationship to Reference 103
Elizabeth Clarke

12 From Print to Online: The Complexity of Licensing E-Reference Resources 111
Michael R. Oppenheim and Roxanne Peck

13 Government Information in the Age of Trump 117
Christopher C. Brown

Part IV—User Populations **127**

14 Environmental Scanning 129
Karen Sobel

15 The Global Reach of Reference 139
Lisa Martin

Part V—Assessment **149**

16 Methods and Approaches for Assessing Reference Services 151
Elizabeth Namei and Sarah Pickle

17 Data in Context: Reconsidering Reference in an Academic Library 169
Harriet Lightman, Geoffrey Morse, and Susan Oldenburg

Index 181

About the Editors and the Contributors 187

Acknowledgments

I want to acknowledge Barbara Ittner, a former editor at Libraries Unlimited, for extending an invitation to develop a proposal for a new book on trends in reference. She shepherded the proposal through the review process, helped shape content and direction, and connected us with prospective chapter authors. Emma Bailey expertly carried out the production process at Libraries Unlimited. I am immensely grateful to Lauren Reiter for her willingness to take on this project with me. I want to thank Lauren for her deep thinking about reference services and for being such an ideal coeditor. This book gave us the opportunity to collaborate with more than twenty talented contributors from a variety of institutions. We thank these very busy authors for finding the time to craft such thoughtful essays. I would like to extend a special thank you to Linda C. Smith for providing the preface. Her participation in this project is especially meaningful to me. She was my advisor at the University of Illinois many years ago and has served as an informal mentor and role model throughout my long career. Completion of this book would not have been possible without the support of our home institution. In particular, I want to thank Barbara I. Dewey, Dean, University Libraries and Scholarly Communications, at The Pennsylvania State University. Dean Dewey and our colleagues in the Schreyer Business Library have enthusiastically supported our project. As always, I want to thank my husband (Craig) and son (Zachary) for their encouragement.

—Diane Zabel

First, I would like to thank Diane Zabel for inviting me to be her coeditor. Diane's reputation in reference and public services and editorial work is unmatched, and I greatly appreciate her mentorship and the opportunity to collaborate on the book. I would also like to thank Barbara Ittner, formerly of Libraries Unlimited, who provided a sounding board and support as we developed the project, and Emma Bailey, who guided us to the finished volume. I am grateful to each of the chapter authors for developing insightful and thought-provoking explorations into reference trends and themes and being willing to share their research and experiences. I would also like to thank Dean Barbara Dewey and the rest of my Penn State University Libraries colleagues for their support. And finally, to Manuel and my parents, thanks for listening.

—Lauren Reiter

Preface

One hundred forty years after Samuel Swett Green described the role of the librarian in providing what came to be called reference service (Green 1876), Anne Houston, Reference & User Services Association (RUSA) President 2015–2016, noted that "RUSA's members are less often called reference librarians than they were in the past, and they do work that is different from what reference work was once thought to be" (Houston 2016, 186). It is evident from a series of four books published in the five years immediately preceding Houston's article that reference is in a time of transition: *Reference Reborn: Breathing New Life into Public Services Librarianship* (Zabel 2011), *Leading the Reference Renaissance: Today's Ideas for Tomorrow's Cutting-Edge Services* (Radford 2012), *Reinventing Reference: How Libraries Deliver Value in the Age of Google* (Anderson and Cvetkovic 2015), and *Repositioning Reference: New Methods and New Services for a New Age* (Saunders, Rozaklis, and Abels 2015). Editors Diane Zabel and Lauren Reiter and the 24 other contributors to *Envisioning the Future of Reference: Trends, Reflections, and Innovations* confirm the continuing importance of reference while illuminating trends that are shaping its future.

The grouping of chapters in several parts enables the reader to consider developments in five important areas: education, skills, and training; evolving service models; collections; user populations; and assessment. Coverage includes reviews of the literature, reports of original research, and documentation of best practice. This book will be of value not only to students and beginning librarians looking ahead to the opportunities and challenges that will shape their careers but also to experienced librarians, library administrators, and library and information science educators seeking to understand possible futures for reference.

Education, skills, and training. In their chapter "New Look, Same Essence: The Enduring Value of Reference Librarianship," Aliqae Geraci and Kelly LaVoice demonstrate through an analysis of recent library position postings that while some classic reference positions remain, reference duties are found across librarian positions with a wide range of titles and responsibilities. These trends have implications for curricula in schools of library and information science (Elizabeth Mahoney, Lauren Reiter, and Diane Zabel) as well as onboarding (Daniel Hickey) and continuing education (Anne Langley) of reference/public service librarians.

Evolving service models. In "Reference Next," noted researcher and educator Marie L. Radford emphasizes the importance of continuing to innovate across all modes of reference service, whether face-to-face or virtual. Chapter authors respond to this challenge by discussing specialized reference services (Corey Seeman), peer-to-peer reference services (Hailley Fargo), and do-it-yourself reference to enable users to find what they need through consultation of online learning objects (Naomi Lederer). Maria K. Burchill and John E. Kenney emphasize the importance of reference librarians as "trusted and empathetic experts" in public libraries.

Collections. For decades the focus of reference collection development involved thoughtful curation of a collection of non-circulating print materials needed to support the work of reference librarians in responding to user questions. The increasing availability of digital content has complicated this curation task while also creating new opportunities for tailoring resources to reflect the interests of a library's user community. Melissa Gasparotto and Manuel Ostos discuss the continuing value of retaining "right-sized" print collections in both academic and public libraries, while Michael R. Oppenheim and Roxanne Peck explore the challenges in licensing electronic reference resources. Elizabeth Clarke demonstrates how reference librarians can add value to open access digital projects by creating LibGuides representing custom collections of primary sources from these projects in response to user needs. While developers of open access digital projects are committed to their ongoing availability, the same cannot be said for all government information in digital form. Christopher C. Brown outlines the threats to various types of government information, approaches to ensuring ongoing access, and the role librarians can play in advocating for preservation.

User populations. In "The Global Reach of Reference," Lisa Martin explores the implications of the shift from a focus on the reference desk as the primary service point to a greater emphasis on serving "dispersed and diverse" users. This may entail development of new skills including cultural competence and universal design. To gain a fuller understanding of user needs, librarians can undertake environmental scanning (Karen Sobel).

Assessment. The growing emphasis on assessment and evidence-based practice in librarianship applies specifically to reference as well. Elizabeth Namei and Sarah Pickle outline a framework for planning an assessment project and identify multiple potential assessment methods, including examples and associated advantages and disadvantages. Harriet Lightman, Geoffrey Morse, and Susan Oldenburg of Northwestern University provide a case study of the ways in which data collection and analysis informed the evolution of reference service models at their institution.

As a student beginning library school in the summer of 1971, I was introduced to reference using the textbook *Introduction to Reference Work* published 50 years ago (Katz 1969). In the section providing an overview of "Reference Service Today," Katz (1969, 11) observed: "Today the single best word for summing up library objectives in general and reference service in particular is *change*. . . . The changes are bound to require new sets of values concerned with library service. Exactly what these values will be remains uncertain, but it is already clear that the librarian will have to fashion new concepts." Fifty years on *Envisioning the Future of Reference* highlights approaches to ensuring that reference remains an integral part of librarianship.

Linda C. Smith

REFERENCES

Anderson, Katie Elson, and Vibiana Bowman Cvetkovic, editors. 2015. *Reinventing Reference: How Libraries Deliver Value in the Age of Google*. Chicago: ALA Editions.

Green, Samuel S. 1876. "Personal Relations between Librarians and Readers." *American Library Journal* 1 (2–3): 74–81.

Houston, Anne. 2016. "What's in a Name?: Toward a New Definition of Reference." *Reference & User Services Quarterly* 55 (3): 186–188.

Katz, William A. 1969. *Introduction to Reference Work: Vol. II. Reference Services*. New York: McGraw-Hill.

Radford, Marie L., editor. 2012. *Leading the Reference Renaissance: Today's Ideas for Tomorrow's Cutting-Edge Services*. New York: Neal-Schuman.

Saunders, Laura, Lillian Rozaklis, and Eileen G. Abels. 2015. *Repositioning Reference: New Methods and New Services for a New Age*. Lanham, MD: Rowman & Littlefield.

Zabel, Diane, editor. 2011. *Reference Reborn: Breathing New Life into Public Services Librarianship*. Santa Barbara, CA: Libraries Unlimited.

Introduction

Despite frequent pronouncements about the death of reference services, it appears that surprisingly librarians are busier than ever. In a profile in the *Wall Street Journal*, James Hagerty (2017), the article's author, found that "even in the internet age, reference librarians still dig up answers that require extra effort, searching old books, microfilm, and paper files, looking for everything from owners of long-defunct firms to 19th-century weather reports. Though online searches are now at the fingertips of most people, many still prefer to call or visit a library. Some can't or don't use computers; others recognize librarians have search skills and access to databases that search engines can't match." While Hagerty's profile focuses on public libraries, academic libraries are engaging in their own conversations about the status of reference services. For example, the Association of College & Research Libraries (ACRL) 2017 conference featured a panel called "Reference: The New Dirty Word?" (Johnson, DeCoster, and Brown 2017). Recent articles in the professional literature have covered topics from "what is reference?" to practical concerns such as "what to do with the reference desk?"

TRENDS IN REFERENCE SERVICES

The time is right for a fresh look at trends in reference and public services librarianship (in both academic and public libraries), including scenarios for the future. While some librarians hesitate to use the word "reference," there is a robust literature on the topic. When developing the proposal for this book, we reviewed the literature and found numerous themes. Several studies documented general trends in reference services, including the following: a decline in reference questions, an increase in online reference services, the de-emphasis of the reference desk, and concerns about the quality of reference services in this environment where reference desks are more likely to be staffed by library workers without the MLS degree. Other articles focused on attempts to improve quality through adding new features to chat reference; developing FAQ pages; highlighting new areas of expertise (such as data management and grant support); delivering pre-emptive reference through the use of course guides, screencasts, and widgets; offering roving service; using social network tools; and having librarians contribute to social question-and-answer services. We also found trends that are more specialized in our review of the literature. Libraries still appear to be struggling with the withdrawal of print reference collections.

Extensive research has focused on chat reference, virtual reference, and integrated systems. The use of new technologies is a prevalent theme, from robotics to crowdsourced reference. The literature also suggests an ongoing need for subject-specialized reference services, such as research consultations, alongside traditional general reference. In this environment of accountability, assessment remains a key theme for managers who are responsible for reference services. The changing roles of librarians require new approaches to the library school curriculum and on-the-job training in libraries. Regardless of evolutions in reference service, the user remains at the center. We found studies focused on information-seeking behaviors of users ranging from today's college students to special populations such as incarcerated people.

SCOPE AND THEMES IN *ENVISIONING THE FUTURE OF REFERENCE*

We envision this collection of essays (many chapters integrating theory, research, and best practice) as a text for graduate programs in library and information science. Because the trends show that academic and public libraries are continuing to explore reference services models, this volume will also be relevant to practitioners and library administrators. Library and information science educators will find this book useful when shaping curriculum.

Beyond the general and specialized themes previously noted, contributors to this volume have identified and expanded upon additional themes. Some interesting observations include the following:

- In their analysis of library job postings, Aliqae Geraci and Kelly LaVoice found that many employers still expect candidates to provide reference service, regardless of whether the term "reference" appears in the announcement. Given this continued demand for reference skill sets, jobseekers would be well advised to develop basic reference competencies. As discussed in Chapter 1, reference education, in turn, is influenced by the demands of employers.
- Daniel Hickey emphasizes that language used in job postings can indicate an organization's commitment to training and professional development. Anne Langley reminds readers that ongoing professional education needs to be a priority for all reference and public service librarians. She proposes some creative and unique approaches, from setting aside Friday afternoons to browse the literature to becoming versed in the technologies that your patrons use or want to use. Similarly, Maria K. Burchill and John E. Kenney emphasize the importance of technology training for librarians working in public libraries.
- Down the road, Marie L. Radford predicts the increasing importance of nascent technologies such as artificial intelligence. The future is already here with Alexa and Siri providing ready-reference assistance, but more research is needed to understand the implications of using these technologies in libraries.
- While we have a fascination with robots, Naomi Lederer reminds us that "Do-It-Yourself Reference" has been around for a very long time. Instead of taking the form of a printed call number map, our finding aids are more likely to be online learning objects. These tools can be as basic as a library web page or as advanced as an interactive tutorial. They can be produced by a librarian or may be created by a vendor as a benefit of a subscription.
- Corey Seeman acknowledges the limitations of self-service in libraries. In cases where users are conducting real-time complex research, the skilled librarian can better address patrons' needs in a timely manner.
- Hailley Fargo points to an evolution of reference desk services, including increased use of a staffing model where reference services are provided by peers in an academic library setting. Part of

the rationale for this model is the idea that the reference desk is a place of learning. Lisa Martin reinforces the blurred lines of reference with her discussion of the integration of reference and instruction. Both Hailley and Lisa note that learning takes place on both sides of the desk.

- Lisa Martin, Maria K. Burchill, and John E. Kenney emphasize cultural competence as an important skill for reference and public service librarians working in both academic and public libraries. Daniel Hickey suggests professional training focused specifically on diversity and inclusion. Marie L. Radford explains that lack of cultural sensitivity can contribute to microaggressions and that strategies for mitigating these behaviors in a reference setting need to be a priority in research and practice.
- Aliqae Geraci, Kelly LaVoice, and Marie L. Radford all note changing roles for reference librarians. Aliqae and Kelly's analysis of job descriptions demonstrate that reference librarians may be called upon for programming, instruction, collection development, and training, mentoring, and supervision of staff. Marie L. Radford describes interesting new roles for reference librarians, such as helping graduate students and faculty manage their scholarly identity.
- Those who forecasted the obsolescence of the print reference collection may have been premature in their predictions. Melissa Gasparotto and Manuel Ostos note that electronic reference sources are not always an adequate substitute for the traditional print. They provide multiple examples in their chapter, from the lack of strong electronic counterparts in disciplines such as area studies to features (such as clumsy ebook platforms and prohibitive costs) that make electronic versions less desirable. Michael R. Oppenheim and Roxanne Peck caution readers that myriad issues relating to the licensing of electronic reference resources may preclude a library from jumping from print to online.
- Open access digital projects can provide an interesting alternative to expensive licensed resources. Elizabeth Clarke's experience in developing robust guides to freely available digital content offers readers a Do-It-Yourself-Reference model, one that would be championed by Naomi Lederer.
- Christopher C. Brown reminds librarians of their fundamental role: being advocates of open access to government information. In his balanced chapter, he notes that concern about the permanence of government information is a historical problem. However, the growth of digital communication (including social media) has brought new challenges to the archiving and permanent record of government information and the reference work that relies on access to this information.
- In addition to tracking trends in our profession, public service librarians need to track trends in their communities. Karen Sobel gives readers the tools with her overview of external scanning practices. Both academic and public libraries can use environmental scanning.
- Data drives the staffing and management of reference services. Harriet Lightman, Geoffrey Morse, and Susan Oldenburg provide a case study demonstrating how data informs decision making regarding changes to service models. Elizabeth Namei and Sarah Pickle have created a blueprint for using quantitative and qualitative data for assessing reference services.

Moving forward, we have detected some interesting examples of unfolding developments relating to reference and public services librarianship. We conducted a cursory review of the literature for the period of June 2018 through May 2019. The debate over the fate of the reference desk is still not resolved. A study of libraries in a large public university system found that various reference models are still employed (Alexander and Wakimoto 2019). However, it is evident that mobile services are here to stay (Guo, Liu, and Bielefield, 2018). We observed librarians experimenting with new and innovative models of reference service. Christina Riehman-Murphy and Jennifer Hunter (2019) have assessed the value of making reference social by throwing research parties as a companion service to traditional reference service. Academic and public libraries can use this fun and effective approach. Librarians at the University of Minnesota and the University of Kansas have broken up research projects into manageable chunks by using research sprints as a strategy for research consultations (Wiggins et al. 2019). In addition to new models of reference service, reference librarians may be embracing new activities. Tibor Koltay (2019) observes that traditional reference strengths, such as the ability to conduct a reference interview, is a useful skill set that may be applied in the data research environment. Even reference librarians are being pulled into data management roles as users demand that support. Health sciences librarians have been involved in the systematic review process for some time. However, this activity is emerging as a new role for librarians supporting other disciplines, including business (Splenda 2019). A review of job postings on the ALA JobLIST site in May 2019 retrieved a posting for a Systematic Review Librarian at an academic library. Libraries have been more sophisticated in tracking reference transactions. Both Mariana Lapidus (2019) and librarians at the University of Louisiana at Lafayette (Plaisance, Breaux, and Harris 2019) have written about the use of reference statistics software to collect customized data on reference transactions. The ability to move beyond hash marks on paper provides librarians with the opportunity to get an in-depth picture of who is using reference services. However, concerns have been raised about privacy issues relating to more detailed record keeping. In a case study, Robin E. Miller (2018) discusses the ethical issues relating to the use of student data for institutional research, including the growing number of academic libraries that are using student data to link library usage to successful student outcomes. Surprisingly, Miller (2018) found that reference consultations are often neglected in this institutional research. Although there are great efforts to gather and use vast amounts of data to analyze reference services, studies show that our users still value the personal touch. In fact, personalized library services have been a theme in recent literature (Bladek 2019; Jameson, Natal, and Napp 2019). Chapter contributors Maria K. Burchill and John E. Kenney remind us that despite changes in the delivery of reference service, "our patrons continue to ask us to be trusted and empathetic experts," a role that we envision for librarians now and in the future.

Diane Zabel and Lauren Reiter

REFERENCES

Alexander, Stephanie, and Diana K. Wakimoto. 2019. "Exploration of Reference Models in a Public University System." *Reference Services Review* 47 (1): 21–36.

Bladek, Marta. 2019. "Latino Students and the Academic Library: A Primer for Action." *The Journal of Academic Librarianship* 45 (1): 50–57. https://doi.org/10.1016/j.acalib.2018.12.001.

Guo, Ya Jun, Yan Quan Liu, and Arlene Bielefield. 2018. "The Provision of Mobile Services in US Urban Libraries." *Information Technology and Libraries* 37 (2): 78–93.

Hagerty, James R. 2017. "Google, Shmoogle. Reference Librarians Are Busier Than Ever." *Wall Street Journal* (Online), November 16.

Jameson, Jodi, Gerald Natal, and John Napp. 2019. "Evolving and Enduring Patterns Surrounding Student Usage and Perceptions of Academic Library Reference Services." *College & Research Libraries* 80 (3): 366–385.

Johnson, Cynthia, Elizabeth DeCoster, and Anne K. G. Brown. 2017. "Reference: The New Dirty Word?" Presentation at ACRL, Baltimore, March 22–25, 2017.

Koltay, Tibor. 2019. "Accepted and Emerging Roles of Academic Libraries in Supporting Research 2.0." *The Journal of Academic Librarianship* 45 (2): 75–80. https://doi.org/10.1016/j.acalib.2019.01.001

Lapidus, Mariana. 2019. "Not All Library Analytics Are Created Equal: LibAnswers to the Rescue!" *Medical Reference Services Quarterly* 38 (1): 41–55. https://doi.org/10.1080/02763869.2019.1548892.

Miller, Robin E. 2018. "Reference Consultations and Student Success Outcomes." *Reference & User Services Quarterly* 58 (1): 16–21.

Plaisance, Heather C., Monique G. Breaux, and Elaine Harris. 2019. "Give Me the Gimlet! Using Qualitative and Quantitative Information to Improve Statistics Reporting of Reference Transactions at the University of Louisiana at Lafayette." *Codex: The Journal of the Louisiana Chapter of the ACRL* 5 (2): 125–152.

Riehman-Murphy, Christina, and Jennifer Hunter. 2019. "Affirming the Research Party Reference Model." *Reference Services Review* 47 (1): 48–59.

Splenda, Ryan. 2019. "Systematic Reviews (SR) in Business & Management: A New Role for Business Librarians." Presentation at the 2019 Academic Business Library Directors Annual Meeting, Boston, April 16–19, 2019.

Wiggins, Benjamin, Shanda L. Hunt, Jenny McBurney, Karna Younger, Michael Peper, Sherri Brown, Tami Albin, and Rebecca Orozco. 2019. "Research Sprints: A New Model of Support." *The Journal of Academic Librarianship* 45 (4): 420–422. https://doi.org/10.1016/j.acalib.2019.01.008

Part I

Education, Skills, and Training

1

Current Status of Reference Education in the Library and Information Science Curriculum

Elizabeth Mahoney, Lauren Reiter, and Diane Zabel

INTRODUCTION

It has been almost a decade since Lisa O'Connor (2011) conducted a comprehensive survey and analysis on the reference curriculum in American Library Association (ALA)–accredited master's degree programs. O'Connor (2011) advocated for the routine analysis of reference education content to keep pace with ongoing changes in technology, user needs, and the information environment and acknowledged the significant challenge for educators in determining not only what to add to the curriculum but what to lose.

When Edgar C. Bailey Jr. (2010) conducted his review of academic librarianship curricula, he found that it was difficult to identify the inclusion of reference in the curriculum due to inconsistent terminology or use of broader terms such as "public services" or "services" to incorporate the reference function. Reference education reflects reference practice, which falls under an increasing number of different names. In a review of the past ten years of literature, Anna Marie Johnson (2018) identified a variety of new work for reference and liaison librarians, including copyright, open access, scholarly communication, and publishing education; data management and data curation; other involvement in faculty research; learning commons; open education; makerspaces; and learning analytics. These activities each comprise a set of knowledge and skills valuable to reference education, and it may be difficult to integrate all of them into a single reference course or specialization. While new pathways for reference librarians suggest a need for specialized courses, reference curricula are moving away from subject-based reference classes. Kristine Condic (2016) investigated the prevalence of discipline-specific reference coursework in MLIS curricula, finding that while offerings in courses on the humanities, social sciences, and sciences have declined, courses in health sciences and medicine have increased over a more-than-50-year period.

Programs moving away from subject-specific offerings may be moving toward courses focused on functional skills or users, driven by the needs of employers and evolutions in reference practice. Via a survey of alumni and faculty of four iSchools (information schools), Laura Saunders (2019) identified 11 core areas of knowledge, competencies, and aptitudes for practitioners. The core skills identified include four hard skills (such as search skills and reference interview/question negotiation); however, the majority were soft skills, including interacting with diverse communities and interpersonal communication (Saunders 2019). Sally W. Kalin (2011) highlighted other soft skills important for reference service, including public service attitude, collaboration, leadership, project management communication, and adaptability. Saunders (2019) emphasized the need for library and information science programs to determine how they will address the need for soft skill development within their curricula and noted the opportunities to weave these skills into role-playing and other types of assignments in reference courses. Developing these skills to educate reference librarians might not need a dedicated course but rather thoughtful integration within courses and throughout the curriculum. Grounding in social justice was also identified as a core competency in Saunders's study (2019). Loriene Roy and Elisabeth Long (2019) explain that incorporating social justice values into the reference curriculum prepares librarians to be advocates for those who are disenfranchised and to be sensitive to community members' needs. The user- and value-focused approach is another direction in the reference education curriculum.

Since O'Connor's study in 2011, the demands on reference education to integrate new skills and content have only increased. Deciding what skills, content, or courses to add, retain, and remove remains a persistent challenge in reference education. Condic (2016) observed that some schools have left behind traditional reference courses in favor of information science courses such as human-computer interaction, information analysis and retrieval, preservation of information, and information economics. The shift toward information science courses may be a result of the "iSchool movement," which began in the late 1980s, with three universities offering graduate library and information science programs. It grew to 24 iCaucus-designated schools by 2009 (Larsen 2009). As of 2019, 37 schools hold iCaucus memberships, with an additional 70 schools participating in the iSchools organization at other membership levels (iSchools Organization 2019). While not all library schools are iSchools and not all iSchools have master's programs in library and information science, the growth of iSchools impacts library and information science programs and may also affect the reference curricula. This chapter will review the offerings of ALA-accredited programs at iSchools to determine if programs are saving room for reference education in the library and information science curriculum.

REFERENCE EDUCATION AT ISCHOOLS

To evaluate reference education offerings at iSchools, data was collected from the American Library Association's Directory of Institutions Offering ALA-Accredited Master's Programs in Library and Information Studies in spring 2019. The ALA's directory provides accreditation status, contact information (including websites), distance education options, areas of concentration or career pathways within ALA-accredited programs, and other degrees/educational opportunities. Schools self-select the areas of concentration or career pathways. One of the options is "Reference and User Services," which was used in this analysis. Data was also collected in spring 2019 from the iSchools Organization membership directory, which identifies iSchools by six membership types (iCaucus, Enabling, Sustaining, Supporting, Basic, and Associate). Schools select their type in this membership hierarchy based on size, resources, and structural limitations of their organizations (iSchools Organization 2019).

The ALA directory showed 61 ALA-accredited MLIS programs in the United States and Canada, of which 36 fall into one of the six iSchool membership types. Of the ALA-accredited MLIS programs with iSchool membership, 25 schools identified "Reference and User Services" as an area of concentration or career pathway. Of the 25 schools, 16 were iCaucus members, 1 was a Supporting member, 4 were Basic members, and 4 were Associate members. While membership type is based on size, resources, and other factors that could potentially affect course offerings, no notable patterns emerged between membership type and reference curriculum.

The presence of reference education and related course offerings was examined on the websites provided in the ALA directory for each of the 25 schools. The majority of these schools had a reference track or concentration, reference included as a requirement within the programmatic core courses, and/or reference courses in another specialized track. All of the 25 schools reviewed had reference education embedded into other courses.

Five of the programs outlined a reference series in a specific track or area of concentration. While programs categorize their reference concentration or career pathway under the catchall term of "Reference and User Services" for ALA's directory, they used a wider variety of terms to indicate a focus on reference in their program materials. For example, "Information Intermediation and Instruction" emerged as a track option alongside the more traditional terms of "Reference Services" and "Research and Information Services." This finding matches Bailey's observation from 2010 that reference services, with their wide-ranging descriptors, can be difficult to detect (Bailey 2010). It also recalls the threat of invisibility noted in Johnson's survey of recent literature of reference and liaison librarianship (2018). While Johnson (2018) discusses the efforts of reference librarians to remain visible in their practice by developing new service offerings, library and information science programs may be following a similar path with reference education. Renaming reference courses as "Information Intermediation and Instruction" may be viewed as an attempt to reinvent and reinforce the relevance of these courses in an information studies environment. Moreover, while reference may not be the clear focus of many of the course offerings at these institutions, since all of the 25 schools had reference embedded in other courses, reference education may be seen to be threaded throughout the program.

Nine schools noted reference as a requirement within the programmatic core courses. Again, these courses use many other terms besides "reference" to assign their public services focus, including titles such as "Basic Information Sources and Services" and "Information Users and Uses." There were 10 schools that listed specialized reference courses within tracks and/or concentration areas. As courses within tracks or concentrations, these tended to be more specialized; however, the type of specialization varied greatly. Some schools offered reference courses related to serving certain populations, such as "Resources for Digital Age Children," and others offered courses focused on instruction and other functional skill specializations, such as "Information Professional's Role in Teaching & Learning." Although the data did include some examples of discipline-based reference courses in required core or track offerings, such as "Art Librarianship" and "Genealogy and Local History," these types of courses were less common than population- or skills-focused specialized reference courses. This finding reflects the declining trend of discipline-based reference courses (Condic 2016) and suggests that programs are focusing on users and skills in reference education.

CONCLUSION

Reference education in library and information science programs continues to experience the primary challenge observed by O'Connor almost 10 years ago. In fact, there are even more areas of reference practice, user needs, and soft and hard skills to consider and incorporate into the curriculum. In this changing environment, iSchools provide an interesting test case to see how schools that are actively evolving to establish a new identity are continuing their role in educating future reference librarians. The data revealed that reference remains a part of library and information science education at iSchools, even when it is disguised or difficult to detect due to varying terminology. The majority of iSchools with ALA-accredited master's of library and information studies programs identified themselves as offering concentrations in "Reference and User Services," and the majority of those schools feature reference in some form in their online program materials. These programs have lowered the visibility of traditional reference but are using new terms to highlight the alignment of reference education with developing user and workforce needs. Amid dynamic shifts in library and information science, iSchools with ALA-accredited programs continue to value reference education by fitting it into the curriculum.

REFERENCES

Bailey, Edgar C., Jr. 2010. "Educating Future Academic Librarians: An Analysis of Courses in Academic Librarianship." *Journal of Education for Librarian and Information Science* 51 (1): 30–42.

Condic, Kristine. 2016. "ALA Library Schools and Subject Reference Coursework: A Short Communication." *Journal of Education for Library and Information Science* 67 (4): 329–332.

iSchools Organization. 2019. "iSchools." https://ischools.org/members/directory/, accessed May 8, 2019.

Johnson, Anna Marie. 2018. "Connections, Conversations, and Visibility: How the Work of Academic Reference and Liaison Librarians Is Evolving." *Reference & User Services Quarterly* 58 (2): 91–102. https://doi.org/10.5860/rusq.58.2.6929.

Kalin, Sally W. 2011. "What Skills Are Needed for the Next Generation of Librarians?" In *Reference Reborn: Breathing New Life into Public Services Librarianship*, edited by Diane Zabel, 281–298. Santa Barbara, CA: Libraries Unlimited.

Larsen, Ron. 2009. "History of the iSchools." https://ischools.org/wp-content/uploads/2017/08/History-of-the-iSchools-2009.pdf, accessed May 28, 2019.

O'Connor, Lisa. 2011. "The Education of Reference Librarians: A Detailed Survey and Analysis." In *Reference Reborn: Breathing New Life into Public Services Librarianship*, edited by Diane Zabel, 317–338. Santa Barbara, CA: Libraries Unlimited.

Roy, Loriene, and Elisabeth Long. 2019. "Incorporating Social Justice in Reference Education." *The Reference Librarian* 60 (3): 226–231. https://doi.org/10.1080/02763877.2019.1597421.

Saunders, Laura. 2019. "Core and More: Examining Foundational and Specialized Content in Library and Information Science." *Journal of Education for Library and Information Science* 60 (1): 3–34. https://doi.org/10.3138/jelis.60.1.2018-0034.

2

New Look, Same Essence: The Enduring Value of Reference Librarianship

Aliqae Geraci and Kelly LaVoice

INTRODUCTION

Technology, social change, economic realities, and shifting patron expectations have shaped the scope of reference work across all types of libraries: academic, school, public, and special. These changes are experienced by reference staff and patrons in the library workplace, studied by researchers in library science scholarship, and can be observed by monitoring library employment. In analyzing a snapshot of recent position advertisements for librarians, the authors seek to understand the current nature of reference work in libraries, how reference librarianship is described by employers in the library recruitment and hiring process, and how reference tasks are distributed within libraries and to librarians of all types. While reference is periodically characterized as dead, dormant, or in decline, the persistence of reference indicators in advertised librarian jobs confirms that this work remains central and enduring to the function of libraries and role of librarians, albeit refashioned with new terminology or camouflaged as a tertiary responsibility.

The American Library Association's Reference and User Services Association (RUSA) defines reference as "reference transactions and other activities that involve the creation, management, and assessment of information or research resources, tools, and services" and transactions as "information consultations in which library staff recommend, interpret, evaluate, and/or use information resources to help others to meet particular information needs" ("Definitions of Reference" 2008). RUSA does not set or recommend qualifications or job titles for reference librarian positions, recognizing that reference responsibilities are incorporated into a wide range of positions and skill sets and deferring to libraries on issues of role distribution and management. In recent years, RUSA (initially founded as the Reference and Adult Services Division in 1972) even considered jettisoning the term "reference" entirely, engaging in an extensive review of the division name in the spirit of acknowledging the expanding scope of tasks and roles embodied by reference librarians across all library types (Houston 2016).

Some researchers studying the evolution of reference and other functional work in libraries have surveyed practicing reference librarians, seeking to capture perceptions of their job responsibilities and changes in duties over time, while others have analyzed position advertisements in order to assess the scope and nature of advertised library needs by quantitative and qualitative means. Both methods also allow researchers to draw conclusions related to positions that may include reference duties but are not primarily classified or titled as reference librarians. Library associations and communities of practice at the local, state, and national levels collect and provide platforms for job advertisements. Many of these organizations host online job posting platforms that provide robust data for researchers.

The authors elected to analyze recent library position postings to the ALA JobLIST service in order to assess the extent of reference positions and responsibilities in national job postings during a snapshot in time: October 2016 to September 2017. While numerous content analyses of position descriptions have been completed over the last 40 years by library and information science (LIS) researchers, the authors hope to capture the contemporary moment in reference librarianship across libraries of all types. The authors aim to move beyond job title as a sole categorization, instead reviewing title language in conjunction with employer-selected functional assignments and employer-authored position descriptions to gain a greater understanding of the perceived value and prominence of reference work in libraries of all types.

LITERATURE REVIEW

LIS researchers have engaged multiple methodologies to identify and assess industry and occupational trends in libraries and librarianship and track changes over time but have primarily relied on surveys of practicing librarians and content analyses of job advertisements to augment the limited, more general occupational and industry employment statistical resources. Surveying practicing professionals allows researchers to capture role and responsibility changes over time that have not yet emerged as new positions with corresponding job advertisements, such as the advent of increased instruction duties or a shift from in-person to e-mail reference services. Reviewing job advertisements shows what skill sets, experiences, and educational requirements employers seek in new reference positions, as well as changes in the number of posted positions in the field. By reviewing studies across methodologies, one can gain a more comprehensive sense of how job duties are conceived and assigned, evolve over time, and are cemented in practice by libraries recruiting librarians with discrete skill sets in functional roles.

Surveys of academic reference librarians indicate an expansion of functional roles to complement continued reference work. Saunders (2012a) surveyed academic reference librarians and found a correlation between a librarian's years of experience and a greater time spent doing reference work, potentially as a result of newer librarians coming in with additional skill sets and spending more time on other responsibilities. Identifying instruction as the next frequent primary duty of reference librarians, Saunders concluded that new responsibilities and skill set requirements are being incorporated into established reference positions. While over 90 percent of reference librarians Saunders surveyed still provided direct patron support, transactional venues have expanded, with a wide range of face-to-face and online communication avenues that go far behind the traditional reference desk (Saunders 2012b). Cardina and Wicks (2004) surveyed reference librarians in academic libraries to examine how job duties and time spent on activities had changed from 1991 to 2001. Consistent with Saunders's findings, the authors noted increases in duties related to technology, including e-mail reference, webpage design, and electronic collection development, as well as a 14 percent increase in supervisory components. They also highlighted shifting terminologies in LIS, as reference librarians indicated "bibliographic instruction" decreased by 15 percent and "information literacy instruction" went up by 15 percent (Cardina and Wicks 2004). Shifting occupational terminologies in LIS to describe teaching responsibilities is well documented; however, new terms used to define reference work (tasks and services or serve as position titles) is less documented in the LIS literature.

LIS research findings that are grounded in content analyses of job postings often align with such survey findings; reviewing both types of studies paints a richer landscape of reference. Wang, Tang, and Knight's (2010) content analysis of academic reference job announcements in *College & Research Library News* from 1966 to 2009 showed a steady growth in reference positions during this time frame, greater than that in other types of positions. The study also highlighted the variety of titles used to represent these positions during this time frame, documenting the increased scope of responsibilities for reference librarians. While some titles remained steady in the postings from 1966 to 2009 (reference librarian, subject librarian/specialist, and public/user services librarian), new titles reflected popular language and duties of the time as well as the growing presence of digital technology in libraries (1966–1969: bibliographer; rare book reference librarian; reference circulation [male] librarian; and readers' service librarian; 2000–2009: instruction & outreach librarian, electronic information librarian, digital information service librarian, and reference/web service librarian [Wang, Tang, and Knight 2010]).

An analysis of job advertisements often looks to educational requirements as indicators of perceived value of specific experience, skill sets, and credentials. Wang, Tang, and Knight (2010) also observed changes in educational requirements, with the majority of contemporary positions now requiring a graduate degree and an additional educational background in a particular discipline. Starr (2004) reviewed library job announcements advertised in *American Libraries* and *Library Journal* in 1983 and 2003, noting a slight decrease in job postings in 2003 that specified an MLS was required and greater mentions of "or equivalent" in education requirements (Starr 2004). Kennan et al. (2006b) also observed a growth of nontraditional librarian roles with reference duties when reviewing two distinct studies that utilized job advertisements in Australia and the United States and found that in 2004 less than half of the positions they examined required "established LIS skills" (Kennan et al. 2006a). This speaks to both technical skill requirements and interpersonal skills required to work in changing LIS environments. Like Starr (2004), Kennan et al. (2006a) note that preparing new librarians entering the field for the wide array of skills they might need for professional librarian positions can be challenging as institutions continue to create new positions utilizing mixtures of skill sets and new technologies.

The fixed nature of position posting periods allows researchers to chart the influence of new technologies on library workflows and personnel management. Xu (1996) reviewed a sample of job advertisements in each year from 1971 to 1990 in four distinct periods, mapped to key library technology developments, finding that the development of automation technologies led to greater similarities in prior work experiences for reference and cataloging librarians. Xu captured time lags between implementation of new technologies and mention of those skill sets as job requirements. Xu also makes an interesting prediction that "routine reference questions" can and will be done by paraprofessionals, giving more time for reference librarians to engage with emerging job duties (Xu 1996, 12). The authors believe reference responsibilities and new positions for non-librarian staff to be an excellent area for additional study, but that is beyond the scope of this specific chapter.

Researchers have also sought to identify the relative presence of reference work in entry-level librarian positions. Detmering and Sproles (2012) gathered listings of entry-level, full-time academic jobs posted between January and December 2010. Of 385 jobs, 192 (49.9 percent) were classified as reference positions (Detmering and Sproles 2012, 546). While this number is less than the 64 percent classified in a previous study coauthored by Sproles (Sproles and Ratledge 2004), the authors suggest this is due to increasing job duties, rather than a decline in entry-level positions, and conclude that employers should offer training and mentoring to entry-level librarians to ensure that they can be successful in their ranges of reference job duties.

The sentiment that reference and other traditional library services are "dying out" was not found in any of the literature examined by the authors. A study by Beile and Adams (2000) examining postings from 1996 found that reference positions accounted for 30.2 percent of the 900 unique positions advertised in *American Libraries*, *Chronicle of Higher Education*, *College & Research Libraries News*, and *Library Journal*; this was by far the largest category in the study (Beile and Adams 2000). A contemporary study by Todorinova (2018) reviewed ALA JobLIST postings from August 2006 to December 2016 and noted that 9 percent of titles included reference (Todorinova 2018).

In 2012, Harper reviewed 70 distinct research studies of library job advertisements, noting that the number of these studies had risen substantially, with 46 studies published during the period 2000–2010 (Harper 2012). While job advertisement analysis is an established method of analyzing trends in a position or occupational type, findings are somewhat limited in scope. Position advertisements are not formal job descriptions and do not generally include a comprehensive description of duties that a new hire will perform, and analyses are best considered within the broader context of LIS research on library service provision, personnel management, labor relations, and funding over time. In that spirit, the authors seek to capture the scope of nationally advertised library positions that include reference responsibilities by studying one year of ALA JobLIST data.

METHODOLOGY

In order to assess the scope of advertised librarian positions with reference responsibilities, the authors reviewed positions posted on the JobLIST website owned by the American Library Association from October 2016 to September 2017. The time period reflects the authors' desire to review full job descriptions for the most recent year available (beyond the year of embargoed postings) in order to assess positions with reference job components, regardless of title.

Discussion with David Connolly, recruitment ad sales manager for ALA JobLIST, revealed that existing data field selections are made by advertising employers (often a supervisor, library or institutional HR department, or a private search firm). During the period from October 2016 to September 2017, which is the focus of this study, the three fields required by ALA JobLIST were State, Country, and Job Category. Employers select *one* of multiple options from a defined list for State and Country, including a Non-US option. *One* job category, or function, can be selected from a defined list, including the option "Other/Not Listed." It is important to note that from August 2006 to December 2015, employers were able to select multiple options for Job Category. While this change does not affect the outcomes of this particular study, it informed the authors' decision to focus on a narrow and recent data slice in which employers selected *the most relevant* function to assign to the posted position and is worth noting in contextualizing these findings with other studies relying on pre-December 2015 data.

The authors elected to use this data source instead of other viable sources such as LIS listservs in part due to the ability to work with existing metadata, such as discrete identifiers for positions, established by ALA JobLIST. However, the authors acknowledge that the fee-based nature of the source necessarily restricts its widespread use by all libraries for all position postings. While the dataset is free of charge to researchers, it is important to note that libraries must pay a fee to post jobs on the site. Pricing for postings, as indicated on the ALA JobLIST website, range from $250 for ALA institutional members to $650 for institutions selecting the Maximum Exposure Premium Job Flash Package (American Library Association 2019).

The ALA JobLIST hosted 2,953 position postings from October 1, 2016 to September 30, 2017. Employers are able to post multiple times for a single position, and duplicate postings encompassed reposted or rewritten positions as well as exact duplicates. In order to arrive at a usable dataset of unique position listings, the authors de-duplicated the initial ALA JobLIST dataset by automated and manual means, reviewing assigned identifiers, title, salary, job descriptions, requirements, and selected job function in order to identify and eliminate repeated positions. In identifying positions posted multiple times with minor changes to titles or descriptions, the authors chose the most recent chronological posting. If significant changes were observed in the position description or other field categories, the authors elected to retain all iterations of the position. After the de-duplication process was completed, the authors then analyzed the remaining dataset in Microsoft Excel by select categorical variables created by the ALA JobLIST process and submission form.

FINDINGS

From the initial 2,953 positions advertised on ALA JobLIST from October 1, 2016, to September 30, 2017, the authors arrived at a working dataset of 2,747 unique position postings. All 2,747 positions included a functional category, selected by the employer from a pre-populated list of 37 functions. Positions categorized as *Administration/ Management* in function were the largest grouping, at 26 percent of the postings. Positions classified as *Reference* accounted for 4.4 percent; *Research* accounted for 3.3 percent; and other "core" library functional areas like *Information Literacy* and *Collection Development* similarly represented single-digit percentages of postings. Postings categorized by *Other* and *Other/Not Listed* together accounted for almost 13 percent.

Of the 2,747 position entries advertised on ALA JobLIST in 2016–2017, 2,514 postings were categorized by "library type," with a clear majority for positions in *Academic Libraries* at 1,648, or 66 percent. *Public Library* postings comprised the second-largest category, with almost a quarter of postings categorized by this type. The remaining available categories, including *Government, Special,* and *School Libraries, Vendor,* and *Publishing,* each comprised between 1 and 2 percent of the postings.

"Traditional" Reference Positions

Given the theme of this chapter and volume, the authors initially looked most closely at the positions explicitly categorized as *Reference,* comprising 122 positions and amounting to 4.4 percent of the positions posted in the year. Of the 115 *Reference* positions that specified a library type, 77 percent were within academic or research libraries, 16.5 percent were within public libraries, and the remainder ranged between less than 1 and 2 percent across other library types (see Figure 2.1).

The vast majority of reference positions posted were full-time positions, with three part-time positions included. States most heavily represented in the position postings include Illinois (13), New York (12), and California (12), with Massachusetts, Texas, and Maryland representing states with 5–10 postings. The remaining states had five or fewer postings, with a single posting outside of the United States.

While only 96 of 123 reference positions posted included a minimum educational category, a master's remains the standard-bearer for reference librarians, with 96 percent requiring the degree as a minimum qualification. Of the 78 percent that selected the minimum experience level category, 18 percent of positions required no experience (see Figure 2.2). Over half required up to two years of experience, with 27 percent of positions requiring between 0 and two years of experience and 28 percent requiring one to two years of experience. Only one position required 7–10 years of experience, and none required more, indicating a limited articulated market for experienced, mid-, or late-career reference librarians.

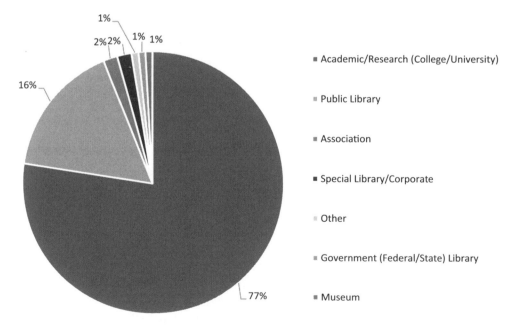

Figure 2.1   Reference Positions by Library Type

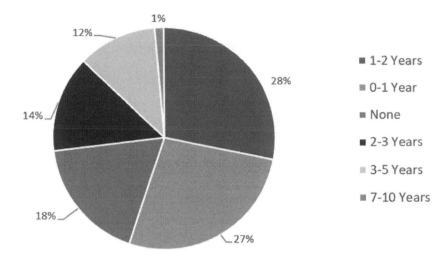

1%

12%

28%

14%

18%

27%

- 1-2 Years
- 0-1 Year
- None
- 2-3 Years
- 3-5 Years
- 7-10 Years

Figure 2.2   Reference Positions: Minimum Experience Required

Few salary ranges are included in the advertised positions, making it difficult to derive much meaning from provided ranges or minimums. About a third of the positions included minimum salary figures, which prevented the authors from adequately assessing compensation for the reference positions posted to ALA JobLIST or those included for other functional categories. Only 27 percent included uppermost salary ranges.

Position titles included a significant number of those explicitly acknowledging the reference role, with 43 containing "reference" in the title and another 14 containing "research."

Position descriptions tended to center or lead with discussions of reference, mention preferred dispositions, and describe modes and locations of reference service:

> *"Seeking an experienced reference librarian with a strong public service orientation to join the Library's department."*—reference librarian, historical society
> *"Provides reference and research consultation services in-person at service desks through individual appointments and via electronic communication (chat email text) including occasional evening and weekend hours."*—engineering librarian, public university
> *"The primary responsibilities of this position is to staff the adult research (reference) desk identify and/or participate in programs and services."*—research and instruction librarian, public library

Research = Reference?

The authors initially hypothesized that the *Research* functional category might contain positions with significant reference responsibilities and considered merging the positions with those explicitly coded as *Reference*. Indeed, about one-third of the 92 *Research* positions included "reference" in the description. In prioritizing the employer-selected functional category, the authors refrained from merging the two categories and instead reviewed *Research* positions separately.

Unsurprisingly, of the 83 percent of positions that included the library-type category, the vast majority of positions (84 percent) were located within an academic/research library, with an additional 9 percent within special library/corporate settings (see Figure 2.3).

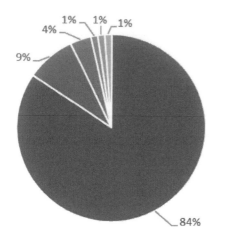

- Academic/Research
  (College/University)
- Special
  Library/Corporate
- Other

- Government
  (Federal/State) Library
- Museum

- School Library/Media
  Center (K-12)

Figure 2.3   Research Positions by Library Type

Three positions were noted as Other, while Government, K-12, and Museum each numbered one position.

As with reference positions, most position postings were for full-time positions. Virginia was the state with the highest representation, with 11 positions, followed by Massachusetts (9), California (7), and New York (7).

As anticipated by the authors, some positions, usually in colleges and universities, appeared to use "research" as a synonym for "reference," reflecting the library's role in supporting student and faculty research:

> *"The Librarian participates in the full range of unit responsibilities including research desk service and individual research consultation."*—research and instruction librarian, private college
> *"Provide reference service and library staff training in research resources. Preferred qualifications [include]work experience in a college or university library providing instruction and research services."*—instruction and research services librarian, private college

However, not all research positions are reference positions. Other positions reflected significant direct research responsibilities, often within a special library:

> *"As part of a firmwide research team, provide substantive research expertise to support the firm's practice areas and business development efforts including strategic research related to markets industries and competitors. Demonstrate strong writing skills and the ability to distill and present research work product in a concise professional manner. Proactively and independently assess research requests and ensure that research meets stated and anticipated needs. . . . Substantive experience in Intellectual Property research strongly preferred."*—research analyst, law firm
> *"Conduct research to support client meetings pitches and RFPs as well as practice and business development projects. Prepare research deliverables with emphasis on translating research data and findings into actionable insights and recommendations."*—marketing intelligence analyst, corporate library

Reference Staffing: All Hands on Deck
In addition to assessing positions explicitly categorized as reference/research in function, the authors also sought to identify the positions that include reference work in some form

or combination. While only a small fraction of the 2,747 positions posted for the year were functionally categorized as *Reference* positions, almost one-third (32 percent) included reference in the job description in some manner, indicating the continued relevance of reference as a function to the position, department, or library. When reviewing position functions selected by the employer, almost all functional categories were represented, with the largest percentage (18.1) were positions primarily coded as *Administration/Management*. Reference positions unsurprisingly were well represented in descriptions containing "reference," at 10.4 percent. The *Other* and *Other/Not Listed* functions combined to total 12.1 percent of the positions, with positions categorized as *Information Literacy/Instruction* (9 percent), *Special Collections/Archives* (6.4 percent), and *Area Studies/Subject Specialist* (6.1 percent) representing between 5 and 10 percent each of total positions mentioning "reference" in the description.

As with the preceding analysis, the majority of positions (73.7 percent) originated from academic libraries, but in this case the second highest group (19.6 percent) originated from public libraries. In keeping with the general pattern observed, almost all were full-time, but a handful of contract (4), temporary (6), and part-time (19) positions were included.

Positions categorized by non-reference functions might still include significant reference responsibility:

> *"Provide reference support and research assistance to faculty students and the campus community by receiving and responding to information requests in person and remotely through phone/email/ chat; promote and provide scheduled and impromptu research consultations; train and mentor reference desk staff on use of applicable programs and best practices for providing high level patron service; . . . assess reference services through review of patron interaction statistics."*—public services librarian, private university, supervisory, *Access Services/Circulation* selected as function

> *"Provides specialized instruction, consultations and reference services in coordination with Instructional Services Unit of the library, and in collaboration with other science and engineering librarians. . . . Participates in providing general reference and research assistance at public service points, including evening and weekend hours."*—librarian for STEM, private university, *Other/ Not Listed* as function

> *"Regular reference shifts and desk coverage and assistance with special collections instruction is required."*—digital archivist, private college, *Digital Projects* listed as function

> *"Provide public assistance at the reference desk and elsewhere as required."*—cataloging librarian, public library, cataloging/bibliographic control

> *"Provide research reference and information assistance to teens and adults. . . . Provide readers' advisory services to teens and adults."*—teen librarian, public library, *Youth Services* listed as function

> *"Areas of liaison activity include teaching, research consultations, academic outreach, creating and maintaining research guides, and scholarly communication; consults with students, faculty and staff about research projects individually or in small groups; and provides subject-specific research and reference services in person and through email online chat conferencing software phone etc."*—assessment librarian, public university, *Other* listed as function

Service Managers and Service Providers

The authors were intrigued by the large percentage of positions containing reference in the description that were functionally administrative/management in nature. The 161 positions showed much greater representation by public libraries (32.4 percent) in addition to the expected academic libraries (62.1 percent). States most represented were California (14.3 percent), Pennsylvania (11.8 percent), Texas (6.2 percent), New York (6.2 percent), and Florida (5.6 percent).

As expected, the duties might encompass the management of reference services or staff:

> *"Maintains high quality reference and reader's advisory services."*—branch manager/librarian V, urban public library system
> *"Provides vision for and directs: Reference & Research Services Department."*—associate dean of public services, public college library

However, some positions also included direct reference work with patrons:

> *"Providing specialized orientations, instructional sessions, and research consultations for faculty, graduate students, and undergraduate students. . . . [Requires] experience providing reference and/or instructional services related to visual arts and/or humanities in an academic or research library environment."*—art librarian (supervisory), disciplinary research library
> *"Provides reference assistance in a variety of settings."*—library director, community college

Some explicitly note that the candidate will manage services as well as participate as an individual contributor:

> *"Oversee and participate in the delivery of traditional, non-traditional, and innovative library services for children from birth to middle school and their families and caregivers, including collection development, children's reference service, readers' advisory, and storytimes as well as emerging non-traditional services such as STEM, maker, and other types of programs that further the mission of the library."*—head of children's services, public library

Limitations and Topics for Future Inquiry

This analysis of job descriptions from October 2016 to September 2017 prompts additional questions for the study of trends in reference staffing to better understand how library workers of all types participate in staffing reference services. The authors would like to further investigate reference requirements for administrative positions to better understand the role of the reference function and distinguish between expected competencies for supervising a function or a de facto and expected occupational skill set. Surveying practicing librarians with supervisory roles and/or hiring managers may provide more insight. The authors anticipate that a more in-depth analysis of position descriptions would surface differences between academic and public library vocabularies that describe the function of reference, nature of reference services, and methods of delivery in their respective settings.

The authors are mindful that significant work in libraries is done by library workers not in dedicated reference or formal librarian roles. Using more regional as well as less expensive or free job postings sources would allow for collection of job descriptions of part-time, paraprofessional, and other staff positions. Analyzing advertisements for these positions could also allow for a deeper understanding of how reference services are staffed as traditional reference librarian positions expand in responsibility and function. While position descriptions reviewed in this study encompass the role of student and staff supervision including reference responsibilities, the data source does not allow for greater research into the qualifications for or training provided to these employees. The broad geographical scope of ALA Job JobLIST provides ample opportunity to compare trends in positions by location, and using this dataset in conjunction with more localized sources would allow for a greater examination of regional employment trends and demands in relation to reference work.

Our findings reflect the positions posted to ALA JobLIST, which is not a comprehensive source of all available library positions. Institutions may choose not to advertise nationally, and less resourced libraries may choose to pursue free outlets for postings. To obtain a greater picture of the total number of staff engaged in reference work, researchers may choose to consult an array of local job postings sites, especially those with lower or no fees for postings. State and metropolitan area library organizations, library and information school listservs, and other providers would increase the number of total reference positions to review. Past studies encompass a range of data collection strategies in this regard.

The authors concur with Harper (2012), who observed a flaw in using job advertisements as a means to determine the desired qualifications for a position because of the lack of researchers' ability to follow up to examine what qualifications successful candidates actually possessed. Position advertisements do not necessarily correspond with an ultimate job description or what the successful candidate ends up doing in the course of their daily work. However, research access to internal personnel and management information in libraries is usually quite limited beyond what can be gleaned from interviews of individuals or formal participation by institutions. Position advertisements may be observed in isolation from the institutional context but may still serve as useful primary sources subject to researcher interpretation and comparison.

CONCLUSION

Reference duties are spread across librarian positions with wide ranges of titles, responsibilities, and functions. A small but core number of "classic" reference positions posted followed expected patterns.

Shifting language to describe traditional reference services is clear, representing both technological and ideological shifts in work. Research was found in titles functionally categorized as reference, as well as in the descriptions of reference services. This term is primarily used by academic libraries. The use of this term may be to encompass the relationship academic reference providers have with active researchers but can also refer to the direct research responsibilities they may have as academics.

It was clear that reference responsibilities are built in positions of all types. One-third of the listed positions include mention of these duties, indicating the enduring importance of the function and the range of roles played by different positions in supporting reference services. More common than "reference positions" are positions where reference is done in addition to other functional roles. Perhaps distributing reference responsibilities across multiple librarians (in contrast to one or more dedicated reference librarians) allows for these professionals to also engage in other key areas of library service work, such as instruction, collection development, and supervisory work. Reference is found in hidden places and baked into many position types within libraries beyond those explicitly categorized as such; simply reviewing a job title will not capture the current scope of reference work and providers. Managers oversee reference but are often also service providers.

As different types of libraries reframe or evolve the reference function, elevate or break down into smaller categories like readers advisory and research consultations, or attempt to distinguish services provided by trained librarians as opposed to paraprofessionals or student employees, it is essential that LIS practitioners and scholars incorporate these categories into our assessment and be prepared to find reference in unexpected places. Early career librarians are best served by a strong grasp of varying terminologies and the ability to frame one's skill set based on the position or library type at hand.

As titles and skill sets continue to shift in the library profession, it remains clear that reference duties are in demand for a wide range of positions. Investing in a solid foundation of reference work will be beneficial to any entry-level librarian or librarian on the market for a new position.

REFERENCES

American Library Association. 2019. "Post Library Job Openings—ALA JobLIST." https://joblist.ala.org/employer/pricing/.

Beile, Penny M., and Megan M. Adams. 2000. "Other Duties as Assigned: Emerging Trends in the Academic Library Job Market." *College & Research Libraries* 61 (4): 336–347.

Cardina, Christen, and Donald Wicks. 2004. "The Changing Roles of Academic Reference Librarians over a Ten-Year Period." *Reference & User Services Quarterly*, 44 (2): 133–142.

"Definitions of Reference." 2008. Reference & User Services Association (RUSA). http://www.ala.org/rusa/guidelines/definitionsreference

Detmering, Robert, and Claudene Sproles. 2012. "Forget the Desk Job: Current Roles and Responsibilities in Entry-Level Reference Job Advertisements." *College & Research Libraries* 73 (6): 543–555.

Harper, Ray. 2012. "The Collection and Analysis of Job Advertisements: A Review of Research Methodology." *Library and Information Research* 36 (112): 29–54.

Houston, Anne. 2016. "Toward a New Definition of Reference." *Reference & User Services Quarterly* 55 (3): 186–188. https://journals.ala.org/index.php/rusq/article/view/5927/7512.

Kennan, Mary Anne, Fletcher Cole, Patricia Willard, and Concepción S. Wilson. 2006a. "Changes in the Workplace: Transformation of the Information Professional?" *Proceedings of the 2nd Research Applications in Information and Library Studies (RAILS) Seminar held at the National Library of Australia, 16–17 September, 2005.* Centre for Information Studies, Charles Sturt University, Wagga Wagga. pp 125–140.

Kennan, Mary Anne, Fletcher Cole, Patricia Willard, Concepción Wilson, and Linda Marion. 2006b. "Changing Workplace Demands: What Job Ads Tell Us." In *Aslib Proceedings: New Information Perspectives* 58 (3): 179–196.

Saunders, Laura. 2012a. "Identifying Core Reference Competencies from an Employers' Perspective: Implications for Instruction." *College & Research Libraries* 73 (4): 390–404.

Saunders, Laura. 2012b. "The Reality of Reference: Responsibilities and Competencies for Current Reference Librarians." *Public Services Quarterly* 8 (2): 114–135.

Sproles, Claudene, and David Ratledge. 2004. "An Analysis of Entry-Level Librarian Ads Published in American Libraries, 1982–2002." *Electronic Journal of Academic and Special Librarianship* 5 (2/3): 1–17.

Starr, Joan. 2004. "A Measure of Change: Comparing Library Job Advertisements of 1983 and 2003." *LIBRES: Library and Information Science Research Electronic Journal* 14 (2). http://libres-ejournal.info.

Todorinova, Lily. 2018. "A Mixed-Method Study of Undergraduate and First Year Librarian Positions in Academic Libraries in the United States." *The Journal of Academic Librarianship* 44 (2): 207–215.

Wang, Hanrong, Yingqi Tang, and Carley Knight. 2010. "Contemporary Development of Academic Reference Librarianship in the United States: A 44-Year Content Analysis." *The Journal of Academic Librarianship* 36 (6): 489–494. doi:10.1016/j.acalib.2010.08.004.

Xu, H. 1996. "The Impact of Automation on Job Requirements and Qualifications for Catalogers and Reference Librarians in Academic Libraries." *Library Resources & Technical Services* 40 (1): 9–31.

3

Beyond the Checklist: Effective Onboarding and Training for Reference Services Success

Daniel Hickey

INTRODUCTION

Every reference librarian or service provider wants to make a positive and meaningful impact on the lives of the patrons they assist. Early career librarians with an internship under their belt and experienced information specialists with expert knowledge can hit the ground running, responding to user communities' information needs and alleviating or expanding the library's service capacity. Regardless of prior experience or natural aptitude, it is critical for supervisors and colleagues to effectively onboard and train individuals who are new to the organization.

Onboarding and training serve two purposes: making new employees feel welcome and ensuring that they become productive as quickly as possible (Laroche and Rutherford 2007, 77). As part of an educating profession, librarians are keenly aware of the importance of onboarding and training as foundational workplace learning opportunities. Barbara Allan in her *No-nonsense Guide to Training in Libraries* delineates how theories of learning and Bloom's taxonomy can be applied to the context of library training (Allan 2013, 22, 27). As the service environments at libraries transform to facilitate new and future-focused forms of scholarship, so too must our onboarding and training programs evolve.

Nearly every ARL Library has some form of socialization program for new hires (Ladenson, Mayers, and Hyslop 2011, 11). In fact, it is difficult to imagine a library that would not offer onboarding and training. However, organizational stressors may disrupt the thoughtful structuring and provision of such programs. Mary Wilkins Jordan (2012, 117) identifies many of the profession's core stressors, for academic and public libraries, as being rooted in public service work. Woodward (2009, 31), meanwhile, focuses on the trend of the shrinking library staff as a complicating factor. Lack of time, large workloads, turnover, absence of legacy planning, poorly defined service models, and outdated documentation may also undermine onboarding and training. For libraries without an effective plan, or at organizations where onboarding and training slip through the cracks, new hires will shower coworkers with questions, causing strain on their colleagues (Laroche and Rutherford 2007, 84).

These complications underscore that structured, consistent onboarding and training are critical for early and ongoing worker success. Klein and Polin (2012, 267) suggest that best practices supplied through practitioner outlets, such as professional societies, often do not provide sufficient guidance to support desired training outcomes. For this reason, it is crucial for supervisors to move beyond generic checklists and outdated training approaches to design trainee-centered programs. Through tested methods such as coaching and deliberate practice, library leaders can impart the knowledge, skills, and competencies required to provide excellent reference services. At stake is not only the patron-focused work at hand but also the integrity of workplace teams and the career satisfaction and success of the recent hire.

BEFORE THEY SAY "YES": SIGNALING TO POTENTIAL HIRES

Helping a new reference librarian understand the local environment and context shouldn't begin on the first day of work. Saks and Gruman (2012, 47) note that the process of acclimating a new employee begins even before the worker enters the organization. Thus, hiring managers and search committees should plan to deliberately advance a dialogue with candidates related to job requirements throughout the recruiting process. As discussed in the preceding chapter, job announcements help candidates gauge their fit with both the position and organization. When crafting language around required and preferred qualifications, hiring managers have the opportunity to signal to candidates what qualities they are looking for in a service provider. Links to strategic plans and mission, vision, and values statements will help applicants develop a vocabulary that resonates with the organization and set a baseline expectation that candidates have reviewed these materials. Evidence that applicants have linked themes and requirements to their personal experience will help in evaluating candidates.

Phone, video, and onsite interviews are another opportunity to convey meaningful information to potential future hires about the service environment. Asking a candidate about their reference philosophy will often lead to generic, textbook responses that do little to illuminate what the individual has done or how they may perform in the future. Sample interview questions to garner deeper insights follow.

- To examine the candidate's ability to reflect and process feedback: *Tell us about the most valuable feedback that you've received on your reference work from a supervisor or colleague. What did you learn about yourself?*
- To examine the candidate's potential for self-directed learning and awareness of their preferred learning style: *Describe a time you had to learn something new quickly to provide effective research support. How did you go about it, and what was the outcome?*
- To examine the candidate's customer service and reference philosophies: *Tell us about a time you didn't feel you gave the best possible reference service. What would you do differently?*

By asking behavioral interview questions that probe the candidate's past actions, rather than hypothetical questions that lead to theoretical answers, search committees will gain insight into how each candidate understands their own capacity to learn on the job.

It's important to acknowledge that interviewing is a two-way street: as the organization evaluates candidates, so too do candidates evaluate potential employers. Hiring managers should be ready to answer questions about how the library supports the growth and professional development of individuals new to the organization. A ready, enthusiastic, and holistic answer—that includes onboarding and training—will give candidates confidence that the library values and prioritizes developing their professionals. When courting candidates, employers should seek to provide specifics to demonstrate that training, onboarding, and professional development are not an afterthought at their organization but rather one of the cornerstones on which employee success is founded.

ON ALIGNMENT

Onboarding and training serve as the most immediate manifestation of the library's investment in professionals that are new to the organization. Recruitment, onboarding, and training are a significant expense to the organization (Laroche and Rutherford 2007, 87). While this chapter describes the components of these programs for new librarians, it is critical that they are informed by and aligned with the articulated values and goals of the organization and profession. To that end, before constructing or revising an onboarding and training plan, managers should take into consideration the following:

- The overarching support for growth, learning, and professional development at the organization
- The formal processes related to performance evaluation and promotion
- The goals setting process for the individual and their department
- The strategic plan and "mission, vision, and values" statement of the library (and any relevant units served)
- Service model(s) and customer service statements
- Guidance gleaned from professional standards, competencies, best practices, and ethics
- Organizational and professional commitments to inclusion, diversity, belonging, equity, and accessibility

Onboarding and training programs that logically dovetail with and mutually reinforce these priorities will help service providers see how their work is part of a larger whole. It is the responsibility of the trainer to highlight and emphasize the interconnected nature of the work at hand.

BUILDING AN ONBOARDING PLAN

Onboarding, often used interchangeably with the word "orientation," can be defined as "all formal and informal practices, programs, and policies enacted or engaged in by an organization or its agents to facilitate newcomer adjustment" (Klein and Polin 2012, 268). Onboarding serves, at its core, to inform, welcome, and guide (Klein and Polin 2012, 269).

Laroche and Rutherford (2007, 87) specify that onboarding is typically more than one day in length and should begin within the first few days of employment. It may take the form of a calendar and checklist and should be constructed by the individual's supervisor before the candidate's first day.

Frequent elements of onboarding:

- Meeting with relevant individuals, teams, and stakeholders
- Reviewing policies, documentation, and procedures
- Meeting with human resources and one's supervisor to discuss performance evaluations, promotion, and supervision
- Reviewing patron populations and communities to be served
- Resolving initial logistical matters (facilities, equipment, etc.)
- Attending work and social events
- Touring facilities

Due to the highly disparate nature of these elements, supervisors should plan to provide a mental framework that unifies and explains the progression of onboarding events. Goals for onboarding, discussed in supervisory one-on-one meetings, can explain the "how" and "why" of an onboarding program's structure.

Woodard suggests that onboarding should go beyond the procedural and logistical and should serve to enculturate and socialize new hires (Woodard 2016, 246–247). Especially in large organizations, reference providers may need to understand and move fluidly between multiple cultures. While learning the culture and developing an understanding of the social dynamics of the organization is important, supervisors should be sensitive to the fact that outside hires will bring fresh eyes and ideas to their role. Soliciting feedback from new hires throughout onboarding and training will help supervisors and managers reflect on how their programs and operations can be improved. While Laroche and Rutherford (2007, 77) suggest an 80-20 percentage split for how the newcomer and existing employees should adapt to one another, acknowledging that mutual adaption should occur is an important insight. While new hires can be a stressor in the workplace, supervisors and colleagues should be careful not to tamp down the creativity, curiosity, and insights they bring to their position (Feldman 2012, 223). Rather, they should harness that enthusiasm to improve the library's services.

Laroche and Rutherford (2007, 87) caution that employers should not assume that all onboarding content has been completely internalized, recommending follow-up and a designated point of contact for questions. To identify where additional reinforcement may be required, supervisors can review the onboarding plan in its entirety upon completion. Hiring managers may also wish to follow up on any important elements of onboarding that have been delegated outside of the supervisory relationship.

BUILDING A TRAINING PLAN

In 1983, Heartsill Young defined "training" for the American Library Association in his *Glossary of Library and Information Science*. Despite any variety of contemporary definitions that can be pulled from the library and information science or social science scholarly literature, this simple definition still best describes the term for the profession:

Training is the "process of developing the knowledge, skills, and attitudes needed by employees to perform their duties effectively and to meet the expectations and goals of the organization. This diverse process, which may be performed by supervisors, fellow employees, and personnel officers, involves planning, preparation, execution, and evaluation." (Young 1983, 231)

Training is distinct from onboarding in that the former does not focus on acclimation to a new and unique context, but rather the proficiencies, competencies, and best practices necessary to accomplish core job duties. Training, by necessity, should address all elements of an individual's responsibilities.

While this chapter primarily focuses on training for research support, it is important to acknowledge the interconnectedness of core job duties: instruction may lead to or be born of reference work; reference often surfaces collection needs and spurs acquisitions. Reference also overlaps fundamentally with cross-department efforts, such as IT support and discovery. Training and onboarding plans should acknowledge this interconnectedness as a strength of the library's service model and should demonstrate how relationships between individuals and departments facilitate information sharing to ensure optimal user experience.

WHAT MAKES A GOOD TRAINING PROGRAM? A MANIFESTO

New hires entering the library may believe the axiom that the vast majority of what they need to know to be successful at their job will be learned on the job. While this may not always hold true, an effective reference training program should aim to bridge the gap between the trainee's preexisting knowledge and experience and what is required to meet the information needs of patrons at the new organization.

An effective training program should be clear and intuitive at the outset, with well-articulated goals and supporting materials. Programs should be consistent across service providers, affording trainees the touchstone of a shared experience and setting baseline expectations for those in similar roles. Agreeing on goals for training is essential. While a training checklist can be a first step (Nims, Storm, and Stevens 2014, 79), SMART goal setting will ensure that all agree on the expected outcomes of the tasks at hand.

Above all, training for new hires must be customized. At the same time as a supervisor or trainer is setting expectations about standardized, quality service, they must also be communicating how training has been crafted to meet the needs of the individual through feedback. The best training programs allow new reference providers the flexibility to experiment, fail, and learn in the process. Customization can be led by the trainer or trainee. A supervisor, for example, may directly observe a trainee's reference work to initially tailor training to the newcomer's ability. Supervisee-led customizations may be sourced from the individual's interests, observation and shadowing of other reference providers, a personal gap analysis, or self-reflection.

Training programs must be socially supportive: Laroche and Rutherford (2007, 95, 97) recommend developing affinity networks (or what librarians might call communities of practice), or a mentor or buddy system, to encourage acclimation and learning. Additionally, training must reinforce a newcomer's sense of purpose (Klein and Polin 2012, 277), linking their work to the mission of the library.

Training must be continuous (Caplan 2013, viii). A "one and done" approach to training ignores the speed at which methods of research and scholarship are advancing and may preclude developing a greater breadth and depth of skill. For this reason, training programs for new hires must interlock with a greater departmental training program, as well as personal, trainee-directed learning efforts.

COMPETENCIES AND CUSTOMER SERVICE

Professional associations for librarians, including the American Library Association (ALA) and Special Library Association, publish guiding documents that define core competencies for research support providers. Most referenced in the literature is ALA's Reference and User Services Association's "Professional Competencies for Reference and User Services Librarians." Trainers should aim to locate reference competencies and best practices at the most granular level. For example, an art librarian may look to the Art Libraries Society of North America's competencies document, while a business information specialist may look to ALA's Business Reference and Services Section's core competencies document. In increasingly flat organizational structures, with supervisors who may not intimately understand the disciplines and populations that their librarians serve, these targeted reference competencies are more important than ever. While such documents can serve as a professional's north star, they must be embellished, expanded, and interpreted through a local lens.

Discussions related to competencies need not focus solely on subjects, technologies, or disciplines. Colbert-Lewis, Scott-Branch, and Rachlin identify four types of competencies for librarians: core to the job, technical, professional, and personal (including soft skills; Colbert-Lewis, Scott-Branch, and Rachlin 2015, 185–186). Their chapter, "Necessities of Librarianship: Competencies for a New Generation," is a must-read for individuals developing future-focused training programs.

The library training literature thoroughly addresses core, technical, and professional competencies. Personal competencies, which can be more challenging to both adopt and evaluate, should not be neglected. An example of a widely accepted personal competency training is those for patrons in distress. As a helping profession, it is important for trainers to balance this need with the idea of emotional labor, which has seen "sustained interest" in the professional literature (Matteson and Miller 2013, 57). Matteson and Miller (2013, 61) found that dissonance between a librarian's natural emotions and the perceived emotional affect required of employees "is associated with increased rates of job burnout and decreased job satisfaction." In highly competitive and stressful research and scholarship environments, training can help resolve the tensions between a reference provider's actual and perceived obligation to validate, address, and advocate for patrons in distress.

Another area of training where great strides are being made is in inclusion, diversity, belonging, and equity. Nicole Cooke (2017, 52) details how "training staff to work with users with special needs or cultural differences" is key to providing equitable service. Cooke (2017, 27–46) identifies diverse populations as follows: race, ethnicity, and national origin; individuals with disabilities; older individuals; individuals with mental illness; individuals with autism spectrum disorder; international and new Americans; immigration status; the hungry, homeless, and impoverished; LGBTQ; and individuals who are or have been incarcerated. Examples of diversity training for reference providers might include how to identify and disrupt microaggressions, bystander training, and so forth. Supervisors may wish to partner with human resources or an office for diversity and inclusion in order to secure an expert on such topics. Reference providers must be prepared to learn about, understand, and assist individuals with different backgrounds and experiences. All too often, key populations who require thoughtful, equitable treatment may be assigned to one specific individual or department. While limiting proficiencies to one person or group is not ideal, for those champions of diverse populations to be effective, broader training and competencies across all reference providers will help them best meet patron's needs.

Reference competencies and best practices should live alongside customer service training (Allan 2013, 153). While any number of corporate models exist for customer service, Julie Todaro and Mark Smith's *Training Library Staff and Volunteers to Provide Extraordinary Customer Service* (2006) provides an excellent exploration of the concept in a library context.

METHODS THAT WORK: DELIBERATE PRACTICE AND COACHING

How do the best trainers impart the knowledge, skills, and attitudes described by Young in his definition of training? Nims, Storm, and Stevens (2014, 79, 84) identify the humble training manual and modules/exercises as the profession's foundational approach. Woodard recommends role playing, drills, action plans, guided practice, and question-and-answer sessions as practical practice strategies (Woodard 2016, 260–262). From the education literature, Allan (2013, 22, 95) incorporates theories of learning as keystones for developing a training program, as well as recommending a design approach to iterate on training offerings.

Practice is a key element of reference training and may take many forms. From the social science literature, the theory of deliberate practice centers immediate, expert feedback and frequent practice as key to helping individuals improve their performance. Ericsson, Krampe, and Tesch-Römer (1993, 367) find that in "the absence of adequate feedback, efficient learning is impossible and improvement only minimal even for highly motivated subjects." To ensure effective learning, trainees need to be given "explicit instructions about the best method and be supervised by a teacher to allow individualized diagnosis of errors, informative feedback," and supplemental remedial training (Ericsson, Krampe, and Tesch-Römer 1993, 367). In the library context, Ericsson's findings suggest that trainers should abandon asynchronous feedback models that temporally sever performance and feedback, despite their convenience, for training to be effective.

The scientific validation of deliberate practice further centers the importance of the trainer. Coaching in a reference context dovetails well with this strategy. Laroche and Rutherford (2007, 94) suggest coaching as one method to develop employees. While coaching was formerly thought of as a one-to-one intervention for an organization's most senior leaders, it is now broadly recognized as an appropriate tool for individuals anywhere on the organizational chart (Tulpa 2016, 34, 39). While no one definitive definition of coaching is endorsed by the American Association of Coaching, it can be broadly defined as relationship in which "a wide range of interventions" are deployed to improve individual performance (Bresser and Wilson 2016, 12–14). Key techniques include "listening, questioning, clarifying and giving feedback" (Bresser and Wilson 2016, 14). Coaching, in a reference context, thus encourages expertly guided reflection, allowing the individual to dissect reference interviews and service interactions for areas to improve.

CONCLUSION: OBLIGATION AND OPPORTUNITY

There is no single "right" way to onboard and train a new reference provider, only more or less effective ones. While a variety of strategies and methods can be deployed, the human and interpersonal aspect of training is most critical to trainee learning and success. It's no mystery why excellent reference librarians are also often excellent trainers: through public service, they have intuitively honed the skills necessary to excel at training.

Onboarding and training set the tone for a new reference librarian's tenure at their workplace. It is incumbent upon the library organization—and most especially library leadership and supervisors—to provide customized and intellectually rigorous training that serves as the foundation for public service excellence and continual staff improvement.

As Woodard (2016, 274) observes, the "act of training itself motivates and builds employee confidence and self- esteem. . . . Training reduces stress and turnover, improves work relationships, and increases adaptability. Without training, reference librarians cannot keep up with change, develop expertise, or learn how to transfer what they already know to new environments." Investing resources—time, money, thought, and emotion— in onboarding and training allows library leaders to proactively shape their staff into expert service providers on the cusp of research and scholarship, thus fulfilling S. R. Ranganathan's 5th law of library science: the library is a growing organism.

REFERENCES

Allan, Barbara. 2013. *The No-Nonsense Guide to Training in Libraries*. London: Facet Publishing.

Bresser, Frank, and Carol Wilson. 2016. "What Is Coaching?" In *Excellence in Coaching: The Industry Guide*, edited by Jonathan Passmore, 3rd edition, 11–32. London: Association for Coaching.

Caplan, Audra. 2013. "Introduction." In *Customer Service in Libraries: Best Practices*, edited by Charles Harmon and Michael Messina, v–x. Lanham, MD: Scarecrow Press.

Colbert-Lewis, Danielle, Jamillah Scott-Branch, and David Rachlin. 2015. "Necessities of Librarianship: Competencies for a New Generation." In *Rethinking Reference for Academic Libraries: Innovative Development and Future Trends*, edited by Carrie Forbes and Jennifer Bowers, 185–200. London: Rowman & Littlefield.

Cooke, Nicole A. 2017. *Information Services to Diverse Populations: Developing Culturally Competent Library Professionals*. Santa Barbara, CA: Libraries Unlimited.

Ericsson, K. Anders, Ralf T. Krampe, and Clemens Tesch-Römer. 1993. "The Role of Deliberate Practice in the Acquisition of Expert Performance." *Psychological Review* 100 (3): 363–406.

Feldman, Daniel C. 2012. "The Impact of Socializing Newcomers on Insiders." In *The Oxford Handbook of Organizational Socialization*, edited by Connie R. Wanberg, 215–229. Oxford: Oxford University Press.

Klein, Howard J., and Beth Polin. 2012. "Are Organizations on Board with Best Practices Onboarding?" In *The Oxford Handbook of Organizational Socialization*, edited by Connie R. Wanberg, 267–287. Oxford: Oxford University Press.

Ladenson, Sharon, Diane Mayers, and Colleen Hyslop. 2011. *SPEC Kit 323: Socializing New Hires*. Washington, D.C.: Association of Research Libraries. https://doi.org/10.29242/spec.323.

Laroche, Lionel, and Don Rutherford. 2007. *Recruiting, Retaining, and Promoting Culturally Different Employees*. New York: Elsevier Butterworth-Heinemann.

Matteson, Miriam L., and Shelly S. Miller. 2013. "A Study of Emotional Labor in Librarianship." *Library & Information Science Research* 35 (1): 54–62. https://doi.org/10.1016/j.lisr.2012.07.005.

Nims, Julia K., Paula Storm, and Robert Stevens. 2014. *Implementing an Inclusive Staffing Model for Today's Reference Services: A Practical Guide for Librarians*. Lanham, MD: Rowman & Littlefield.

Saks, Alan M., and Jamie A. Gruman. 2012. "Getting Newcomers on Board: A Review of Socialization Practices and Introduction to Socialization Resources Theory." In *The Oxford Handbook of Organizational Socialization*, edited by Connie R. Wanberg, 27–55. Oxford: Oxford University Press.

Tulpa, Katherine. 2016. "Coaching within Organizations." In *Excellence in Coaching: The Industry Guide*, edited by Jonathan Passmore, 33–51. 3rd edition. London: Association for Coaching.

Wilkins Jordan, Mary. 2012. "We Are All Stressed Out! Now What? Looking at Stress in Libraries." In *Leading the Reference Renaissance*, edited by Marie Radford, 113–124. New York: Neal-Schuman.

Woodard, Beth S. 2016. "Training and Continual Learning for Reference Staff." In *Reference and Information Services: An Introduction*, edited by Linda C. Smith and Melissa A. Wong, 244–280. 5th edition. Santa Barbara, CA: Libraries Unlimited.

Woodward, Jeannette. 2009. *Creating the Customer Driven Academic Library*. Chicago: American Library Association.

Young, Heartsill, editor. 1983. *The ALA Glossary of Library and Information Science*. Chicago: American Library Association.

4

Continuing Education for Reference/Public Service Librarians

Anne Langley

INTRODUCTION

Reference/public service librarians are the tires of the library car, if you will. These librarian tires are the part of the car that makes direct contact with the road—where the road is the people who most often use or need the library for their research, teaching, and learning. We have to make sure the tire treads are deep and the rubber is new if we don't want the car to get a flat tire or to slide off the road in a storm. These librarians have a particularly immediate need to be informed and to keep expanding their knowledge since they work directly with users. Because there is so much change in our profession, in higher education, and in practically everything the library does, continuing education is the only way to stay relevant and helpful to those we support. And yes, our role is a supportive one. That means that we have to include ongoing deep study of the people we support and institutions we are embedded in, while staying abreast of changes in our own field that affect in small and large ways how we provide that support.

Continuing education includes daily observances, regular activities or workshops, and mindful assessments. It includes sharing with and learning from colleagues near and far. It means the learner needs to be constantly observing and inquiring of those we support and serve: for example, by asking questions such as, How do users interact with and create information that is different from yesterday, or last week, or two years ago? How can librarians save users time, but especially how can librarians teach them to be independent and discerning users and creators of information? We need to continually ask ourselves what we are doing that hampers how users learn and do research. We need to ask what we are doing right that we can share with others in our profession or extend to other places in our libraries or institutions.

Continuing education must include what is considered to be more traditional: through focused specific courses of learning, which not only are relevant to your own areas of work and/or expertise but also must be more broad and far reaching. By seeking out knowledge that is tangential yet relevant, continuing education can yield new and sometimes revolutionary directions for your own practice and those of the profession at large. This multipronged approach is sure to carry reference/public service librarians into the future as relevant, library professionals who competently embrace the needs of our users and seek productive solutions to new problems and situations that arise.

There are multiple opportunities and options to plot out your own continuing education or to provide for them at your own institution and beyond. This section goes more in depth into both formal and informal education options in a number of different areas.

PEDAGOGY, INSTRUCTIONAL DESIGN, AND SO FORTH

Many of our professional organizations offer excellent education opportunities in pedagogy and instructional design for reference/public service librarians. The Association for College and Research Libraries (ACRL) has multiple courses and webinars, as do many local, state, or consortial organizations. Your own institution may offer workshops in these areas, and there are national associations that offer continuing education (CE) credits or workshops, meetings, and presentations in this area. Seek out and take advantage of these often free or cost-effective opportunities to improve your own pedagogy and instructional design.

SUBJECT EXPERTISE

If you are in a role or aspire to be in a role that requires subject expertise, there are many opportunities to learn about, or learn more about, the subject(s). There are the more obvious ones such as obtaining degrees in a subject (rather extreme, and not entirely necessary) or taking introductory courses in that subject (more reasonable and often all you need). Some universities and colleges allow librarians and staff to take classes for free, or at reduced rates, or allow auditing. Not only do you gain basic subject expertise, you also learn first-hand how students (including you) and faculty interact with the learning management system, and with the library and librarians. One thing to keep in mind, however, as you seek subject expertise—you are not seeking to be a practitioner in that subject. Your primary focus will need to be on how, why, and when do students and researchers in these subjects interact with information—focus on the information produced by not only their area but also those of related areas. For example, you don't need to be an expert of Russian grammar or know how to draw complex chemical compound structures. You just need to know where and how best to efficiently find and use the information resources that support the work of that discipline or field.

There are some fields where there are continuing education opportunities specifically designed for librarians. One of these is Science Boot Camp for Librarians, started in 2009 by the University of Massachusetts system libraries. These boot camps are now held in multiple places across the United States every year. They provide much-needed continuing education opportunities for science and medical librarians seeking to add to their own knowledge or learn about new areas of science and medical research. There are now other boot camps for librarians in various disciplines, including the social sciences, innovation- and collaboration-themed boot camps, and more. The concept of each boot camp is built around providing new information, immersion, and a shared experience for networking.

KNOWLEDGE OF LIBRARY, DEPARTMENTS, FACULTY RESEARCH, SCHOOLS, COLLEGES, AND INSTITUTIONS

The more you know about the inner workings at your own institution, the better you can reach and serve the students, faculty, and other researchers you support. If you have subject liaison responsibilities, make a point of talking to the faculty in the departments you serve on a regular basis about their latest research or any new pedagogical approaches they or others in the department may be incorporating. Walk around the building—poke your head into offices, make appointments, ask if you can attend departmental meetings as an observer. Go to departmental talks and visiting researcher presentations. Annually, or more often, peruse the web pages of colleges, schools, departments, and individual faculty members. Take note of changes from year to year. Read the annual reports of the departments, schools, colleges, and institutions to learn about where there will be new focus and pay attention to what is unspoken—what is being de-emphasized? See if you can attend university governance meetings. You don't have to attend every one—you may not even be allowed to—but you can peruse the minutes or notes or past agendas. See what is relevant for you and how you support the departments. Think about how the library and you in particular can support what they are doing or planning to do.

Make sure you do the same for your own library and for those near you geographically, or those whom you strive to be like. Go visit other departments and ask them what they are doing differently, what are the new challenges they are facing, or how they have solved them. Read your library's annual report. Make sure that your work is in tandem with that of librarians in other departments and that you learn from them what is changing in their unique areas of librarianship. What are the challenges facing special collections and archives? What can you learn from your colleagues about the issues they encounter and how do their professional societies think about how to find solutions? What can work in one area of the library that can enhance and inform your own area.

TECHNOLOGY TOOLS FOR INTERACTING WITH, ACCESSING, AND SYNTHESIZING INFORMATION

There are many options available to you to expand your education in technology tools. Librarians not only use tools in their own work; they also often teach these tools to the users they support. Your own library technology team may offer workshops on new tools, or the institution's learning and staff development office often provides training in new or often-used technology. Your institution may provide access to an online library of training tools, such as Lynda.com. Take advantage of these often free opportunities to expand your repertoire. You never know when it will come in handy as a reference/public services librarian.

Beyond the walls of the university, there are many options to expand your knowledge. Many library and information science schools offer additional training in technology tools and their application in higher education or more specifically in a library.

There are specific vendors who offer onsite training opportunities for you and sometimes for your users. Invite them to campus or talk to them at a conference. The more you know about the inner workings of a database or tool, the better you can help the patrons learn how to get the most out of a product.

Some other technology tools may come in handy for you to learn about to support your faculty and students. Researchers are increasingly using software such as GIS, R, or other statistical analysis tools. Learning how researchers use these technologies for quantitative and qualitative research is vital to how best you can serve them.

LEGAL AND GOVERNMENTAL CHANGES AFFECTING INFORMATION

There are many legal issues that affect how users interact with libraries and that govern what libraries are allowed or required to do. These issues include: copyright, intellectual property, research data management, and the White House Office of Science and Technology (OSTP) memo. This particular area of continuing education is often overlooked but is very necessary. You have a professional and ethical obligation to stay abreast of how regulations and laws affect library work and library users. For example, the Office of Science and Technology memo sets the public access requirements for federally funded science research. I would go so far as to state that we all have a professional duty to become advocates for legal issues that affect our library work. This will require continuing education throughout your career. If you move from one institution to another, you may need to investigate the laws governing libraries, especially state institutions if the move is to another state.

You can do this by reaching out to your state library and spending time on their website. Local library associations often have sessions on related topics at local meetings, so take the time to become involved locally and not just in your national organizations.

Nationally, there are many agencies in Washington that advocate for the needs of libraries. The Association of Research Libraries (ACRL), American Library Association (ALA), and many others all have lobbying and policy departments or staff. Keep abreast of the key issues that may affect your library and your own practice through regular perusal of their publications, websites, announcements, or even social media venues.

VENDORS AND PUBLISHERS: CHANGING BUSINESS MODELS

The world of publishing is constantly in flux. There are library-supportive vendors and publishers and others who are not so friendly to us and to our users. One area of continuing education is that of learning more about the information providers and their relationships with our profession. What they do directly affects so much of what we do. The costs of information, or of providing access to information, have a huge impact on our ability to provide for the information needs of our users.

LEADERSHIP AND MANAGEMENT IN THE PROFESSION— WHETHER OR NOT YOU ARE A MANAGER

This area of continuing education is rife with opportunities for librarians. Not only do most institutions offer management and/or supervisory training, but many library and information sciences associations, entities, consortia, and many others offer opportunities for learning about supervision, management, and leadership.

While you may think that you will not be or even want to be a supervisor or a manager, or even a leader in the profession, the opportunity will indeed arise, if it hasn't already, for you to manage student workers or interns or to oversee a big project with group members from across the library or even the university or within a professional association. We all will need to supervise someone, manage a group, or lead an initiative at some point in our career. So make sure you take advantage of any opportunity to learn more about how to do so—the earlier in your career, the better.

Early in my career, three of the best training workshops I attended were as follows: how to manage conflict, how to facilitate, and how to deal with difficult people. These three workshops shaped and informed every position I have had. There is not one week that goes by that I don't have to deal with or help someone else deal with a difficult person, manage conflict, or facilitate a discussion in a meeting or event.

For deep, extensive leadership or management programs, seek out programs offered by ALA, ARL, ACRL, and a variety of other entities. Some institutions offer internal internships or programs that follow a leader for a period of time and learn from them. Seek these programs out if you think you may be interested in a very intensive program.

THE LIBRARY PROFESSION

Throughout your career, you will need to keep ahead of what is going on in our profession. There are many ways to gain this type of continuing information. Become a member of at least one local and one national association. Attend professional meetings, locally, regionally, or nationally at least every other year. Read professional journals and association publications regularly—at the very least, look through the table of contents to see what are the topics editors are choosing to publish. Are there any ideas you can adapt to your own institution or areas of responsibility?

Early in my career, I began to devote Friday afternoons to scanning the literature, looking at web pages, and deep diving into articles about what was going on in our profession. Sometimes I learned how colleagues were doing and where they had moved to, I discovered options for continuing education opportunities, or I found people I wanted to reach out to, to learn more in depth how they solved a problem at their own institutions. Colleagues near and far are always happy to have someone call or e-mail them to ask questions about a presentation or an article or a book. Not only is it flattering, but it is yet another chance to help improve the profession through sharing best practices or to learn what not to do. Learning from other's mistakes is just as useful as taking an idea and adapting it to your own situation. Make regular time in your own workweek to assess what is going on in the field. Put it on your calendar. Stick to it. You will be more knowledgeable and more productive, with regular review of what is happening around you and farther afield.

SCHOLARLY COMMUNICATION

Open access (OA), open education resources (OER), digital scholarship, institutional repositories (IR), copyright and intellectual property awareness are just a few of the ever-important topics that sit under the umbrella of scholarly communication; you need to, at the very least, understand their importance to research and scholarship for the faculty and students you support. Their rising importance to academia, and the need to educate ourselves and our institutions about their importance, means that you will have to carve out time to learn the basics in each of these areas.

There are many places to find continuing education opportunities on issues of scholarly communications. The Scholarly Publishing and Academic Resources Coalition (SPARC) is a national entity that has focused for many years on raising awareness of—advocating for—and supporting new ventures in all things related to scholarly communication and open access to information in all of its forms. SPARC holds meetings and hosts presentations in a variety of spaces throughout the year.

There are journals and conferences devoted to multiple areas of scholarly communication, and almost every national conference offers sessions on some aspect of scholarly communication. Your library may have its own office of scholarly communication or have a scholarly communication librarian or digital projects group charged with overseeing the work of the library in this area. Visit a departmental meeting, or take a librarian to lunch and ask them what are the key issues you would need to know before you work with faculty and students in this area.

WORK TOOLS FOR COLLABORATION, PROJECT MANAGEMENT, WRITING, AND PRESENTING

Similar to technology tools and supervisory techniques, management and leadership, collaboration, project management, and others are key skills, which you may not have learned in library school or on the job but will help you succeed as a productive, creative professional. Many institutions and library consultant firms offer continuing education opportunities in these areas.

Keep an eye out for business or professional writing courses, presentation, and public speaking skills; even attending Toastmasters International or learning about Robert's Rules will help you throughout your career. All librarians will need to write reports, present information locally or at a conference, and manage projects, either individually or with colleagues; be sure you gain the skills necessary to do so, all of which are vital components of your continuing education journey.

VOLUNTEERING TO PARTICIPATE

Don't forget that you can increase your knowledge and experience through volunteering to participate or lead on internal, external, state, national, or international committees, work groups, and so forth. Much can be learned when participating on groups or committees, where you will start out having little knowledge or experience. Space management and renovation, strategic planning, reorganization, website re-working are just a few of the areas where you can gain extensive knowledge outside of your work responsibilities. In fact, for many of these, especially the space, strategic planning, and reorganization topics, this may be the most useful and often only way to gain meaningful training or education in these areas of library work.

WHATEVER YOU THINK IS RELEVANT OR TANGENTIALLY RELATED TO WHAT YOU DO, OR WHAT YOU WANT TO DO

Sometimes continuing education can take you far afield from librarianship. For one of my books, I decided I wanted to include case studies. I looked far and wide for an article about how to write them for librarians and there were none. So I had to reach beyond the professional literature and find other sources of how to write one. I looked in business literature, found what I was looking for, and adapted what I learned to fit our profession. Think about what you want to do now or later in your career, learn to do what is needed to bring greater understanding of the work you are doing, make use of technology that may help you be more efficient, and know where the holes in our profession are or how we do things a certain way. Think broadly about who or what profession already does similar things—go learn from them and bring back to our field what you learn.

SELF-ACTUALIZATION THROUGH STUDY, PRACTICE, OBSERVATION, AND WRITING OR TALKING ABOUT WHAT YOU LEARN

As a final suggestion, you can also undertake to extend your education and knowledge by writing, presenting, or experimenting on something that you either know is a gap in the profession or want to learn more about. Sometimes you may encounter something entirely new that doesn't exist anywhere in any field yet. Consider exploring further and writing about what you learn. You may be creating a new theory or approach that will help you and our profession. I think this could be called the Montessori Method of continuing education—learn while doing.

Having done this myself with all of these forms, I can advocate this as a way to become if not an expert then at least close to being one in the profession. When I set out to write a book on collaboration, there weren't any books or articles talking about how best to do collaboration in our field. While collaboration was a buzzword used by many speakers and leaders in many presentations I had attended in the early 2000s, there was nothing to read about it or its practical applications in libraries. So I decided to write a book about it. I read as much as I could about collaboration in other fields, I observed what worked and what didn't in my own professional experiences, and I reached out and talked to practitioners about their own collaborative experiences. I sat and thought, and thought some more, and came up with what seemed like universal principles about collaboration, and wrote. And wrote some more, and got some help writing, and created my own continuing education opportunity for myself and, I hope, for others. The crowning affirmation of how valuable this has been is when, during an interview after my presentation, one of the participants referred to my book on collaboration and said he had studied it in his library school. Through wanting to learn more in depth myself, I had furthered not only my own learning and practice but that of future librarians. Be bold, think big, and share what you think and what you have learned with the rest of us.

CONCLUSION

These are not the only areas to expand your knowledge and expertise as a reference/public services librarian. You will, I'm sure, find other creative ways to learn and grow in a world that is never stagnant. It is an exciting time to be a librarian, and with so much changing around us, we have a professional responsibility to take active part in the changes. Use our experience and knowledge to help librarianship grow in the best ways to ensure our profession can help keep good information practices going and growing now and into the future.

Final word of advice: keep good track of your continuing education activities, whether they be formal or informal. Make sure to include a listing of them in your annual self-evaluation and make sure they occupy a prominent section in your curriculum vitae or resume. Your present supervisor and future employers have a vested interest in knowing that you have committed yourself to life-long learning and having evidence that you are a productive and creative asset to them and the profession. Plus it is fun: always an important component of learning.

Part II

Still Evolving Service Models

5

Save the Time of the Reader: Using S. R. Ranganathan's Fourth Law as the Vision for the Future of Library Reference Services

Corey Seeman

INTRODUCTION

S. R. Ranganathan's monumental 1931 work *The Five Laws of Library Science* remains one of the most powerful and inspirational works in our field. Even though he might not have envisioned the digital library of today, his work remains a beacon that guides librarians into a new world order. While each of the laws is as relevant and meaningful as they were when his work was first written, one law might have more weight in the way that I see librarian roles in this digital age. The fourth law, "save the time of the reader," captures both the image and primary goal of the library of the future. This stands as a critical principle for the future of libraries, especially in regard to reference services that we provide to our communities. I first explored this topic in a presentation given at the 3rd Global Conference on Emerging Trends for Business Librarianship (Seeman 2017). We can look far beyond the topic of business librarianship and see promising applications for all academic libraries.

Ranganathan's fourth law is one that often focuses on technical services, especially in the context of creating catalogs and the organization of information. Through these resources, we create users who are more self-sufficient in finding what they need. Without these resources, our users wouldn't be able to find books, articles, reports, or anything else in any of the media that we collect to make available to our communities. While the creation of self-service tools like catalogs is a significant investment that libraries make to save the time of our users, they are by no means perfect. We organize information the way that we understand it. The self-service library user is successful when they search for books or data in the same descriptive conventions that libraries use. But does it work for business researchers or even others in the academy? Does the patron's visioning of information align with the way that we structure it in our physical and digital libraries? Often, the answer is no.

A better way to save the time of the reader is through direct support and assistance. The popular approach to the increasingly digital library is to allow and enable patrons with the ability to browse and search more on their own. Our current model too often is one that removes the librarian from the equation, allowing the patron to search on their own. But there are many fields where this is not viable. In my own area of business, researchers have the perception that there is an abundance of information, yet they become frustrated when their desired items appear elusive. Equally frustrating is the appearance of similar or redundant information that may not be that consistent when compared closely. These information issues are especially common for entrepreneurial researchers, who are working in new and narrow markets that are not as well defined or described. This chapter reenvisions S. R. Ranganathan's fourth law as a guide for reinvigorating reference services in the 21st century. We can save the time of our researchers by being service-oriented and responsive to their research needs. Through a strong service ethos, we can better understand our users and, in turn, help them find the information and works they need. Most important, we can use this orientation to help craft the library of the future, one that will reengage our patrons and our community.

As librarians in the Information Age, we are continually struggling to find our role and our place in supporting the communities we serve. It is very possible that the answer, as many libraries have shown, comes not from serving but from teaching. This ties very closely with the speculation that our work is dwindling as students, faculty, and other community members are able to find items in a self-sufficient manner. However, there are studies, including an important one by Bandyopadhyay and Boyd-Byrnes (2016), that note that despite shrinking reference numbers there is still a strong need for mediated assistance for library services in the digital age. What is also important to consider is that not every search is the same. When a patron knows what they are looking for, they often can find that item. However, when they do not know where to begin, a self-service approach might not be a good place to begin. So in many ways, while patrons can get access to a great deal of resources independently, it may also be difficult for them to know where to go for information. This is the role that librarians can play to support the research needs of patrons. Direct support and assistance of researchers can make a big difference in their ability to get work and research done effectively and efficiently.

THE CHANGING WORLD OF LIBRARY REFERENCE AND COMMUNITY NEEDS

> *Business has always been subject to uncertainties and change. It is affected by the elements, by wars, by mass movements, by changes in the wants and desires of consumers and by government regulation. Above all, competition tends continually to modify the business structure. New methods, new products and new processes introduce new elements that undermine the supremacy of one industry or firm or even a whole system of doing business. And the trend toward increasing regulation of business by governmental bodies here and abroad must not be ignored. In short, one generalization that truly applies to all business is: Change is continuous and inevitable.*

The preceding statement was written for the introduction of an important book about libraries. The quote seems to belong to a book written over the past five to ten years. Surprisingly, the quote comes from a work that is much older. The quote is from Edwin Coman's introduction to his 1949 book, *Sources of Business Information* (Coman 1949).

The reference to the state of business, or even to business librarianship, is just as relevant and valid today as it was when the book was written 70 years ago.

It is very easy to think about change only from the librarian's perspective. The very nature of our work has changed a great deal as we have moved from a print-centric collection to a mixed-medium collection, to one that is ever increasingly electronic. And while it is easy to think that libraries are just going through more change now, the reality is that we have been going through shifts and changes for years and years. As Edwin Coman wrote about business, our change will likely continue into the future. But the bigger concern is this—will libraries be ready to meet the challenges of today and tomorrow?

We are living in a period of great change in higher education. This has a large impact both on the experience that students are receiving and in the way that services and resources are delivered to them and other community members. For many academic libraries, our facilities, and our services, are delivered in a way that seeks to balance between our traditional role as repository of resources and the new demands and needs of this information age. It is as if librarians are trying to keep one foot firmly established in two boats that appear to be moving in different directions. This balancing act will lead to difficult decisions for librarians who seek this path forward, especially with diminishing resources and greater community expectations.

Librarians are fantastic about envisioning change when they are leading the way. We have done a great job of embracing the new electronic environment in a hybrid fashion with traditional print volumes and physical media. Because we collect for the "long term," we are likely far more conservative than we might otherwise be. This possibly leads to a situation where we are likely still behind where our patrons are and where they likely wished we were. This also possibly leads to a situation where we still buy items for our collections based upon the aspirations we have for our students, our faculty, and our community rather than based upon their particular needs. Change without a sense of urgency, real or otherwise crafted, may be very slow and deliberate.

Sometimes change occurs due to external factors, conditions that are beyond a library's control. Change might be more dramatic under these circumstances. This is the situation that librarians at the Kresge Library of the University of Michigan's Ross School of Business found ourselves in when we lost our physical collection space and our student study and work space in a single summer (Seeman 2015). As a result, we had to quickly consider what services we could continue to offer and which ones that we had to let go. The resulting library is not recognizable to anyone who remembers what it looked like before. However, we rallied around to ensure that we could still meet the needs of the schools where we had the ability to do so. Without a print collection and a large student space, our service options were fewer than they had been.

When we consider academic libraries, we are often envisioning large spaces with row after row of tables where our students are hard at work. If it is a residential campus, maybe students are seeking peace and quiet. If it is a commuter campus, maybe students are seeking a place to utilize the time between obligations. In either case, it might be a place where students can gather to work on group projects or study together in groups. It is also possible that students are working with library collections, though that seems to be less and less common.

For many of our patrons, libraries may function as a useful working space. As long as they have creature comforts and their needs are met, they are content. These might include a place to do the following activities: work or play on their laptops or devices, charge electronic devices, study or do work, relax, sit, collaborate, or do just about anything else. These are not inherently library-related functions and can be provided for a campus or community by many different groups. And while librarians (myself included) relish seeing large headcounts of people in the building, there is a missed opportunity to make a connection with the campus in a meaningful way that cannot be easily replicated by others. The key there is the way that we work with our patrons, our faculty, and our students in helping them find the material that they need for their research. The reality is that the work of reference or research assistance for our community is far more complicated than it once was. We should no longer be focused on what is available in our library or via our network. We need to look beyond the traditional limits of the library if we are to truly make a difference for our patrons and support their research. This is fundamental in the way that we are changing the role and function of the library. While it may wreak havoc with our sense of tradition and our routines, it does provide our patrons with a great service that enables them to face the bigger questions.

This vision of the library as a facilitator of or a connector to resources both inside and outside is important in providing great reference services. Stability and control often accompany our traditional libraries, especially on campus, and are as rigid as the shelves of books and tables awaiting students to work. We kid ourselves that students are in the space because they want to engage with our physical objects. That is definitely the case for many of our patrons, but it seems very unlikely, in higher education, that the majority of students are doing any interaction with the physical objects. So if students are using the library as a place to study, there are other entities on campus that can perform that function. Many schools create study areas that are outside of the library and are effectively operated by ensuring that the wifi is working and that the electricity is on. Is it a library responsibility to do these two things? One might say the answer can be found in Dr. Ranganathan's five laws.

DR. RANGANATHAN'S FOURTH LAW

When Dr. Ranganathan laid out his five laws back in 1931, he planted the seeds for a real user-focused library and has inspired librarians ever since. The five laws are identified as the following:

- First law: Books are for use.
- Second law: Every person his or her book.
- Third law: Every book its reader.
- Fourth law: Save the time of the reader.
- Fifth law: The library is a growing organism.

In many regards, these laws are just as valid now as they were when Dr. Ranganathan first recorded these thoughts nearly 90 years ago. The laws are exceedingly well thought through and capture the work that we do to support the information needs of the communities that we serve. They are primarily focused on ensuring that we have the materials and resources (mentioned in the laws as books) that our community needs. These laws do not cover the changing roles and functions of a library, though you could make the argument that the fifth law is about growing and changing with the times. But the focus, I believe, is on ensuring that we have resources in our libraries that our patrons need. In exploring these laws, one law stuck out in regard to the way that our entire service operation has been set up. The fourth law captures what our service ethos is at the library and provides a path forward for reinventing reference services in the modern digital library.

The fourth law is fairly simple and straight forward. It states, "Save the time of the reader"; it is normally associated with technical services and material processing. In the world of libraries back in 1931, when Dr. Ranganathan first proposed these laws, libraries were typically organized by closed stacks systems where patrons needed to use card catalogs to explore these collections. If collections are well documented and described, items may more easily be found (or discovered) and used. If materials are described with appropriate subject headings and bibliographic data, then they will be easily discovered. But there is something else here that has drawn me to the fourth law. And this is where we get a sense of what reference needs to look like in the 21st century.

Saving the time of the reader can manifest itself in many different ways. While we can teach students to better understand the resources and how to determine the credibility of the information, the challenge is how to help the student become self-sufficient in a relatively short amount of time while they are in school. It is difficult to consider that any student could be as strong a searcher as a librarian who has years' experience in this very area. This is particularly true in business librarianship. And while the casual researcher can find items on their own, trying to assess quality, bias, and validity is often problematic. And as we all know from the kitchen, bad ingredients make for a bad dish. Trying to steer students and faculty into these "better ingredients" can be difficult.

What we have in the profession is that the questions coming to the library are not the same as the ones answered at the reference desk years ago. We no longer have people reaching out for basic information. There are a great many reference sources freely available on the Internet that are perfectly valid and viable resources. Should a student need information about a movie, IMDB is an excellent resource. Should a student need information about a particular athlete or sports team, Sports Reference (https://www.sports-reference .com/) is a tremendous resource. Should a student need to know when a certain person was born, Wikipedia tends to be very functional and easy to use. So the questions that would have come to the reference desk 30 years ago have gone away. No longer do librarians need to learn how to use myriad reference works like they might have when studying in library school. Librarians now use the same sources that students might have used on their own.

As a result of this shift, many libraries have chosen to close reference desks or replace librarians with student employees, who are equally adept at answering directional questions. This does not even come close to capturing all the questions that are central on the minds of our patrons. Given that many people can find the answers on their own to straightforward questions, there is not much of a need to save the time of the reader. However, this is where we can add value by providing a higher level of attention and care for our patrons. We can provide clarity as patrons navigate or attempt to navigate through their research. Librarians can absolutely assist patrons when answers do not come as easily as their requests become more challenging. This is the role that the librarians are uniquely qualified to serve on their campuses.

SUPPORTING STUDENTS AT THE POINT OF NEED: ONE LIBRARY'S FUTURE OF REFERENCE SERVICES

If we can assume that many questions that historically would come to the reference desk are being answered independently, we are left with a fundamental problem. What do we do with the reference desk and the reference services? This also begs the question, What do we do with the reference collection, a weighty and expensive investment in both space and money that many libraries make year in and year out? With the changes that have taken place in the modern library, many libraries have modified their traditional service models to address evolving user needs. While these decisions to eliminate traditional reference services have been well thought out and address the demonstrated needs in individual libraries, librarians might be stepping away from the patron at the time when they may need more assistance than ever.

From observations at many different academic libraries over the past decade, we have noticed a number of trends that have removed the librarian from the public view and public service functions. Among the many different work changes that have taken place are the following:

- *Creating a shared service point with circulation.* The premise behind this is that most of the questions are directional and it wastes librarian time to answer them.
- *Creating a shared service point with technology support.* This is a model that is commonly used in information commons and other combined service operations.
- *Removing librarians from the information or reference desk altogether.* With this change, you can relieve a librarian and use a staff position or, more commonly, a student worker.
- *Making interactions with librarians as needed on an appointment-only basis.* This enables people with more complicated questions to reach out if they need to.
- *Shifting the roles of the librarians to be more instructional.* In this model, librarians shift their focus from direct support of research as their primary concern to teaching research skills and information literacy.

It is very likely that none of these tasks could be taken on had we not seen a shift in the way that students and community members interact with the library. And while these represent some rewarding new roles and functions for academic libraries, does this approach by librarians meet the needs of the campuses that we serve? Self-service has changed many aspects of our lives, and it seems that libraries might not be any different. Consumers see this trend every day. For example, airline kiosks may allow passengers to use an automated system (rather than relying on a staffed help desk) to make changes to a reservation. More and more services are taking this approach. Rather than having a dedicated person available to answer simple questions, why not automate this function as much as possible? Given the direction of technology and AI (artificial intelligence), it is very likely that this self-service approach will continue to expand in all areas of life.

While we have come up with ways to answer the easy questions, have we figured out how to respond to the more complicated ones? This seems like a strange question to ask, but it is central to our work at the library in supporting student and faculty research. I would like to explore this a bit as we consider that we can see two basic types of questions from our community. In a known item search, a patron is seeking an article or a data source or something specific that is beyond their research. With known item searches, the notion of self-service works particularly well. So if someone is looking for an article or a report, it is very possible that they can fulfill their own needs. However, when someone is looking for an unknown item, they have very different needs and abilities. We live in an age where there is data everywhere, but it may not be exactly what we need. Maybe a patron is looking at a narrow area of an industry where there simply is not a great deal of attention currently paid. Maybe they are looking at an entrepreneurial area that is too new to be written on exclusively. Maybe they are looking at an economic sector that is relatively small, an area where no one is gathering data for wide distribution. Maybe they are seeking information that would be proprietary and not publicly available.

This is the conundrum in business research, especially in support of experiential learning. A great deal of business education is done with the standard business case. These are well-thought-out teaching objects where a problem is presented and data is provided along with a list of participants. There are often a set of questions that are also provided to ensure that students are thinking in the right direction. The students, in preparation for the class, canvas the case over and over again to understand everything about that particular problem. When they are put on the spot in class, they hopefully have a good enough understanding of the case to be able to answer the faculty member's question about the case. Good cases also have teaching notes, so faculty understand how to guide students to the outcome that matches the case's learning objective.

In the world of academic libraries, there are a few aspects of the business case method that are problematic. First, cases provide all the information that the student needs in order to participate in class discussion. Cases are self-sufficient learning tools that have an educational mission and they are intended to be used accordingly. Second, business cases provide very particular outcomes for companies or organizations in a specific point in time. There are cases that reflect how companies might respond to incidents or challenges that took place years ago. Third, since the cases are self-contained, there is generally no library component needed to support the students. Cases rarely have additional readings to help students better understand the situation or the solutions being proposed. Furthermore, students rarely need to conduct secondary research to understand a case study presented for class discussion. Finally, cases represent points in time with different protagonists and problems. While they can help provide information on how to operate under many conditions, cases might not be great preparation for what happens when you find yourself in unknown territory.

An alternative teaching method used by many business and professional schools is experiential or action-based learning. This is a major component in the way that business education works at the Ross School of Business at the University of Michigan. While the students use a great deal of cases during their time at Michigan, the major educational component of the Ross student is the completion of an action-learning project. At a meeting in the Ross School of Business recently, Dean Scott DeRue discussed the need for students to manage through ambiguity and complexity. With standard business cases, the problems, supporting documentation, and data as well as guiding questions are all there. In many ways, it could represent a complicated version of a Sudoku or Crosswords puzzle, complete with answer key. These are great for learning exercises, but they only represent a sampling of the variety of issues that come up in the day-to-day life of a manager. This is where experiential learning comes into play. Not only is it good for the student, but action-learning projects provide a tremendous opportunity for libraries to make new connections with the communities that they serve.

At Kresge Library Services, our librarians have been supporting experiential learning projects at the Ross School of Business for nearly 20 years. As experiential learning programs have expanded across the school, we have continued to support them and have shifted staffing to meet the needs. This strong embedded librarian program has become the central element in our service proposition to the school and the main reason why we have been able to thrive despite a dramatic reduction in the physical size of our library since 2013.

With most experiential programs at Ross, students are pulled together into groups of between four and six to a team. They work with a sponsor agency (that might be a company, nonprofit, NGO, or governmental agency) on a particular project that is of great interest or concern for that entity. Among the recent projects that we have supported, the problems that they have been charged to solve include the following:

- A nonprofit arts organization exploring fundraising improvement and operational efficiencies
- A consumer goods firm looking at expanding their product line in Peru
- A business school from Eastern Europe looking to expand services to their local entrepreneurial community
- NGO grappling with recycling and waste in the Pacific Islands
- A social enterprise trying to determine new markets for products exported from Africa
- A larger commercial bank trying to grapple with fintech changes and mobile payments in India
- A hospital in the developing world trying to better manage communication between the main facility and supporting clinics
- An online educational entity looking to support students in remote locations with easily transferable classes that may be taken for credit

Unlike business cases, the students start off with little more than a problem description that occasionally is outdated by the time the project starts. This is in sharp contrast to the standard business case that has a well-defined question and the information needed to determine the correct path to take. These experiential learning exercises are the opposite. They move and shift as the students learn more or as the sponsor's needs change. While this can frustrate students, it does mirror the way that organizations respond to different stimuli. In business and other organizations, you cannot always move forward without being impacted by other events and needs. This is the ambiguity that is critical for students to understand in order to become effective managers.

In support of their work, Ross students are assigned faculty advisors (typically two faculty members), who guide and grade their final projects. The projects run 7 weeks for daytime MBA students or up to 14 weeks for other programs. Daytime MBA students, during the 7-week program, have no other classes competing for their attention and it is scheduled during the first year of study (in the two year program). Students in the longer 14-week programs often will be taking other courses during that time period. The student teams have a number of learning partners assigned to support them (though this varies depending on the degree program). For MBA students involved in the key program, multidisciplinary action projects (MAP), each of the 80-plus teams is assigned learning partners that include a communications coach (typically a business communications faculty member), a peer advisor (second year MBA students), centralized support for any primary research they are hoping to conduct, and a librarian. The librarians play a pivotal role in the project as we guide them through available resources, within our licensed databases and beyond.

While this work is critical for teams, some teams will get all the data that they require from their sponsor (especially if the project is exploring internal efficiencies). However, this is certainly not always the case. There is a great deal of disparity among teams in the data that they need and the data that is available. If the students can leverage the librarians to get a sufficient amount of data to draw a conclusion, then the teams can put forward solutions to their sponsors that reflect sound judgement based on the best available information. This is only possible because of the dedicated connection with the librarian (Berdish and Seeman 2011).

The most important aspect of our work as embedded librarians is that Kresge librarians work with the same team over the course of the project. This avoids the need for students to repeatedly explain what they need and the scope of their project. This allows subsequent questions to be answered more quickly, a great benefit to the team. The number of teams supported by a librarian will vary, but we try to keep assignments equitable and balanced among the reference librarians. There are times during the academic year when librarians can be supporting upward of 20–30 teams at a time, though with varying needs. It is the administrative responsibility of the library director to ensure that there is balance among the librarians and the teams that they are supporting.

With the expansion of action-learning support at the Ross School of Business over the past 10–15 years, we have shifted our staff to accommodate this priority. Figure 5.1 shows how many teams Kresge librarians have supported in experiential learning programs.

This chart does not include all of our student interactions, just the number of teams that we have supported at Kresge Library Services. It also does not include the smaller projects that are class-related that do not have external sponsors. In order to fully support these action-learning projects, we have changed a few positions in the library and have grown the corps of reference librarians since I joined the library over 13 years ago. We are continually looking at converting staff positions into librarian positions in order to accommodate this growth and reduce the number of teams supported by a single librarian. Having fewer teams to support will create a situation whereby the librarian may be more helpful in supporting team projects. When a librarian has many teams to support, providing each of them with strong support can be challenging.

Where we see the value is in the connections that we make with students during this program. MBA students typically have very few library needs during the core curriculum's first 21 weeks. For these classes, there are typically no research assignments and most of the work assigned to students is from cases, textbooks, simulations. However, the last seven weeks of the core curriculum is MAP and that is where students go from having all

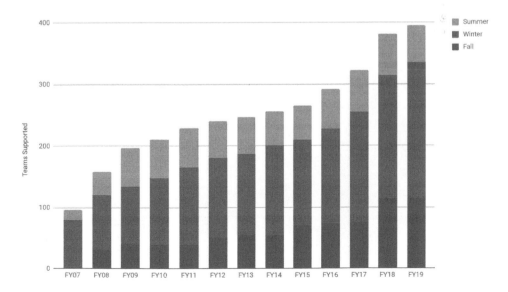

Figure 5.1   Kresge Library Services Action Learning Support FY07–FY19

the information they need for their assignments to having virtually none of it. So while students may have waited 21 weeks before interacting with a librarian, the connection actually works well because it is taking place at an established point of need. While we can go over library services and research support during student orientation, if students will not use the skills or the concepts for the better part of five months, then there is relatively little value to this type of interaction.

There are two ways that we know that we have made a very positive impact on the program. First, we score among the highest learning partners by the students who are surveyed at the end of the program. While it might be driven by low expectations of what librarians can do (given that we rarely work with students prior to the program), it is likely a result of the demonstration of solid work during the program. From our 2016 survey, we were able to extract these comments about librarian support:

- *We made a lot of difficult requests of Dee, and she was fantastic.*
- *Celia is the best. We wouldn't have been able to do this project without her.*
- *[Joel was] extremely responsive, and was willing to spend a lot of time on our requests. A surprisingly valuable resource.*
- *Halley was amazing! She was so quick and responsive to our requests. She was invaluable to our team.*

Second, and more anecdotally, we see great instances of students on our MAP teams reaching out when they are faced with additional questions and projects during their time at the Ross School of Business. This stems from the "ultimate question" of whether you would recommend that service to a friend (Reichheld and Markey 2011). We have seen this universally adopted by students as they move into their subsequent projects and courses. While repeat business is purely anecdotal, it does let us know that we have made connections with our students.

This second element actually represents a tremendous path forward for Kresge Library Services. To demonstrate this, I would like to use a different set of laws. Zingerman's is a world-class delicatessen in Ann Arbor, Michigan, that has grown into an entire suite of businesses covering quality foods. Their reputation for quality and service has enabled them to create a training operation where their philosophy may be shared and taught. Ari Weinzweig is the founding partner of Zingerman's and the coauthor of the 2010 book *A Lapsed Anarchist's Approach to Building a Great Business* (Weinzweig, Nagy, and Stiner 2010). In this book, and in their training, the authors refer to their 12 natural laws of business. The ninth law is one that has the most impact on my philosophy: "success means you get better problems" (ZingTrain 2016). This has a clear connection to what we do at Kresge Library Services and how our success has contributed to our growth as a unit despite a large space contraction. With the success that we have had with MAP and other experiential learning programs, we have gotten broad attention and questions. Our ability to solve the research needs of students makes them more likely to reconnect when they find themselves with another information need. Our ability to support student teams means that administrators will seek to include us when new programs are being launched. While reference questions are declining in other libraries, our reference interactions are increasing because we have made this connection. And as Zingerman's ninth law would indicate, each success means that people will present us with more difficult questions. And that is what librarians should be promoting across the schools that they support. And unlike providing a place for students to work, collaborate, and charge their devices, no group can do this work as well as librarians.

A PUBLIC-SERVICE APPROACH TO THE FOURTH LAW

The approach that we have taken at Kresge Library Services is exactly Dr. Ranganathan's fourth law—"save the time of the reader." This has provided a connection with our community that is quite strong and has crystalized our role and function at the school despite changes to the library. It would be very possible for our librarians to stress the need for information literacy programs at the start of any degree program. However, at the beginning of any program, that can be esoteric and abstract. This is especially true in many business curricula, where the assignments are self-contained learning objects and the need for additional resources or information assistance is minor.

To this end, the reference ethos at our library is all about saving the time of the reader so that they can spend their time on analysis of the resources to present the best solutions for the company, agency, organization, or other body. There are many different ways to save the time of the reader. First, we can help them find resources they need, especially if they are starting out with a project or learning about an industry. Second, we can help them track down articles they cannot locate. Seemingly, many librarians might see this as a technology problem where a better link resolver or other plugins might work effectively to help the students. But as most librarians know, the search for an article can be messy. So who better than a librarian to navigate those waters. Third, we can help them understand the value of particular resources. This is an information literacy skill that can be done on the fly. As a student or patron is exploring conflicting information, we can help them interpret what they are reading so they can draw the best possible conclusion. Fourth, we can provide reference services to ensure students spend more time doing analysis. While finding data and reports and other information resources might be quicker now than had been historically the case, it invites the faculty to encourage or demand a higher level of analysis. If the data acquisition phase can be reduced, then the data analysis phase can be expanded. Fifth, the librarian can help the patron find information well beyond the walls of the library. We are routinely searching through our licensed material to support teams, but also exploring resources well beyond. This is particularly important when looking to support questions related to global development or very narrow or entrepreneurial subjects. Librarians are excellent searchers, and we can find things that many researchers cannot easily find. This is where we can provide value by winnowing down a seemingly limitless set of readings into a group that address the subject.

While we can train students to better understand the trappings of modern research, it becomes increasingly unlikely that we could ever train our students to be as adept in searching as librarians. Thinking about any subject specialty, such as business or economics, it is increasingly difficult to envision a scenario where students would be able to answer difficult questions with the training that can be provided in a relatively short amount of time. So rather than preparing students for all the potential questions that they might be getting over the course of a day or week or term, librarians need to be available to assist them at their point of need. That is a much more powerful connection that we can make with our community and one that will assist the students in producing a higher quality product. If we can save the time of the reader, then we can allow them to focus more on the question at hand. Our role can be not only to help identify resources but also to provide understanding of what is and what is not available.

Most fundamentally, librarians can demonstrate expertise that will be a highly sought after commodity in higher education. If a library can demonstrate this skill and value to the community, then university or school administrators might be less likely to question the value of the librarians and what they are contributing to the school. While this can be a great deal of work for the librarians and the library staff, it has paid dividends repeatedly as program administrators, faculty, and students alike see the value of the library and support its role and place in the academic enterprise.

CONCLUSION

Researchers in all areas (especially business) benefit from librarians who are engaged with their work and understand students' directions. At Kresge Library Services, our role is clearly connected to supporting students' research needs and aspirations. While our students are sometimes interested in learning how to do the research themselves, most of the time they focus their energies on analysis. Working with them through these projects has been tremendously satisfying and beneficial to the library unit.

While much of the resources that libraries acquire are electronically available, the easy ability to acquire readings and data by students and faculty does not necessarily translate into people having all the data that they need. Library information is organized and arranged and presented in a way that we understand it. But it may not be in the way that the user is approaching the problem. The self-service library user is successful when they search for the data in the same basic conventions. However, many business researchers use information and search for it in a very narrow and different manner. So in many regards, their work does not lend itself to the self-service model. We need to understand the use, their needs, and create an empathetic and helpful approach. The best way to do this is not to teach them how to think like a librarian but for us to listen to what they need and help them find it. That is how we make a meaningful connection to our community, one that attracts more attention from other members of our community.

Saving the time of the researcher happens at two critical junctures. First, we need to have systems reasonably in place to find materials. We would be poorly serving our community if they could not find items on their own. However, as we struggle to make everything easy to track down and find, there is a law of diminishing returns as we move toward a completely automated system of self-service research. Second, we need to make ourselves available to the researcher in a manner that works for them. What is an essential element to our program is the notion of connecting with an individual librarian. This alone enables a relationship to build over the life of the project and one that enables the librarian to better meet the research needs of the student or the faculty member.

As we consider the future of academic librarianship, it is very clear that we have made great strides and changes over the past 20 or 30 years as we welcomed the strong adoption of electronic resources into the mix of traditional print resources. While this has greatly enhanced our patrons' ability to retrieve items more effectively and independently, there is too often an assumption that patrons do not need our assistance. When patrons are doing more straightforward research, this might indeed be the case. However, as the scope of their projects grows more complicated, this is a great opportunity for librarians to assist their students, faculty, and other community members in finding the information they need. The future of reference service is very much the past, connecting our readers to the resources that enable them to complete their projects. We should strive to ensure that they have more time to do the analysis by providing critical support and assistance in the data and information collection phase. If we can save the time of the reader, then we can make a profound impact on their work and their ability to do greater work.

REFERENCES

Bandyopadhyay, Aditi, and Mary Kate Boyd-Byrnes. 2016. "Is the Need for Mediated Reference Service in Academic Libraries Fading Away in the Digital Environment?" *Reference Services Review* 44 (4): 596–626.

Berdish, Laura, and Corey Seeman. 2011. "Kresge Library's Embedded Librarian Program: A Student-Centered Approach." In *Embedded Librarianship: Moving Beyond One-Shot Instruction*, edited by Cassandra Kvenild and Kaijsa Calkins, 153–164. Chicago: Association of College and Research Libraries.

Coman, Edwin T. 1949. *Sources of Business Information*. New York: Prentice-Hall.

Ranganathan, S. R. 1931. *The Five Laws of Library Science*. Madras, India: Madras Library Association, and London: Edward Goldston.

Reichheld, Frederick F., and Rob Markey. 2011. *The Ultimate Question 2.0: How Net Promoter Companies Thrive in a Customer-Driven World*. Boston: Harvard Business Press.

Seeman, Corey. 2015. "The Ethereal Library: Thinking Creatively When You Have No Space to Think," In Proceedings of the Conference for Entrepreneurial Librarians. https://libjournal.uncg.edu/index.php/pcel/article/view/1186.

Seeman, Corey. 2017. "Save the Time of the Reader: Using S. R. Ranganathan's Fourth Law to Build the Business Library of the Future." Presentation at the 3rd Global Conference on Emerging Trends for Business Librarianship, Ahmedabad, India, November 21–22, 2017. http://hdl.handle.net/2027.42/139587.

Weinzweig, Ari, Ian Nagy, and Ryan Stiner. 2010. *A Lapsed Anarchist's Approach to Building a Great Business*. Ann Arbor, MI: Zingerman's Press.

ZingTrain. [c. 2016]. Zingerman's 12 Natural Laws of Business: Now Yours to Harness! http://info.zingtrain.com/zingermans-12-natural-laws-of-business.

FURTHER READING

Bhatt, R. K. 2011. "Relevance of Ranganathan's Laws of Library Science in Library Marketing." *Library Philosophy & Practice* (July): 23–29.

Carr, Patrick L. 2014. "Reimagining the Library as a Technology: An Analysis of Ranganathan's Five Laws of Library Science within the Social Construction of Technology Framework." *Library Quarterly* 84 (2): 152–164.

McMenemy, David. 2007. "Ranganathan's Relevance in the 21st Century." *Library Review* 56 (2): 97–101.

Rimland, Emily. 2007. "Ranganathan's Relevant Rules." *Reference & User Services Quarterly* 46 (4): 24–26.

Walter, Scott. 2012. "Ranganathan Redux: The "Five Laws" and the Future of College & Research Libraries." *College & Research Libraries* 73 (3): 213–5.

6

Reference Next

Marie L. Radford

INTRODUCTION: WHAT'S NEXT FOR REFERENCE?

This chapter takes a speculative look at some trends that will have a growing impact on reference services. First, I take a quick look at innovative initiatives found in the library literature that foreshadow a vibrant library future and then discuss four of my recent research directions: intelligent personal assistants (IPAs), including smart speakers such as Alexa or Siri, crowdsourced reference, scholarly identity (SI) support, and understanding and mitigating microaggressions for service excellence to marginalized populations.

Checking out the current literature on reference service innovations, there are some tantalizing hints about what might be in store at a library near you. *Eek! The robots are coming!* According to Calvert (2017), it is inevitable that robots and devices that use artificial intelligence (AI) will be taking a larger role in libraries in the years to come. Robots are already being used in some libraries, performing functions such as shelf reading, retrieving large boxes, and serving as personal assistants or guides for library users. As these technologies grow in sophistication, soon we will see more applications, for example, robots retrieving and reshelving books, media, and other items of varying sizes, plus assisting users with physical disabilities.

Another promising futuristic application for the early technology adopters among us is virtual reality (VR) that uses computer-generated simulations of a digital world, which you can interact with via headsets and peripherals. Figueroa (2018) interviewed librarians on their use of VR in school, public, and academic settings. He observed,

> Throughout this period of growth and expansion, libraries and librarians have once again demonstrated their adaptability to new information formats and user needs with projects that reflect the various directions VR has moved. Whether it is classroom use of Google Expeditions, new educational spaces and lending programs on academic campuses, or a demonstrated commitment to equitable access to this new technology in public libraries, librarians have taken on VR as a new way to engage their users. (Figueroa 2018, 26)

For examples of six VR projects within health science libraries, take a look at Lessick and Kraft (2017). Projects they describe include crafting interactive games for learning tasks, using dashboards for a data literacy program, creating a next-generation repository for nontraditional scholarly products, and more. The authors "hope these imaginative virtual projects will illuminate new ideas and inspire other librarians to consider, utilize, develop, and spread new technology solutions that reshape library services, making them more responsive, nimble, and effective" (Lessick and Kraft 2017, 408).

It does not take a crystal ball to predict that, due to the ubiquitous spread of smart phones and tablet computers, there will continue to be an increase in the use of and demand for mobile services that can be accessed anytime and anywhere via pocket connectivity. Guo, Liu, and Bielefield (2018) surveyed 138 members of the Urban Libraries Council and found that about 95 percent of them have one or more mobile websites, catalogs, or apps. These are of two types: traditional library services adapted for access from mobile devices or totally new services created for mobile device/platform use (Guo, Liu, and Bielefield 2018, 79). An example of how mobile apps might be used in reference services is provided by Kani (2017), who did a feasibility study of the use of the Evernote app as a method of collaborating and capturing citations during a research consultation at an academic library.

NEXT QUESTIONS—VOICE-ENABLED SMART SPEAKERS (A.K.A. INTELLIGENT PERSONAL ASSISTANTS)

My fascination with reference work present and future has always had a focus on the encounter between librarians and users. I have studied reference questions and the questioning process, with an eye to how we can improve our understanding, build positive human relationships, and provide accurate answers (e.g., see Radford and Connaway, 2005–2008; Radford et al. 2011). The universe of ways for people to seek information through questioning is expanding with the advent of intelligent personal assistants, a.k.a. voice-enabled smart speakers (e.g., Alexa, Siri). These devices are finding a consumer market, and estimates are that Alexa is now available around the world in about 80 countries. It is estimated that millions of IPAs have been purchased, with features that vary by region (Amazon 2019). Looking ahead to our technological future, these devices are likely to continue to multiply rapidly, corresponding to the intensifying acceptance of smart phones and Bluetooth and advances in AI and machine learning. There is not much literature on these devices in the library and information science (LIS) field (see, however, Hennig's [2018] *Siri, Alexa, and Other Digital Assistants: The Librarian's Quick Guide*). Calvert (2017, 170) notes that AI applications for libraries range from IPAs that now deliver simple questions and answers with programmed responses (e.g., directional questions) plus a future that will hold advanced assistance from "an autonomous device that incorporates human-robot interaction at a higher cognitive level." My research team completed an initial exploratory study that is beginning to investigate the implications and impact of IPAs on children's use and potential learning, especially with an eye to thinking about considerations that surround the potential use of IPAs in libraries. Allen and Sarang (2018) note that when this technology was placed in the children's room of a public library, users became interested. Others believe that libraries are situated to provide introduction to IPAs and their skills, including school libraries (Hennig 2018; Hoy 2018; Scardilli 2018). Our initial literature review also revealed that all is not sweetness and light and that there may also be a dark side to the use of these devices. We found that there were concerns about the accuracy of the information provided (Boyd and Wilson 2018), privacy (Enis 2018), and security threats (Chung et al. 2017). Children in particular may be at risk, as they are an especially vulnerable population whose privacy and safety are of paramount importance, with one article dubbing IPAs as "creepy" technology (Yip et al. 2019). Additionally, children can have difficulty with Alexa understanding them and can be confused about human versus machine-based feelings (Elgan 2018).

We found a huge gap in the LIS literature, especially the need to discover more about how children are using these devices and what might be potential uses for IPAs with this pre-literate group. We know that children have questions (sometimes incessant questions that may exasperate busy parents, caregivers, or librarians). Could IPAs be of value to help answering their questions? What might be the benefits and downsides to consider?

For our exploratory work, we discovered that Amazon has a customer review site for Amazon's Echo dot Kids/Alexa,[1] their product designed for children. We took a look at 200 customer reviews (100 positive [P] and 100 critical [C]) from 1,505 total reviews (1,029 P, 476 C) to see what parents/caregivers were saying about how children were using Alexa. We found an already-existing list of codes from Common Sense Media (2017) and NPR (2018) and qualitatively applied them to the reviews, using the constant comparisons method (Charmaz 2014). So, what do parents/caregivers report about children's use of Alexa in these reviews? Our analysis of customer reviews revealed, in descending order of frequency, that children were using Alexa to play music, hear stories, get information/answers, connect with others inside the home, and play games. Parents/caregivers said that children are active users of Alexa (e.g., singing/dancing to music), as opposed to passive users of television or other screens where they watch videos. One said that her son was "dancing so hard it feels like the chandelier is going to fall down." As noted in the literature, other parents/caregivers said that children experience problems that included (in descending frequency) playing music, hearing stories, playing games, getting information, connecting with others inside/outside the home, and controlling lights/electronics. Children were, in some cases, unable to request particular songs or had voice recognition issues that might be frustrating. One review stated, "I have had several instances where my child was in tears because she felt that this Alexa didn't like her because she wouldn't do the right thing." The children were seemingly viewing Alexa as a person (generally a female due to the feminine voice), not a machine, and expecting human behaviors.

These initial preliminary results both hold tantalizing opportunities for voice-enabled devices, especially for pre-literate or beginning readers who are unable to look information up in books or via computers, and raise important questions about safety and privacy concerns, as well as gendered anthropomorphic consequences when children feel upset by Alexa's response or lack of response. A few innovative libraries have already begun using IPAs to answer fact-based and current event questions. Questions that my team is seeking to explore next include the following: How are, and how should, libraries use IPAs in services to children? What concerns exist? What is the potential for IPAs in addressing children's information needs, including children with disabilities? What is the potential for use of smart speakers for reference services? Will these devices prove to be beneficial or deleterious to future library service?

NEXT COLLABORATION—CROWDSOURCING

Reference has typically been a one-on-one experience, with one librarian assisting one library user. Crowdsourced social question-and-answer (SQA) platforms, such as Yahoo! Answers, invite the crowd of experts and others to join together to give more complete answers. How might libraries use social reference or crowdsourced reference to engage users in our community of practice? Our research team explored the current state of virtual reference service (VRS), compared to SQA sites, endeavoring to discover how VRS could become more collaborative and tap more effectively into librarians' subject expertise. We also tried to find out whether VRS could be more sustainable through collaboration with SQA services (Radford, Connaway, and Shah 2011–2014; Radford et al. 2017). We conducted 102 in-depth phone interviews with 50 VRS librarians and 52 VRS/SQA users and coded them using the critical incident technique (Flanagan 1954) and the constant comparisons method (Charmaz 2014). Findings suggest that librarians welcome collaboration with one another, including when a question is within their areas of expertise, which surprised us. They believe that collaboration can lead to great answers rather than merely good answers. One librarian said she engages in consultation when "you've exhausted the resources that you are aware of and you don't want to be a dead-end for the patron." Another commented, "We kind of play off of each other so we come up with new things to try. I think it's successful because we understand the need, the question, and trying different sources and keywords. It's been my experience that if you bring in another reference librarian on a question, they won't quit either." We also discovered, to our delight, that librarians were open to the idea of crowdsourcing questions beyond the librarian community, provided that the person answering the question from the crowd had expertise and credentials. We concluded that given tight resources, librarians should consider innovations, such as crowdsourcing, suggested by SQA sites, that might enhance our potential to raise the quality and quantity of referrals and greatly increase collaboration within, as well as beyond, librarians and non-librarian experts to improve the overall user experience.

NEXT SERVICES—SCHOLARLY IDENTITY SUPPORT

With today's increasing scrutiny on scholarly productivity and the value of libraries, there is a growing (and a bit stress-inducing) emphasis on metrics and altmetrics for demonstrating impact, especially in academic circles. My research team is exploring a newly emerging role for reference librarians to support SI practices that enable librarians, faculty, and students to use social media platforms (Academia.edu, ResearchGate, ORCID, Twitter, etc.) both to promote their work and to learn about the work of others (see Radford et al. 2018; Radford et al. 2019). For this project, we defined SI work as scholars' efforts to build and promote their reputation, networks, and research through use of digital tools and academic social networking sites.

It does not take a crystal ball to see the "writing on the screen," that these practices will continue for the foreseeable future, although I cannot guess which platforms will become most prominent or how much metrics will continue to drive tenure, promotion, and hiring decisions. As a result of a finding from the dissertation of Stephanie Mikitish (2017) that studied the value of academic libraries for PhD students, I became aware that doctoral students desired help with creating and managing their digital scholarly identity. I wondered in what possible ways academic librarians could provide SI-related assistance as part of their suite of services to PhD students and faculty. So, my team set out to investigate ways that academic librarians could help scholars navigate this evolving and potentially treacherous landscape through an exploratory series of 30 interviews with 10 faculty, 10 doctoral students, and 10 academic librarians. We based our investigation on a theoretical framework using Goffman's (1967) impression management, face work, and face threats constructs. We asked about participant's needs when managing SI, about effective practices, and about advantages and pitfalls of SI involvement. Also, we asked the academic librarians about their personal SI work and what services they were already providing to faculty and PhD students at their institutions.

The interviews were qualitatively analyzed by a team of four coders, using the constant comparisons method (Charmaz 2014), developing and enlarging a set of codes using NVivo software. Our 30 participants were predominantly female and Caucasian, with about half being 26–34 years of age, although the librarians, recruited from the ACRL listserv, were a bit older. Faculty and PhD students were social scientists, recruited from the communication discipline. When asked which platforms they were using for SI work, they reported that Twitter, Facebook, Research Gate, Instagram, and Academia.edu were used in descending order, from 77 percent (n = 23) to 50 percent (n = 15). Three major themes arose in the analysis: benefits of SI work, drawbacks of SI work, and library service roles. Benefits included connecting with other researchers, disseminating academic activities, sharing/exchanging materials with other researchers, and facilitating tenure/promotion. For example, one PhD student commented, "I can connect with people who share similar research interests with me through those academic websites. I can see their research interests and papers. Whenever I use those online tools it gives me feelings like I'm part of these people and makes me feel like I belong." Drawbacks included time constraints, concern with for-profit business models, context collapse, confusion, and concern over damage to reputation. On confusion, one librarian said, "The landscape is now so crowded that it's difficult to choose, select, and create a consistent and comprehensive identity." Our participants also brought up ethical considerations that included danger of commodifying people via "branding," copyright peril, privilege and power dynamics, and data capture. To illustrate the concern (and some ambivalence) over for-profit models, one librarian said, "I think part of it is that I feel some hesitation to engage with ResearchGate and Academia.edu based on their corporate ties and for-profit business models. I know Twitter and Facebook are the same, so it's not a consistent feeling, but I worry about the profit motivations of ResearchGate and Academia.edu."

We discovered that all 10 of our librarian participants were already engaged in providing SI support to faculty and PhD students, including offering workshops, giving orientations to altmetrics and the scholarly landscape, and providing information on digital tools. Additionally, nine out of ten were helping users to package content. One librarian described their workshop as being "about tools and strategies for managing scholarly profiles, deciding where to publish, avoiding predatory publishers, metrics/altmetrics, social media." PhD students had not really thought about the library as a source of help but, when asked, two wanted help with individual consultations, two wanted an orientation to altmetrics and the scholarly landscape, and one wanted help creating a personal website. The faculty members desired help with copyright, open access, and information on digital tools. One faculty member said, "The biggest [barriers] are the publisher agreements that say what can or can't be posted. Ideally [I] would want to be able to post everything."

Future directions for this project will involve an analysis of Twitter activity of academics, since that platform was the top site used for their SI work. We also plan to further explore relationships and services with academic librarians and to develop materials to assist with discovering and using digital tools. Hinchliffe (see Radford et al. 2019) notes that as soon as we publish anything, we already have an online identity. Our choice is whether or not we want to have an unmanaged online identity or a managed one. She also notes that we create our digital footprint but that others create content about us that constitutes our digital shadow. Scholars need help with these issues! Forward-looking librarians definitely have a role to play in demystifying SI work and in educating users about their footprints and shadows, as we journey forward in our digital future.

NEXT STEPS FOR SERVICE EXCELLENCE—MITIGATING MICROAGGRESSIONS FOR EQUITABLE SERVICE

There is an extensive amount of writing and research on the components of the reference encounter that help to promote service excellence. What more could we do to make our services more open and welcoming to all users, especially those from underrepresented communities? I have engaged in years of investigations of interpersonal communication dimensions that lead to successful and satisfying interactions from library users' perspectives, as well as from librarian viewpoints, which culminated in *Library Conversations: Reclaiming Interpersonal Communication Theory for Understanding Professional Encounters* (Radford and Radford 2017). To continue to improve our services in the future, I wondered what have we not considered, especially given noted gaps in library services to marginalized populations.

My previous research involving analysis of live chat virtual reference transcripts, interviews, focus groups, and surveys applied Goffman's (1967) theoretical framework of face work and face threats. My work identified behaviors and practices that either facilitate or create barriers to reference success. I've come to believe that microaggressions are a particular type of face threat barrier. Microaggressions are intentional or non-intentional verbal, nonverbal, or environmental slights or insults to individuals of marginalized groups (see Belluomini 2014; Sue et al. 2007). According to Sue et al. (2007), there are three types of microaggressions: micro-assaults, micro-insults, and micro-invalidations. These are generally communicated verbally (e.g., racial epithets), nonverbally (e.g., dismissive body language, such as an eye roll), or environmentally (e.g., displaying offensive symbols, such as a swastika; Giraldo-Kerr 2014).

I wondered how microaggressions happened in library service contexts. What types of microaggressions do library users experience in face-to-face (FtF) or online settings? What guidelines can libraries and librarians follow to mitigate this behavior? My research team investigated these questions through transcript analysis and focus groups. We first examined a set of 1,710 live chat sessions (randomly selected from 2006 to 2016) from OCLC's Questionpoint, focusing on 148 that contained relational barriers. The team qualitatively coded the transcripts using NVivo software to develop and apply a typology of codes, understanding that microaggressions are subtle and difficult to identify. We found no identifiable microaggressions in 97 percent (n = 1,655) of the 1,710 transcripts and no demonstrations of overtly discriminatory behavior by librarians. However, we did find that 3 percent (n = 55) included microaggressions, the largest proportion being verbal microaggressions, followed by nonverbal, and a few that were environmental. To illustrate a verbal microaggression, one live chat librarian was asked about legal resources for divorce in California, at a time when marriage equality was legal, and replied, "Also keep in mind that California is a community property state so most property and debts acquired during your marriage needs to be divided up between you and your husband." This was coded as a microaggression, since although the librarian had no way of knowing that information, the assumption was made that the divorcing couple must be heterosexual, with a level of economic status to own property. Of course, the user might have been in a heterosexual marriage and might own property, but if that had not been the case this could constitute a potential insult. An example of a nonverbal microaggression might be hanging up abruptly, and environmental microaggressions generally occurred when librarians inadvertently created a hostile environment by ignoring a user's question or their confusion over technical instructions. As another example, one of my master's students, Kevin Chung, recently had an experience in which he was offered Chinese resources when inquiring about ESL materials in a live chat. He said that this was disconcerting since he had not asked for Chinese resources and that since his last name was part of his e-mail address the librarian had assumed he wanted those specific resources without asking.

As a second part of this research, we conducted five focus groups (two with undergraduates and two with librarians). We had 28 participants from marginalized populations in the United States (including black/African American, Latinx, LBGTQ, and Asian individuals). Both the student and librarian groups had much to say about environmental, nonverbal, and verbal microaggressions that they have experienced in library settings. As an example of an environmental microaggression, one participant, who identified as a queer person, said, "[My library] lists all of LGBT history under sexual deviancy, next to literature about prostitution or stuff like that. . . . We don't even have that extensive of LGBT history in our library, and it's not uncommon for LGBT history to not be documented or to be documented incorrectly in library systems. . . . It seems unfortunate that we have to document our own history because the library system is failing to do so." Another student reported a nonverbal microinsult as follows:

> Me and my friends would stay in the library after school. We were mostly Black and Spanish. We didn't do anything bad, but sometimes we were talking or laughing, and the librarian would stare at us. We felt uncomfortable. Being watched like that felt similar to walking into a store & being watched. . . . White kids were also in the library with us and they weren't watched like that. It was like there was extra security on us, everyone else was just regular security. The librarian would walk more rounds around our area. She watched us more closely. This was all very nonverbal, and that felt more uncomfortable. I felt her gaze. It wasn't just side-eye.

From the librarian focus groups, examples were given of microaggressions by users, colleagues, and institutions (e.g., library policies, professional organizations, librarianship culture). While at the desk, a user told one of the participants, "No, I'll wait for a real librarian." Another had similar experiences where "someone can look at me and decide—I think sometimes it's the fact that I'm an Asian-American woman and I'm very young, and they made the assumption that . . . I could not possibly be well-qualified enough to help them." Two participants noted that "there are so many more [microaggressions] . . . from colleagues" than from students. Participants addressed tone policing, when a person of color is reprimanded for or has to curb their vocal inflection. Focus group participants were told that they seemed "angry," "overly aggressive," and "intimidating." One recalled,

"I spent a tremendous amount of energy, to the point where I'd be physically exhausted, trying to phrase—trying to figure out how to choose my words and deliver them in a way that would be accepted, right? So that my message was received. So, I spent a ton of time formulating the way that people talk in academic libraries so that people would hear what I have to say."

From this research, we developed a set of suggested guidelines for mitigating microaggressions as follows:

From the literature:

- Present resources from various perspectives (Ettarh 2014; Sue 2010).
- Avoid assumptions of identity or ability (Ettarh 2014; Sue 2010).
- Be aware that nonverbal invalidations transfer to VRS (Belluomini 2014).

From our research findings:

- Treat all users/colleagues with respect.
- Raise awareness of microaggressions in FtF and virtual contexts.
- Construct and implement service guidelines that incorporate voices of users and librarians from marginalized populations.
- Respond with open questions when unsure.
- Avoid wording implying identity assumptions.
- Suggest specific alternative resource (not just "look elsewhere").
- Allow time for user reply.
- Listen to feedback on information needs and calls for help.
- Provide needed information without implying this is a hassle.
- Suggest generalized resources for broad questions.

My team's research found that microaggressions of all types may occur in library encounters whether virtual or FtF. Even well-meaning individuals may not be aware of how their behavior might impact others. It is important to raise awareness of these behaviors and implement effective training and guidelines to ensure that future reference services are more welcoming and inclusive for all users, respecting their individual identities.

CONCLUSION

There is ample evidence that librarians will continue to push boundaries to improve reference services using ground-breaking practices, some of which are already in place today. One expected constant for the foreseeable future is the continued use of all modes of reference services, including virtual modes, such as live chat and e-mail reference. Bowers Sharpe and Norton (2017), in their longitudinal study that looked at 15 years of e-mail service, found that volume of e-mail use has remained very steady over time. They discovered that e-mail questions are more closely mirroring the type of queries that are received in FtF encounters, including growing numbers of research-related questions. It is important, as these services have matured and are now considered traditional, to continually innovate to better match the ways that users want to engage with library services and to make access discoverable and convenient. Rich and Lux (2018) profiled Bowling Green State University's implementation of a pop-up chat widget that was embedded in webpages, catalogs, and databases that resulted in more than double the number of chat questions, from students who were on or off campus. They will come if we build access that is point of use, multimodal, and on demand. In a study of how new roles in reference and liaison academic librarians are shifting, Johnson (2018, 91) concludes that our goal of "connecting people to information hasn't changed, but that the methods employed have and will need to continue to change." The future is surely to be an exciting one, especially if we are not content to merely react to (or resist?) all the changes that are expected (and unexpected) and if we seek to embrace these transformations as change agents.

ACKNOWLEDGMENTS

Thank you to my Cynergy research team members Mary Chayko, Lynn Silipigni Connaway, Diana Floegel, Vanessa Kitzie, and Stephanie Mikitish for participating in the projects described in this chapter. Thanks also to Sarah Barriage and Daniel Houli for their continued participation with IPA work, to Gabriella Shriner for helping with the literature review, and to Diana Floegel for assisting with references and formatting.

NOTE

1. The customer review site for Amazon's Echo dot Kids/Alexa product is available at the following link: https://www.amazon.com/Echo-Kids-smart-speaker-Alexa/product-reviews/B077JFK5YH/ref=cm_cr_getr_d_paging_btm_next_2?ie=UTF8&reviewerType=all_reviews&filterByStar=positive&pageNumber=2

REFERENCES

Allen, Susan, and Avneet Sarang. 2018. "Serving Patrons Using Voice Assistants at Worthington." *Online Searcher* 42 (6): 49–52.

Amazon. 2019. "Supported Alexa Featured by Country for 'International Version' Echo Devices." https://www.amazon.com/gp/help/customer/display.html?nodeId=202207000.

Belluomini, Ellen. 2014. "Microaggressions and the Internet." *New Social Worker*. https://www.socialworker.com/feature-articles/technology-articles/microaggressions-and-the-internet/.

Boyd, Matt, and Nick Wilson. 2018. "Just Ask Siri? A Pilot Study Comparing Smartphone Digital Assistants and Laptop Google Searches for Smoking Cessation Advice." *PLoS One* 13 (3). https://doi.org/10.1371/journal.pone.0194811.

Bowers Sharpe, Krista, and Christina Norton. 2017. "Examining Our Past, Considering Our Future: A Study of Email Reference, 2000–2015." *Internet Reference Services Quarterly* 22 (4): 133–165.

Calvert, Philip. 2017. "Robots, the Quiet Workers, Are You Ready to Take Over?" *Public Library Quarterly* 36 (2): 167–172.

Charmaz, Kathy. 2014. *Constructing Grounded Theory: A Practical Guide Through Qualitative Analysis*, 2nd edition. Thousand Oaks, CA: Sage.

Chung, Hyunji, Michaela Iorga, Jeffrey Voas, and Sangjin Lee. 2017. "Alexa, Can I Trust You?" *Computer* 50 (9): 100–104.

Common Sense Media. 2017. *The Common Sense Census: Media Use by Kids Age Zero to Eight*. San Francisco: Common Sense Media. https://www.commonsensemedia.org/research/the-common-sense-census-media-use-by-kids-age-zero-to-eight-2017.

Elgan, Mike. 2018. "The Case against Teaching Kids to Be Polite to Alexa." *Fast Company*, June 24, 2018. https://www.fastcompany.com/40588020/the-case-against-teaching-kids-to-be-polite-to-alexa

Enis, Matt. 2018. "Voice Activated," *Library Journal*, April 3, 2018. https://www.libraryjournal.com/?detailStory=voice-activated-technology-focus.

Ettarh, Fobazi. 2014. "Making a New Table: Intersectional Librarianship." *In the Library with the Lead Pipe: An Open Access, Open Peer Reviewed Journal*. http://www.inthelibrarywiththeleadpipe.org/2014/making-a-new-table-intersectional-librarianship-3/.

Figueroa, Miguel. 2018. "In a Virtual World: How School, Academic, and Public Libraries are Testing Virtual Reality in Their Communities." *American Libraries* 49 (3/4): 26–33. https://americanlibrariesmagazine.org/2018/03/01/virtual-world-virtual-reality-libraries/.

Flanagan, John C. 1954. "The Critical Incident Technique." *Psychological Bulletin* 51 (4): 327–358.

Giraldo-Kerr, Anna. 2014. "6 Things to Learn about Microaggressions." *The Huffington Post*, June 19, 2014. http://www.huffingtonpost.com/anna-giraldo-kerr/six-things-to-learn-about_b_5512057.

Goffman, Erving. 1967. *Interaction Ritual: Essays in Face-to-Face Behavior.* Chicago: Aldine Publishing Company.

Guo, Ya Jun, Van Quan Liu, and Arlene Bielefield. 2018. "The Provision of Mobile Services in US Urban Libraries." *Information Technology & Libraries* 37 (2): 78–93.

Hennig, Nicole. 2018. *Siri, Alexa, and other Digital Assistants: The Librarian's Quick Guide.* Santa Barbara: Libraries Unlimited.

Hoy, Matthew B. 2018. "Alexa, Siri, Cortona, and More: An Introduction to Voice Assistants." *Medical Reference Services Quarterly* 37 (1): 81–88.

Johnson, Anna Marie. 2018. "Connections, Conversations, and Visibility: How the Work of Academic Reference and Liaison Librarians Is Evolving." *Reference & User Services Quarterly* 58 (2): 91–102.

Kani, Justin. 2017. "Evernote in the Research Consultation: A Feasibility Study." *Reference Services Review* 45 (1): 67–78.

Lessick, Susan, and Michelle Kraft. 2017. "Facing Reality: The Growth of Virtual Reality and Health Sciences Libraries." *Journal of the Medical Library Association*, 105 (4): 407–417.

Mikitish, Stephanie. 2017. "Information Engagement: How Social Science Doctoral Students Seek, Filter, Access, and Organization Information." PhD dissertation, Rutgers, The State University of New Jersey.

NPR. 2018. *The Smart Audio Report.* NPR and Edison Research. https://www.nationalpublicmedia.com/wp-content/uploads/2018/07/Smart-Audio-Report-from-NPR-and-Edison-Research-Spring-2018_Downloadable-PDF.pdf.

Radford, Marie L., and Lynn Silipigini Connaway. 2005–2008. "Seeking Synchronicity: Evaluating Virtual Reference Services from User, Non-User, and Librarian Perspectives." http://www.oclc.org/research/activities/synchronicity.

Radford, Marie L., Lynn Silipigni Connaway, Patrick Confer, Susanna Sabolsci-Boros, and Hannah Kwon. 2011. "'Are We Getting Warmer?' Query Clarification in Live Chat Virtual Reference." *Reference & User Services Quarterly* 50 (3): 259–279.

Radford, Marie L., Lynn Silipigni Connaway, Stephanie Mikitish, Mark Alpert, Chirag Shah, and Nicole A. Cooke. 2017. "Shared Values, New Vision: Collaboration and Communities of Practice in Virtual Reference and SQA." *Journal of the Association for Information Science and Technology* 68 (2): 438–449.

Radford, Marie L., Lynn Silipigni Connaway, and Chirag Shah. 2011–2014. "Cyber Synergy: Seeking Sustainability through Collaboration between Virtual Reference and Social Q&A Sites." http://www.oclc.org/research/activities/synergy/default.htm.

Radford, Marie L., Lisa Janicke Hinchliffe, Kristen Mapes, and Lynn Silipigni Connaway. 2019. "Re(-Casting) Call: Sculpting Services and Strategies for Cultivating Online Scholarly Identity." Presentation at ACRL, Cleveland, OH, April 10–13, 2019. http://dx.doi.org/10.17613/jtw6-pp40.

Radford, Marie L., Vanessa Kitzie, Stephanie Mikitish, Diana Floegel, Gary P. Radford, and Lynn Silipigni Connaway. 2018. "Investigating Practices for Building an Ethical and Sustainable Scholarly Identity with Online Platforms and Social Networking Sites." In *Proceedings of the 81st Annual Meeting of ASIS&T, Vancouver, 2018*, 404–413. Silver Spring: Association for Information Science and Technology.

Radford, Marie L., Vanessa Kitzie, Stephanie Mikitish, Diaa Floegel, and Lynn Silipigni Connaway. 2019. "'People Need a Strategy:' Exploring Attitudes of and Support Roles for Scholarly Identity Work Among Academic Librarians." In *ACRL 2019 Proceedings, Cleveland, 2019*, 594–605, Chicago: American Library Association.

Radford, Marie L., and Gary P. Radford. 2017. *Library Conversations: Reclaiming Interpersonal Communication Theory for Understanding Professional Encounters.* Chicago: ALA Editions.

Rich, Linda, and Vera Lux. 2018. "Reaching Additional Users with Proactive Chat." *Reference Librarian* 59 (1): 23–34.

Scardilli, Brandi. 2018. "The IoT Space: New Ways to Connect to People and Things." *Information Today* 32(7).

Sue, Derald Wing. 2010. *Microaggressions in Everyday life: Race, Gender, and Sexual Orientation.* Hoboken, NJ: John Wiley & Sons, Inc.

Sue, Derald Wing, Christina M. Capodilupo, Gina Celeste Torino, Jennifer M. Bucceri, Aisha M. B. Holder, Kevin L. Nadal, and Marta Esquilin. 2007. "Racial Microaggressions in Everyday Life: Implications for Clinical Practice." *American Psychologist* 62 (4): 271–286.

Yip, Jason C., Kiley Sobel, Xin Gao, Allison Marie Hishikawa, Alexis Lim, Laura Meng, Romaine Flor Ofiana, Justin Park, and Alexis Hiniker. 2019. "Laughing Is Scary, but Farting Is Cute: A Conceptual Model of Children's Perspectives of Creepy Technologies." In *CHI 2019, Glasgow, 2019.* https://doi .org/10.1145/3290605.3300303.

7

Do-It-Yourself Reference

Naomi Lederer

INTRODUCTION

The 21st-century library has constituents who never set foot physically on site. Some universities have a library that does not exist as a physical location but only virtually. Library users who use the physical library also use online resources—it is almost impossible these days to find a card catalog, so the user who simply wants to read a specific book will need to use the library's website to obtain a call number and location. Online resources mean that electronic publications in the library collection can be used 24 hours a day. Archives and special collections have growing numbers of digital items, which enable users to look at them without having to travel to a physical location.

Most libraries are neither open nor staffed all hours of the day. In addition, physical locations may be closed for holidays or other occasions and may have fewer hours during parts of the year. Yet, while the physical location may not be open, the electronic library is still humming away. For those who have access to the Internet, the 24-hour electronic library is a valuable resource that can be tapped into at any time. Dictionaries, encyclopedias, articles, and books are available at their fingertips or voice command. The library provides access to electronic books, electronic journals, databases, digital collections, information about loan periods, programming, collections, exhibits, speakers, use of various library resources such as study or meeting rooms, interlibrary loan, available technology (printers, tablets, laptops, chargers, and other devices), locations, hours, policies, and contact names and/or numbers. Users can use the catalog remotely to look up call numbers so that they can more efficiently use the building, something important when transportation, parking, work schedules, course schedules, and/or family care are part of the mix.

Unfortunately, accessing, understanding, and making the best use of these resources can be complicated. It seems as if every vendor of electronic material has to create quirks and difficulties that can confound the uninitiated and annoy those who have grown accustomed to a previous iteration when they modify the software. This is where do-it-yourself reference can be a lifesaver.

DO-IT-YOURSELF REFERENCE

Do-it-yourself reference has existed since the first building directory was placed out for the public to see or the first bibliography was printed for pick up and use. It is the piece of paper with call number locations listed on it with the floor and/or specific area of the building where items are found. It is the map that shows restrooms, water fountains, computers available for public use, where to check out materials, and so forth. It is the guide that shows how to determine if the library owns a serial and which years are owned. It shows how to find a book, government publication, film, microformat, map, or other format. It is the list of resources available on a topic. It is the card at the end of a row of shelves that informs users what call numbers are found in that range. It is the sign overhead or on a wall that indicates that this is the reference section, this is the periodical room, or where atlases are kept. In other words, it is anything that helps users locate what they need to do their research without e-mailing, using a chat service, or talking face to face with library staff. In libraries with self-checkout, a user might never have to interact with anyone in order to get what is wanted or needed.

To serve constituents, libraries in the 21st-century need to provide guidance online in order to help their users find what they need in an expeditious manner. At the same time, people have different online access speeds and may have different accessibility needs so guide designers must carefully consider how their products work with different platforms, including those based on text reading of a page.

This chapter is not going to focus on the use of multiple specific tools that can be used to create learning objects. Specific software is a moving target because of updates and fixes. At other times, online objects stop functioning when a browser has an update. The focus is on the broader picture of online learning objects.

WHAT IS AN ONLINE LEARNING OBJECT?

An online learning object will be defined here as a teaching or learning resource that is available electronically on the web. It may or may not be interactive. It may teach general skills or a specific skill. Its intended audience may vary, but because it is on the web it is available to anyone with web access, unless the learning object is behind a firewall of some kind, for instance, within a learning management system.

The term will be used broadly here within the context of libraries, ranging from brief lessons covering one kind of task to lengthy documents that provide comprehensive coverage of a topic. An example of a brief lesson is one that covers how to find out if the library owns a book. A comprehensive lesson would be one that exhaustively describes every resource available at a library that is potentially relevant for research on a specific topic.

Some learning objects integrate quizzing, games, or other activities that serve to reinforce a lesson or skill. Learning objects may include photos or other types of images such as screenshots of catalogs or databases. They might be a FAQ (frequently asked questions) list with answers to repeated queries. A learning object can include activities and assessments with responses shared with the librarian and/or a course instructor, depending on the software used to create it.

Examples of learning object formats include the following:

- basic web pages (LibGuides, a proprietary software that is currently popular will also be discussed)
- podcasts

- videos (sometimes placed on YouTube, but may be embedded on a library page)
- presentation slides (e.g., PowerPoint)
- infographics

The chapter's Suggested Readings section has a list of select resources that can be used for inspiration and suggestions for creating objects, including software. The resources don't necessarily need to be read in detail, but they provide guidelines and useful practical applications as well as learning theory to consider when creating a do-it-yourself reference. Look for books in your library catalog by the following subjects to find additional ideas: "instructional systems—design" and "web-based instruction."

FOCUSING ON LIBRARY CONTEXT

Do-it-yourself reference is going to be relevant and needs to be customized as long as libraries are in differently shaped buildings with different content. The strength of good libraries is that they adapt to meet the needs of their constituents, so it is highly unlikely that some kinds of guides will ever be generic—locations of materials, for instance, must be specific to an individual building—and not just for place but for time because materials can get shifted. Ownership of databases may change depending upon the current budget or because the provider went out of business.

CREATING LEARNING OBJECTS

Before creating a learning object, it is important to consider whether it is needed. The creator of the potential resource needs to have an affirmative answer to at least one of these questions:

- Do local users need this guidance?
- Are there remote or distance users who need this guidance?
- Have multiple users asked questions about how to find this kind of information?
- Is there a course that is covering the topic?
- Is the topic of interest to people in this community?
- Is there a new version of the library catalog or frequently used database?
- Have the specifics for logging in remotely changed?
- Is there a piece of equipment that has its own challenges (e.g., microformat readers)?
- Is special software (or browser version) required for downloading or reading ebooks?
- Are there special collections that require users to have a preliminary understanding before accessing them?
- Is there a special event that requires explanation or context?
- Is content elsewhere too site-specific?
- Does a potential resource found elsewhere lack helpful annotations?
- Is the other page confusing or misleading?
- Does the other site have more than one rotten link? (Do a sample check.)

Determine if there is something elsewhere that could be pointed to or copied with permission (give credit to the originator). Other sites can be a great place to point out to your users. Read through them carefully to make sure that they have helpful information, clearly presented.

There needs to be an audience for the resource and it is important to consider the primary audience. Will the audience be first-year students or seniors? Graduate students?

K–5, 6–12 students? Adults who have never used your facility before? An audience whose first language isn't the one you are going to be writing in? Anyone who is using your library? This will assist you in how you construct your object. You may decide to focus on the use of images if language is going to be a potential barrier. You may decide to have your learning object available in more than one language, provided you have a reliable translator. In these instances, be sure to have settled the text of your guide before asking for a translation. It is important to have the same and accurate information on each version for as long as possible.

You will also want to consider whether or not the object is to have a long tenure on your site or a brief one. This impacts your ability to customize. If it is an object that will only be used for the short term, it can be highly specific. The images can be current and exact. Keep in mind that there is short term and there is *short term*. Do you really want to be spending your valuable time on something with a brief shelf-life? You need to weigh the cost and time benefit of what you are doing. A basic web page has the benefit of being easy (provided you have learned how to create them) to do so the cost/benefit can be recovered almost immediately. A visually driven tutorial may require hours of staff time to create, so using it for something with only short-term relevancy may not be a good use of library resources.

DESIGNING LEARNING OBJECTS

It is important to have pedagogical reasons for how you design your learning object. They need not be based on a theory to be successful, but you should put serious thought into how you are pulling the content together. When you have examples, what do you choose? If you can have a generically useful example, that can be helpful in some contexts, but subject-specific examples will be more useful when creating learning objects for a topic.

Related topics lend themselves to matching patterns. For example, the author of this chapter has guides for doing research on different literary authors on her English Language & Literature site. Researching one literary author is similar to researching another, so the recommended research sequence is the same. Using the template of a previously created page, the author can quickly design a new one. Customization is what makes the new page valuable: the relevant call number(s), terms to use in the library catalog, exact volumes in reference books of literary criticism, focused journal(s), where to find articles (with hints for different databases, as relevant), and sites found on the web, annotated. The new guide can be created faster than starting from scratch.

Other subjects have their own complexities. Nevertheless, an earlier page can be used as a template often enough, so looking for a framework to start with is worthwhile. Of course, if you are just starting out you will not have one of your earlier pages to use. In that case, a careful design means that in the future you may be able to use that first one as a jumping-off point.

Examining others' guides can provide ideas for you. Look for guides that have a research strategy element to them. A random collection of resources is not helpful to a researcher who is trying to figure out what to do first. Make it clear where the researcher should start. Furthermore, even an excellent external guide will not have information on where books and journals can be located locally. Note in your annotation for the site that users should check their local catalog for holdings and to use interlibrary load for items that are not owned.

UPDATING LEARNING OBJECTS

Commit to updating long-term objects. If broken links are not corrected or removed, it looks bad and frustrates your users. If the snapshot of your home page is what it looked like in the past, it isn't going to help your users today. If you are not going to update, either don't create the object in the first place or make every effort to ensure that your object won't become dated any time soon. Eventually, it will become dated—that is inevitable—but if you strategize, you will only need updates when, for example, your library gets a new library catalog system, adds a more relevant database, or cuts a database that you were using as an example: in other words, external reasons, not because you hadn't carefully considered your learning object in the first place.

There have been a lot of online learning objects that went well beyond a basic web page that have come and gone because of the reasons mentioned previously that render the objects unusable. So basic is good. You might be considered a tad unimaginative and not cutting edge, but the number of cutting-edge—even award-winning—online learning objects that were used for two years or less is astoundingly high. The hours spent putting these objects together? Enormous. Some of the tutorials have been fantastic and deservedly award-winning. However, an out-of-date or unusable learning object is impractical, and it must be replaced with current guidance in a timely fashion. If you have plenty of time and resources for updating learning objects on a regular schedule that should be at least every two years, depending upon the type of learning object (e.g., if it includes the number of results from a catalog or database search, it will need more frequent updating), by all means create ones with a complicated back end.

The author operates under the belief that making things as timeless as possible is best. Web pages (now in Lib Guide format) that she first created in 1996 (think creating pages entirely in Notepad) are still up and used very often. There have been updates, additions, and modifications (as well as use of FrontPage and Dreamweaver, as directed to use over time), but the core strategies have not changed. It is interesting (and productive) to add new content as new resources become available, instead of revisiting old ground to make unnecessary improvements.

WEB VERSUS LIBGUIDE

When the author sees a LibGuide with stacked tabs at the top, she knows immediately that she will not be linking to that guide, not even to one tab on it. Where is the user to start? The top? The bottom? Is there any kind of sequence? How are these guides linked together? This popular software does not make it clear to the user where to start. Depending on the page designer or externally determined design, a LibGuide can have up to three columns. It can be difficult to determine a research sequence when the boxes have different lengths in different columns. Pedagogically there should be a research sequence that fits the subject of the guide. Sometimes you start with one kind of resource; other times you start with another.

A LibGuide is not the same as a straightforward web page. It isn't merely a question of copying material from a web page to a LibGuide if you have older, but still valuable, content. The format impacts how you arrange materials, and there needs to be a lot of thought as to how the page looks and how things are presented. Boxes are useful ways to divide content into sections. However, printing LibGuides from the public view (problem verified as still present as of mid-November 2019) splits the page into odd configurations. The left and right columns of a three-column guide can appear on different pages from the center. Longer boxes have the lower part cut off at the foot of printed pages, so content is lost. It is annoying when the medium is interfering with the message. If there needs to be a long section, it should be possible to print all of it. The author has had students show up in her office with printouts of her (former) web pages, so online guides are used in print format by some users. It makes the author shudder to think about her guides being printed now. Maybe the software vendor will fix that travesty. One hopes sooner, rather than later. Also, a function that only works properly on select browsers is not user friendly.

Another frustration with LibGuides is that images must be loaded one by one, which can be time consuming. There are times to include images—either for pedagogical reasons, because showing is a faster way for users to see what the resource looks like, or because it makes it more interesting to look at because there are pictures to break up the text.

An advantage of LibGuides is that they update immediately on the fly and can be corrected from wherever the page owner happens to be as long as there is Internet access. It is possible that LibGuides are popular because they are fixed in many ways. There are librarians who have no interest in design and this product makes creativity unnecessary. For those who have brief guides with little content, LibGuides work just fine. For example, the book listings with the cover use a lot of space and really lengthens a page, which can blur the reality of a short list, but it makes a long bibliography use up a lot of screen space.

An important detail when using LibGuides (or any other web resource) is to create a user-friendly URL. A bunch of numbers and letters is going to be difficult for users to copy. Try to be as descriptive as possible with the fewest letters: main URL from library, subject, page.

IMAGES IN DO-IT-YOURSELF

A great place to find royalty-free images is on government sites. Some images on the sites are under copyright, so check each one closely, but there is a wide variety and the quality tends to be high. Always be willing to remove an image if you have accidently put up a copyrighted one. Put terms in your browser for images related to your topic and add "site:gov" to your search to find these.

Check with your database vendor to see if snapshots of screens are acceptable. The author has never heard a vendor say no, but that day may come. One vendor with a database that features copyrighted images provided the author with images to put on her page promoting it. The statements on copyright were so emphatic—as were telephone conversations with vendor staff—the author cropped in her own photographs into the materials showing how to use the database. Showing what the interface looked like online was acceptable. Showing a single one of the images in it was not.

VENDOR TUTORIALS

A growing number of vendors are providing online guides to using their databases, so if you do not have time to create your own, that is an option. Some may even create tutorials by request if enough librarians ask. However, keep in mind that these tutorials often emphasize the vendor's name and not the content of an individual database, so be sure to have an annotation with content customization with your link to these. The author has encountered people who refer to individual databases by the vendor name, and this is misleading to an enormous degree. We have over 40 individual databases for one vendor; trying to help a student who "searched vendor X" is not going to be a speedy conversation. Which one? Be specific.

SUBJECT GUIDES—ANNOTATE!

Annotations are essential. Write annotations for every link off site and for every library database for which you have time to customize. Why? How else will users know which link they want to select? A list of resources is useless unless there is some indication as to the content found therein. As a user, do I want to click on the first link? The fourth? The tenth? The twentieth? Lumped together under one heading is not providing helpful guidance. Am I going to find scholarly journal articles, newspaper articles, magazines, blogs, or something else? In this list of links to photographs—of who, what, when, where, larger historical event, and taken by whom?

In the annotation, describe the content of the site—what is found there. Is it an overview of the topic? Are there photos? Manuscripts? Is it a bibliography covering specific years? Are items in pdf? Images? Audio? Who is the audience for the source? How do you use it? The author has pointed to sites aimed at younger audiences than hers and uses the annotation to explain why it is nevertheless useful for undergraduate or graduate students. Alternatively, a site might have a very complex vocabulary and a hint that having a dictionary handy is helping your audience. You want to provide your users with reasons they want to go to the site. What makes it different from the other links you are listing?

If your intuition is telling you that the site is useful but you cannot think of how to describe it, or you are in a rush when creating your page, take direct quotes from the site (use quotation marks to cite properly—you are setting an example to your users that plagiarism is not acceptable). The "about" or "about us" will have what you need in many cases. Another quick text to grab is the site's own description of the content. If it has been well described you might as well use it, with quotation marks, of course.

TUTORIALS THAT MOVE AND/OR ARE INTERACTIVE

An advantage to basic learning guides is that many, most, or ideally all screen readers for the visually impaired can read them so the creator need not do more than provide descriptive alternative text for images. Tutorials that rely on moving images and audio should be made accessible to differently abled users via subtitles for those who can't hear the audio and via audio descriptions for those who can't see. You may need to come up with completely different but comparable tutorials for some audiences. Venn diagrams used to visualize Boolean logic is going to require something that is a bit more helpful verbally beyond "two circles overlapping."

Manual dexterity should also be a consideration. Even people with average levels of dexterity can have difficulties getting a cursor over a tiny link, and public computers with multiple users may not have the fine-tuning capabilities of a computer operated by one gentle user. Therefore, if you are creating a tutorial that requires users to click on parts of the screen, make sure that the clicking area is large enough (and far away enough from other click options) for users to access. The author has run across sites where the slightest movement of the mouse and a link is no longer an option. Think centimeters or inches for users to click on, not millimeters.

If you are using audio, as in a podcast that is audio only, or a tutorial that is a mix of image and sound, it needs to be clear. Practice speaking your text or be willing to rerecord sections of the presentation multiple times to get it right. This is where software that allows for sectional changes is highly desirable. Ask questions or read reviews before purchasing a new software. In the future, there may be more quick, easy, and inexpensive ways to record and upload audio, but you still need to avoid background noises and other sound distractions. You want to show your library's best face, and a sloppy recording does not demonstrate professionalism.

Keep the tutorial short. While research varies on the ideal, you can't go wrong with 2–5 minutes per concept. A tutorial should have a very brief introduction describing what it is teaching or explaining (in case someone accidentally clicks on a different tutorial than desired) and then quickly get to the lesson itself. You already have your audience. Don't bore them with a long introduction.

Tutorials should include practical advice. For example, sometimes a user needs to try multiple times with different word combinations before getting a good set of search results. Demonstrations or tutorials that work perfectly on the first try are misleading. This creates a risk of users becoming quickly frustrated when their first efforts do not give them satisfactory results. If it takes an experienced librarian more than one try to get a desirable outcome for a given topic, it is going to take the novice user at least that many times. Therefore, make it clear that multiple searches are nothing to be ashamed of and are standard practice. Also, if applicable, end the tutorial with a quick reminder that there are people in the library available to help.

CONCLUSION

While this book is looking forward, it may appear that this chapter is looking back in some ways by spending time on basic web pages. However, in a time of budget cuts and library staff with multiple responsibilities, it is essential that any do-it-yourself reference be as accurate and timely as possible. If an object is created using a special software that has since been updated (sellers are out to make money, not help their customers to best monetize their assets) or the browser updates or a hacker damages it, and it becomes useless, that means wasted time, effort, and money (staff time costs money). Because every library is different, customization of material will remain essential; even online-only collections have different arrangements.

Librarians have been forward thinkers for years. Every time you see a catalog record with the height of the book in centimeters, you know that libraries were going metric in the United States years ago, when most of the rest of the world was on it and the rest of the United States refused to change. However, when it comes to do-it-yourself reference, sometimes the most basic way to describe or teach something is best. If someone doesn't have the right program installed in their computer or the latest version of a high-end software or browser, that fancy tutorial is a blank image on the screen to them. A basic print or basic online resource can be a best choice for describing complicated databases and concepts. Think of all those files and tutorials that cannot be accessed today because the software is no longer supported! It is easier and faster to update the simpler formats because starting from scratch is not always going to be a timely option. Thus, basic do-it-yourself reference is genuinely forward-thinking in the 21st century.

SUGGESTED READINGS

Bender, Sara, and Karlie Hill. 2016. "Pedagogical Considerations for Effectively Teaching Qualitative Research to Students in an Online Environment." *Journal of Effective Teaching* 16 (2): 93–103.

Dziuban, Charles, Patsy Moskal, Liza Parker, Maria Campbell, Colm Howlin, and Connie Johnson. 2018. "Adaptive Learning: A Stabilizing Influence across Disciplines and Universities." *Online Learning* 22 (3): 7–39.

Kingsley, Tara L., Jerrell C. Cassady, and Susan M. Tancock. 2015. "Successfully Promoting 21st Century Online Research Skills: Interventions in 5th-Grade Classrooms." *Reading Horizons* 54 (2): 91–134.

Koh, Joyce Hwee Ling. 2017. "Designing and Integrating Reusable Learning Objects for Meaningful Learning: Cases from a Graduate Programme." *Australasian Journal of Educational Technology* 33 (5): 136–151.

Smith, Susan Sharpless. 2010. *Web-based Instruction: A Guide for Libraries*, 3rd edition. Chicago: American Library Association.

University of Illinois at Urbana-Champaign University Library. n.d. "Learning Objects." Accessed January 2, 2020. http://guides.library.illinois.edu/learningobjects

Yarbrough, Jillian Ruth. 2018. "Adapting Adult Learning Theory to Support Innovative, Advanced, Online Learning—WVMD Model." *Research in Higher Education Journal* 35: 1–15.

8

Peer-to-Peer Reference Services in Academic Libraries

Hailley Fargo

INTRODUCTION

One emerging trend in academic library reference work is to build peer-to-peer programs where undergraduate students, employed by the library, support their peers during the research process. This new model extends reference services for the academic library into new territory, supports students at a point of need; offers help in a common, peer language; and provides a meaningful employment experience for the students providing the reference support.

This chapter will explore the theoretical frameworks used by librarians and practitioners who have built and implemented peer-to-peer reference programs, highlight examples of current peer-to-peer reference programs, and provide best practices for those interested in starting their own program. This chapter will also address some concerns associated with implementing a peer-to-peer reference model, such as the referral process and quality of service.

THEORETICAL FRAMEWORKS BEHIND PEER-TO-PEER REFERENCE PROGRAMS

A strong peer-to-peer reference program in an academic library should be intentional and grounded in a theoretical framework that guides its creation and implementation. The following section will explore three frameworks: peer-assisted learning (PAL), situated learning and communities of practice, and student employment as a high-impact practice. Since there is overlap between these frames, academic libraries often use multiple frameworks to build their peer-to-peer reference program.

Peer-Assisted Learning

PAL is when a peer helps another peer learn and, in the process, they also learn through the act of teaching. In this situation, the peer providing the support is not a professional teacher (Topping 1996, 322). In PAL environments, the interactions between peers should have the following key values:

- All participants should learn something throughout the interaction.
- This interaction between peers always complements, never supplements, professional teaching.
- All participants gain new knowledge through the interaction.
- All learners should have access to PAL.
- Peer mentors should be trained and assessed by professional teachers, who work with the mentors throughout their time assisting learners (Topping and Ehly 2001, 114).

Along with these key values, PAL is often described as being grounded in Lev Vygotsky's concept of *zone of proximal development*. In the interaction, an experienced peer mentor is working with a novice student researcher and both "stretch" to meet each other in the middle. The two students can speak to each other as peers and both will learn something they might not have learned on their own. "For all participants, they might never have truly grasped a concept until they had to explain it to another, embodying and crystallizing through into language" (Topping and Ehly 2001, 124). This shared language can be a powerful tool in learning a new concept or skill through peer help. Additionally, the authority gap between the mentor and the student is much smaller than between a teacher and student; this smaller gap can be helpful in explaining a new concept and creating a low-stress situation to ask questions.

Having to explain concepts and ideas to peers has tremendous benefits for the peer mentor. Topping goes as far as to say that "just *preparing* to be a peer tutor has been proposed to enhance cognitive processing in the tutor—by increasing attention to and motivation for the task, and necessitating review of existing knowledge and skills" (1996, 324). Peer mentors in academic libraries have noted that their role within the library has led to increased confidence in their information literacy skills and in their conducting research for their own projects (Allen 2014; Faix 2014; O'Kelly et al. 2015; McCoy 2011). In addition to increasing information literacy and research skills, being a peer mentor can help students not only "learn the subject better and deeper, but they also learn transferrable skills in helping, cooperation, listening, and communication. [Peer learning] encourages personal and social development" (Topping 2005, 643). These are all skills that students will need beyond their time as an undergraduate and the ability to practice those skills regularly is valuable. These skills can help contribute to a student's personal growth and allow them to reflect on their experiences to see potential future directions (Beltman and Schaeben 2012, 39).

Beyond the skills gained being a peer mentor, another benefit of creating a peer-to-peer model with the PAL framework is that these interactions can help create an environment of social constructivism, where it is understood that knowledge is created and developed in communities (Elmborg 2002, 457). This community-focused aspect of these programs can also be viewed through a situated learning and communities of practice lens.

Situated Learning and Communities of Practice

Situated learning is where a learner gains new knowledge in a specific context where that new knowledge can be applied. This is a social process where experts and novices come together to share knowledge. In these situations, the experts help bring the novices more fully into the community; in a meaningful way, learners learn by doing. Jean Lave and Etienne Wenger (1991, 40) discuss how situated learning is "an analytical viewpoint on learning, a way of understanding learning" that is distinct from intentional instruction. Much of Lave and Wenger's work draws on ideas around apprenticeship and the ways in which a novice learns alongside experts.

Similar to PAL, Lave and Wenger (1991, 49) draw on Vygotsky's zone of proximal development but want to extend this idea further, to emphasize the social nature of these situations and the changing dynamics between the experts and novices. When applying situated learning to peer-reference programs, the situated learning happens between peer-reference assistants and the library employees who train these students. Together, they form a larger community of practice.

All situated learning happens within communities of practices, which are defined as "groups of people who share a concern or passion for something they do and learn how to do it better as they interact regularly" (Wenger-Trayner and Wenger-Trayner 2015). This community of practice is also "in relation with other tangential and overlapping communities of practice" (Lave and Wenger 1991, 98). Communities of practice exist everywhere, especially in an academic setting where people are coming together to learn. Students who provide peer-reference support are part of a community of their peers providing that support and also bring their other communities of practice into their role as a peer-reference assistant.

When starting a peer-reference program, the initial community of practice is the peer-reference assistants and the library employees who support and train them. Over time, this community of practice grows with new cohorts of peer-reference assistants. The more experienced peer-reference assistants will grow into mentor roles to support their new peers learning the job. This access to learning opportunities is an important element of a community of practice, along with having the ability to interact with "old-timers, and other members of the community; and to information, resources, and opportunities for participation" (Lave and Wenger 1991, 101). When a student is learning how to provide peer-reference, they might spend time shadowing more experienced peer-reference assistants to learn about the types of questions they will be asked and how to support their process in this position.

Communities of practice work well when there is a leader who helps steer the direction, training situations, and conversation. Especially in a peer-reference program, it is important to have a coordinator who sees the big picture and finds meaningful ways for student employees to interact with one another and the library in order to ensure success in their role. The last framework to consider when building a peer-reference program is around this idea: to transform student employment in the library into a high-impact practice opportunity.

Student Employment as a High-Impact Practice

In higher education, value is placed on student engagement experiences where undergraduate students commit time to explore and learn, outside the classroom, and gain the skills they need to succeed. One type of student engagement experience is high-impact practices: educational situations meant to foster learning and student growth. Research done around high-impact practices suggests that participation in these activities can "increase rates of student retention and student engagement" (Kuh 2008, 9). Kuh believes these activities "require daily decisions that deepen students' investment in the activity as well as their commitment to their academic program and the college" (2008, 14). Some examples of high-impact practices include first-year seminars, learning communities, undergraduate research, internships, and service learning (Kuh 2008, 9–11). While student employment is not technically an official high-impact practice, librarians Rosan Mitola, Erin Rinto, and Emily Pattni (2018) argue that when done correctly, student employment in the library aligns with the characteristics of high-impact practices and should be treated accordingly.

Along with the student devoted time to participating in a high-impact practice, Kuh (2008) also mentions that these experiences must have interactions with faculty and peers, allow for formal and informal feedback, establish connections to the campus and broader communities, foster diversity, and provide transferrable skills to those who participate. When building a peer-reference program, coordinators should think about ways to include these elements in the training, continual training, and community building of the program. In reviewing the past 20 years of LIS literature around library student employee programs, Mitola et al. (2018) looked to see if any of these characteristics could be found. They discovered that library student employee programs do a good job of asking student employees to devote time and energy into their position and ensure that there is a lot of faculty and peer interactions but were coming up short in providing mentoring, informal and formal feedback, and diversity initiatives (Mitola, Rinto, and Pattni 2018, 362–363). If you are building a peer-reference program with the goal of creating a high-impact practice for your students, careful consideration should go into the training and continued learning in order to ensure these six characteristics are intentionally integrated into the program.

PEER-TO-PEER REFERENCE PROGRAMS, IN PRACTICE

With these theoretical frameworks in mind, it is important to see how peer-to-peer reference programs are built in academic libraries. This section will explore a few examples in the LIS literature of peer-to-peer programs, as well as the peer-to-peer reference program created and implemented at Penn State University, University Park campus.

There are many libraries who have tried different variations of peer-to-peer reference. One example that frequently rises to the top is the LibRAT (Library Research Assistant Technician) at California Polytechnic State University San Luis Obispo. Bodemer (2014, 170–171) describes how the program was created to provide support in the residence halls and eventually moved into the library to provide reference and to assist librarians in one-shot instruction. The Michigan State University has peer research assistants, who provide reference support in "Engagement Spaces" located within their residence halls (Marcyk and Oberdick 2017, 165). Grand Valley State University has gone as far as to remove professional staff from some public services so students entering the building see their peers and know they can assist them (Meyer and Torreano 2017, 39). These examples demonstrate how libraries can set up these programs in a variety of ways, in order to respond to the context and needs of their library, institution, and students. While there is not a one-size fits-all model for developing peer-reference programs, it can be helpful to see the variety of ways librarians have implemented these programs.

In response to the growing trend of using PAL in libraries, the *Peer-Assisted Learning in Academic Libraries* book was published in 2017 to bring together a collection of academic libraries employing this method. Editors Erin Rinto, John Watts, and Rosan Mitola highlight 14 institutions using PAL in some form. A third of the book focuses on peer-to-peer reference programs while the rest focuses on integrating student employees into instruction and outreach initiatives.

Penn State Libraries' Peer Research Consultants

In 2016–2017, the Pattee & Paterno Libraries at Penn State University, University Park campus, had 17 service desks throughout the building to answer patron questions. This staffing model had a few issues; first, many of the desks were overseen by different library departments or by a unit that was a collaborator with the library. This caused an inconsistent staffing pattern in terms of who staffed the desk, their hours of operation, and expectations. In addition to the inconsistent staffing pattern, each department trained employees differently and this led to uneven knowledge across desks. When a student at the desk did not know the answer, they might have sent the patron across the library to a different desk, perhaps without knowing if a different desk could assist the patron. This lack of communication caused the "bouncing patron," with some patrons moving to multiple desks without getting their initial question answered. Finally, through data collected at the desks, the Pattee & Paterno Libraries were seeing a decline in reference questions asked, along with most questions being asked in the afternoon, evening, and weekend hours.

These factors culminated in the formation of a committee that provided a vision for a new service model. The major goals of this service model were to decrease the number of desks throughout the building, find ways to professionalize library student employment through the creation of a peer-reference program, and bring together similar services that would have the same hours of support in a shared space, called The Search Bar.

In fall 2017, The Search Bar opened as a suite of peer-to-peer services located centrally within the Pattee & Paterno Libraries. The Search Bar is open 64 hours a week when classes are in session and houses writing tutors, technology tutors, and peer research consultants (PRCs); ideally, these peer-to-peer services intersect and are interconnected as they support their peers. Our vision for The Search Bar is to eventually have a hybrid tutorial service where a student comes in for research help and, while the PRC leads the session, the writing tutor and technology tutor sit in to offer support in their areas of expertise. This vision allows for a space to be created in the library where our students are learning together, sharing new knowledge together, and are empowering one another.

As the plans for The Search Bar were coming together in summer 2017, the author of this chapter, along with two other library colleagues, created the first iteration of our peer-reference program and training. In creating and defining the work of the PRC, seven learning outcomes were written to guide training and assessment.

As a PRC, you will be able to

1. define what reference is and your role in the reference process;
2. lead a reference conversation and interpret the information need of the patron;
3. collaborate and work effectively with peers from diverse backgrounds and abilities in order to provide reference service and better understand the experiences of your peers;
4. use foundational[1] library resources in order to support the research needs of your peers;
5. demonstrate (and teach) your peers on different parts of the research process such as

   a. building or narrowing a topic
   b. conducting and refining keyword searches
   c. understanding the makeup of databases
   d. helping peers understand the type of information they are looking at (online and in print) and what sort of access the library has to this information

    e.   evaluating information

    f.   explaining how citations are created

6. respond to reference questions in a variety of mediums (in-person, online, e-mail, phone, etc.);

7. judge a reference situation to determine the limit of expertise and will be able to identify the correct referral process. For a referral handoff, the PRC will be able to clearly communicate the student's information need and the steps already competed in The Search Bar.

Others that have built similar programs have found that creating learning outcomes, philosophy statements, goals, or scope statements can be a useful way to ground a new service (Baugess et al. 2017; Marcyk and Oberdick 2017). From those learning outcomes, a rubric was established that allowed coordinators to "test" the PRCs part way into the first semester. This rubric was one way to check in with the PRCs and ensure they were providing quality service to their peers and also help the coordinators identify gaps in the training program.

In hiring the first round of PRCs, the team opted to hire students who had previously worked in the library. This allowed the PRCs to hit the ground running when the Search Bar opened and provided the coordinators an opportunity to build a training program that supplemented the students' current knowledge on using library resources. Similar to Michigan State, "Targeting library student employees who already had some necessary skills and general comfort with library resources proved to be a winning strategy" (Marcyk and Oberdick 2017, 108). Along with a heavy training schedule in fall 2017, the PRCs also had continual training, in the form of digital badges, dissect a database worksheet wherein students answered questions about the scope of a database, purpose and search functions, and monthly staff meetings.

Beyond the training, reflection was also a major component of the PRC program. This is a common technique used by others including the Research Assistance Program at Indiana University Libraries (Courtney and Otto 2017, 157) and by the Peer Research Navigators at Christopher Newport University (Wallis 2017, 194). Reflection activities can be embedded in a variety of places including staff meetings and as a survey that is filled out after working with a student on a reference question. For the PRCs, this written documentation was used by coordinators in a variety of ways: to understand what was happening during the first semester in The Search Bar, to see what questions were being asked, to understand how our PRCs felt about this new position, and to track the growth of our PRCs as they became more confident in their position.

Both The Search Bar and the PRC program continue to see changes. Training has been adapted to fit the needs of the new PRCs and conversations continue with the other peer services in the Search Bar on the best ways to support our students. Our hope is to continue to develop this program and begin to assess long-term impacts of our PRCs.

BEST PRACTICES

If there is interest in developing a peer-to-peer reference model at an academic library, the following are some best practices to ensure that an intentional and meaningful program is built from the start. This section also provides commentary on some critiques of creating a peer-to-peer reference model, including concern over the quality from undergraduate students.

Create Learning Outcomes to Guide the Training and Assessment of a Program

Developing goals, learning outcomes, philosophy, or scope statements for your peer-reference program helps not only to ground your program but also to define what success looks like. These guiding statements can be crucial to get buy-in and support from library colleagues while also sharing the vision for your program. Additionally, having outcomes and assessment ensures a meaningful work experience for students because you are able to check in and see if the program is on track.

The learning outcomes or goals will create the foundation for your training program. "It is essential that students are well-prepared for the demands of their position and are able to deliver high-quality learning experiences to their peers" (Rinto, Watts, and Mitola 2017, 10). This might require a robust training program at the start to get your students up to speed but then will require regular training check-ins, in order to ensure that all students feel confident in providing support to their peers. One way to get buy-in from colleagues is to find opportunities for subject librarians or other library employees to be a part of training. By bringing in colleagues and leveraging their expertise for training sessions, the students get to know more people in the library and gain new knowledge about library resources. The training program will inevitably change over time, as you gain an understanding of what your students need to be successful in their role.

For those concerned about the quality of service of students providing reference help, a strong training program and confidence in the ability of our undergraduate students can help quell concerns. A hands-on training program that allows for regular check-ins with the peer-reference assistants allows coordinators to make sure questions are getting answered effectively. In studies done by Keyes and Dworak (2017) and Stevens (2013), both found that undergraduate students are capable of answering questions that are comparable to paraprofessional staff or librarians. This shows that peer-reference assistants can help us extend our reference landscape and provide valuable just-in-time service to their peers.

Think Strategically about How the Peer-to-Peer Model Fits within the Larger Reference Landscape at the Library

A peer-reference program is not created in a vacuum and when implemented this program will need to fit within the already-existing reference landscape. Student employees who provide reference service complement, not supplement, service provided by subject librarians. Peer-reference assistants help to *extend* reference to patrons and provide a new avenue for their peers to receive help and learn more about library resources. In carving out a space for peer-reference assistants, a referral process should be defined as early as possible. It should be made clear when and how a student will refer their peer to another tier of help—subject librarian, professional staff, and so forth. Again, library context will guide what this referral process might look like. For example, Michigan State's Peer Research Assistants share subject librarian information with the students they help (Marcyk and Oberdick 2017), and Hope College has positioned their reference desk next to the librarians who would handle referral for a smooth hand-off (Hronchek and Bishop 2017). Once a referral process is in place, it should be communicated with library colleagues and peer-reference assistants and reviewed on a regular basis in order to make changes, if necessary.

Be Willing to Commit the Time and Resources Necessary

Building a peer-reference program takes time and energy. If an academic library is considering creating a peer-reference program, they should make sure they have staff willing and ready to devote the necessary time needed. In addition to the time it takes to kick-start a program, the coordinators will need to account for time each week to supervise and mentor student employees, build and deploy training, and assess the progress. To make a program sustainable, it is important to have more than one person overseeing the program. Through reviewing the literature and the author's own personal experience in building a peer-reference program, one should account for 15–20 hours to on-board the students, and a substantial amount of time in the beginning to prepare the training materials, instruction, and examples. While the time will decrease as the students are trained, coordinators will still need to spend time each week mentoring and providing feedback to the peer-reference assistants. Libraries who do not provide their staff with the necessary time to run these programs will likely see the service provided by the peer-reference assistants suffer.

Commitment to Create a Meaningful Experience and Value the Student's Expertise

Finally, in starting a peer-reference program, coordinators should make sure that providing a meaningful experience to student employees is a driving factor in supporting this program. We know that these sorts of programs have the potential to give our student employees transferrable skills such critical thinking skills, leadership, communication, and time management (Beltman and Schaeben 2012; Charles, Lotts, and Todorinova 2017; Melilli, Mitola, and Hunsaker 2016) as well as a better understanding and use of library resources (Allen 2014; McCoy 2011). If we want our programs to have this sort of impact, we have to commit to building this program and supporting our students along the way.

In building these programs, we also need to let our student employees know that we support them and value what they bring to the table and to our larger reference landscape. In libraries, we often praise and promote the subject and functional expertise of our librarians and staff. Our student employees should not be any different; "we should also value our students' expertise and the experiential knowledge they bring into their role as peer mentors/leaders. They know how to be a student at your institution and this expertise should be celebrated the same way we value subject and functional expertise" (Fargo 2018). By creating a peer-reference program, you take one step in showing students their voices and experiences matter to the library. Student employees respond well to these sorts of program, will often step up and into leadership roles, and can provide the insight we need to make our programs stronger and to make sure our patrons are well supported.

CONCLUSION

In the article "Teaching at the Desk: Toward a Reference Pedagogy," James K. Elmborg (2002, 455) argues that the reference desk can be a meaningful spot for teaching, potentially more influential than the classroom. A peer-to-peer reference desk is no different; there is incredible opportunity to create this desk as a meaningful spot for teaching and transformation, for both the student providing the help and the student seeking the help. Many academic libraries have found this to be a successful model, both for their student employees and for the students they serve. As reference and academic libraries continue to change and grow over the next several years, peer-to-peer services will continue to play a role in helping to transform these areas.

NOTE

1. Foundational is defined as knowing how to use the discovery layer, the catalog, the "Try These First" databases (Gale Virtual Reference, Opposing Viewpoints, CQ Researcher, Access World News, and Academic Search Complete) and having a general understanding of how our subject-based Lib-Guides are organized and how they are used to help a student find discipline-specific databases and subject help.

REFERENCES

Allen, Seth. 2014. "Towards a Conceptual Map of Academic Libraries' Role in Student Retention," *The Christian Librarian* 57 (1): 7–19.

Baugess, Clinton K., Mallory R. Jallas, Meggan D. Smith, and Janelle Wertzberger. 2017. "Peer Research Mentors at Gettysburg College." In *Peer-Assisted Learning in Academic Libraries*, edited by Erin Rinto, John Watts, and Rosan Mitola, 135–146. Santa Barbara: Libraries Unlimited.

Beltman, Susan, and Marcel Schaeben. 2012. "Institution-Wide Peer Mentoring: Benefits for Mentors." *The International Journal of the First Year in Higher Education* 3 (2): 33–44.

Bodemer, Brett B. 2014. "They CAN and They SHOULD: Undergraduates Providing Peer Reference and Instruction." *College & Research Libraries* 75 (2): 162–178.

Charles, Leslin H., Megan Lotts, and Lily Todorinova. 2017. "A Survey of the Value of Library Employment to the Undergraduate Experience." *Journal of Library Administration* 57 (1): 1–16. https://doi .org/10.1080/01930826.2016.1251248.

Courtney, Michael, and Kate Otto. 2017. "The Learning Commons Research Assistance Program at Indiana University Libraries." In *Peer-Assisted Learning in Academic Libraries*, edited by Erin Rinto, John Watts, and Rosan Mitola, 147–164. Santa Barbara: Libraries Unlimited.

Elmborg, James K. 2002. "Teaching at the Desk: Toward a Reference Pedagogy." *portal: Libraries and the Academy* 2 (3): 455–464. https://doi.org/10.1353/pla.2002.0050.

Faix, Allison. 2014. "Peer Reference Revisited: Evolution of a Peer-Reference Model." *Reference Services Review* 42 (2): 305–319. https://doi.org/10.1108/RSR-07-2013-0039.

Fargo, Hailley. 2018. "They CAN and They SHOULD and It's BOTH AND: The Role of Undergraduate Peer Mentors in the Reference Conversation." *In the Library with the Lead Pipe*, December. http:// www.inthelibrarywiththeleadpipe.org/2018/they-can-and-they-should-and-its-both-and/

Hronchek, Jessica, and Rachel Bishop. 2017. "Undergraduate Research Assistants at Hope College." In *Peer-Assisted Learning in Academic Libraries*, edited by Erin Rinto, John Watts, and Rosan Mitola, 191–205. Santa Barbara: Libraries Unlimited.

Keyes, Kelsey, and Ellie Dworak. 2017. "Staffing Chat Reference with Undergraduate Student Assistants at an Academic Library: A Standards-Based Assessment." *The Journal of Academic Librarianship* 43 (6): 469–478. https://doi.org/10.1016/j.acalib.2017.09.001.

Kuh, George D. 2008. *High-Impact Educational Practices: What They Are, Who Has Access to Them, and Why They Matter*. Washington, D.C.: Association of American Colleges & Universities.

Lave, Jean, and Etienne Wenger. 1991. *Situated Learning: Legitimate Peripheral Participation*. Cambridge, United Kingdom: Cambridge University Press.

Marcyk, Emilia R., and Benjamin Oberdick. 2017. "The Peer Research Assistants at the Michigan State University Libraries." In *Peer-Assisted Learning in Academic Libraries*, edited by Erin Rinto, John Watts, and Rosan Mitola, 165–178. Libraries Unlimited.

McCoy, Erin H. 2011. "Academic Performance among Student Library Employees: How Library Employment Impacts Grade Point Average and Perception of Success." *Christian Librarian* 54 (1): 3–12.

Melilli, Amanda, Rosan Mitola, and Amy Hunsaker. 2016. "Contributing to the Library Student Employee Experience: Perceptions of a Student Development Program." *The Journal of Academic Librarianship* 42 (4): 430–437. https://doi.org/10.1016/j.acalib.2016.04.005.

Meyer, Kristin, and Jennifer Torreano. 2017. "The Front Face of Library Services: How Student Employees Lead the Library at Grand Valley State University." In *Students Lead the Library: The Importance of Student Contributions to the Academic Library*, edited by Sara Arnold-Garza and Carissa Tomlinson, 39–55. Chicago: ACRL.

Mitola, Rosan, Erin Rinto, and Emily Pattni. 2018. "Student Employment as a High-Impact Practice in Academic Libraries: A Systematic Review." *The Journal of Academic Librarianship* 44 (3): 352–373. https://doi.org/10.1016/j.acalib.2018.03.005.

O'Kelly, Mary, Julie Garrison, Brian Merry, and Jennifer Torreano. 2015. "Building a Peer-Learning Service for Students in an Academic Library." *portal: Libraries and the Academy* 15 (1): 163–182. https://doi.org/10.1353/pla.2015.0000.

Rinto, Erin, John Watts, and Rosan Mitola, editors. 2017. *Peer-Assisted Learning in Academic Libraries*. Santa Barbara: Libraries Unlimited. https://www.abc-clio.com/ABC-CLIOCorporate/product.aspx?pc=A5126P.

Stevens, Christy R. 2013. "Reference Reviewed and Re-Envisioned: Revamping Librarian and Desk-Centric Services with LibStARs and LibAnswers." *The Journal of Academic Librarianship* 39 (2): 202–214. https://doi.org/10.1016/j.acalib.2012.11.006.

Topping, Keith J. 1996. "The Effectiveness of Peer Tutoring in Further and Higher Education: A Typology and Review of the Literature." *Higher Education* 32 (3): 321–345.

Topping, Keith J. 2005. "Trends in Peer Learning." *Educational Psychology* 25 (6): 631–645.

Topping, Keith J., and Stewart W. Ehly. 2001. "Peer Assisted Learning: A Framework for Consultation." *Journal of Educational and Psychological Consultation* 12 (2): 113–132.

Wallis, Lauren. 2017. "Information on My Own: Peer Reference and Feminist Pedagogy." In *The Feminist Reference Desk: Concepts, Critiques, and Conversations*, edited by Maria T. Accardi, 189–203. Sacramento: Library Juice Press.

Wenger-Trayner, Etienne, and Beverly Wenger-Trayner. 2015. "Introduction to Communities of Practice." https://wenger-trayner.com/introduction-to-communities-of-practice/.

9

Public Library Reference Services in the 21st Century

Maria K. Burchill and John E. Kenney

INTRODUCTION

The patrons of today's libraries, big or small, academic or public, ask one thing of reference and information services (RIS) staff. They ask for our empathetic expertise. Exactly what that expertise is varies by the location, the specialization, and the size of the library in which the patron finds themselves. RIS staff may specialize in one field or they may wear many hats, with experience in all of the following: customer service (both remote and/or in person), cataloging, collection development, outreach and program development, readers' advisory, access services, instruction; the list goes on (Petek 2017, 138). This need for versatility has become more common as staff shortages in the public sector and budget constraints make it nearly impossible to have a single, dedicated professional responsibility. The question the authors pose is, at the heart of our vocation, have our patrons' expectations changed in the new millennium? The answer is multifaceted. Patrons continue to be the reason RIS staff are employed on the floor or at an information desk. While technology has evolved, and will continue to do so, so too has the patron's comfort with the vast data available at their fingertips, whether they know how to use it well or not. It is their expectations of staff service and the techniques staff use to divine those expectations that remain largely what they were when the profession began.

Patrons want quality service and access to the latest materials. New technology and new media afford staff unique opportunities to learn on the job, opportunities which in turn make better librarians better able to serve patrons (VanScoy and Bright 2017, 110). Additionally, the behaviors we display both in person and online heavily influence the patrons' overall satisfaction with the proverbial reference transaction (Tyckoson 2017, 177).

For this chapter, the authors conducted a survey of articles published on reference and information services, access services, and the like over the last two decades in order to define more clearly areas of change in public RIS services for the foreseeable future. This allowed a better understanding of the challenges public library staff face in their duties at their libraries. Because large public library systems are often at the forefront of change and research, the authors informally interviewed staff from mid-size and rural public libraries to understand the RIS trends in less populous areas across the United States. The literature and the interviews largely support our theory that, while the technology we utilize to serve our patrons has undergone dramatic changes, our patrons continue to ask us to be trusted and empathetic experts.

21ST-CENTURY REFERENCE SKILLS

Does the Traditional Reference Interview Apply Today?

The reference interview is considered a core competency to delivering excellent customer service at a reference desk, over the phone, online, or while roaming. The customer or patron is at the heart of all library services. This attitude is a dramatic shift away from a focus on the preservation or completeness of a public library collection. Being accessible and willing to help are now the main tenets of the vocation. Librarians across the country are promoting the merits of customer service models more commonly found in the retail sector (Ax-Fultz et al. 2016; Weinstein and McFarlane 2016). Libraries like Anythink in Colorado have enjoyed increased fame as their communities come to understand that they are their libraries' focus and raison d'etre (Anythink Libraries 2009). In 1996, the American Library Association (ALA) published (and thereafter periodically updated) their *Guidelines for Behavioral Performance of Reference and Information Service Providers*. Within this document lay the steps of the hallowed reference interview, steps RIS staff attempt to follow to conform to best practices across the United States and around the world. These steps remain largely the same as they were decades ago (Selby 2007, 2). Following the guidelines not only is practical when trying to divine the title of a book that is blue but also has a positive, emotional impact on the patron. The patron then leaves the transaction with (and sometimes without) the information they sought. In either case, they form an opinion on the quality of service and decide whether or not they will return (Tyckoson 2017, 177). Briefly, those steps are as follows:

- visibility/approachability
- interest
- listening/inquiring
- searching
- follow-up

Within these steps, ALA addresses staff behavior as a major factor in the outcome of the transaction (ALA, 2008b, para. 1). Staff at most libraries follow them instinctually, without thought, in order to fulfill the mission of the interview, which is to satisfy the patron. Precision, while admirable, is not always necessary or required by management. This is often because management understands that natural conversation takes over as a rapport is established. Rapport can be built quickly or it can take time and familiarity with a patron. Service quality, regardless of precision, at the information desk (if you still have one), online, or while roaming, is one of the primary reasons a patron returns to the library over and over again (Tyckoson 2017, 177).

Online Service

The aforementioned tenets of the reference interview apply in the world of digital reference services as well. The challenges of delivery, however, vary depending on whether the service is conducted by chat, by messaging, or over e-mail (Selby 2007, 5). Customer service can be particularly tricky when conducting a digital reference interview. An understanding of a patron's body language and speech pattern is fundamental to the successful in-person transaction; however, physical cues are lost when delivering services remotely. Instead of body language and speech pattern, staff must rely on typed language and speed (Selby, 2007, 10). The International Federation of Library Associations (IFLA) identifies the ability to multitask, as well as a familiarity with the messaging or e-mail client as being among key skills that staff need to conduct a successful online transaction (International Federation of Library Associations 2015, 4). The speed with which an interview is conducted and results returned varies greatly between live chat sessions and e-mail reference questions. Some time may be spent sorting out serious questions from spam in an e-mail session, and some questions may require more research time than is appropriate for a chat session. Chat, on the other hand, is fast paced and requires maintaining near-constant contact lest the patron mistake the staff person for an AI (artificial intelligence) device or think that the staff is ignorant. Care must be taken to make the patron aware of these factors in order to provide the best service. Juggling multiple questions in a chat session can be especially difficult. Connections can be lost or patrons can become frustrated with the time it takes to search. E-mail reference has the benefit of being offline and in a more professional written form. Thus, information can be recorded, sent, and saved with minimal risk of loss or errors. E-mail reference is adopted widely by libraries of all sizes across the United States. Other chat options, like chatbots, which appear to be up-and-coming, may offer a critical entry point to online, simultaneous services for smaller libraries because the chatbot may be pre-programmed with answers to the most common questions a library may receive (Vincze 2017, 6). Key factors that will continue to affect adoption of chat services in the next few years in smaller libraries will be budget, staffing, and familiarity or comfort with available software, all of which are constant considerations for staff and managers when instituting new services.

While interviewed directors and staff emphasized that they felt the steps of a typical reference interview have not changed significantly in generations, they acknowledged that the types of questions are dramatically different. It's not new to declare that patrons rely more heavily on Google and other search engines than they do on an old-fashioned phone call to their local librarian. Interviewed staff felt that patrons' reliance on the librarian for those types of questions has declined steadily. One director recalled when the number of users and the amount of time spent on an online resource such as Dialog, was measured carefully and search terms were selected from Library of Congress Authorities and crafted in the Boolean style. These days, staff noted that keyword searching often suffices, but there is a growing need for deep, technical knowledge of multiple devices, operating systems, and programs, as well as a continued familiarity with new and old titles for readers' advisory. These types of requests easily trump more traditional resource research or in-depth reference questions, at least for the staff in the middle-sized and rural libraries we interviewed. Many felt that the definition of a "reference" question needed to be revised given our patrons' changing information needs. Typically, a reference question is defined as

> information consultations in which library staff recommend, interpret, evaluate, and/or use information resources to help others to meet particular information needs. Reference transactions do not include formal instruction or exchanges that provide assistance with locations, schedules, equipment, supplies, or policy statements. (ALA, 2008a, para. 1)

Staff agreed that directional questions should be uncounted and unreported in yearly use statistics. However, they thought that technology questions, including equipment operation and those that required any form of technical instruction, should be counted among the total annual reference statistics (Central PA District Directors 2018).

Regardless of the questions asked, or the definition used, whether conducting a reference interview in person or online, we found the steps to a successful reference interview remain largely unchanged. Staff behavior is the main factor in determining success. Being approachable and maintaining communication ties, while showing interest, are factors that affect the patron's overall satisfaction with the transaction.

IMPACT OF TECHNOLOGY

Librarians are working to overcome the difficulties of training staff on new software and hardware. C-Net, WebJunction, *Library Journal*, and other professional websites offer articles and opportunities for continuing education that focus on training in new technology. Keeping abreast of the latest developments is a necessity for reference and information services staff in the 21st century (King 2018, 30). Staff who take time (or are given time) to investigate the newest databases, devices, software, and hardware will be better poised to assist patrons with their questions in future reference interviews. Given the variety of questions, devices, and resources, staff should be encouraged to approach technology with all of their natural curiosity, not to mention their patrons, in mind. They should ask themselves the following questions: How does or will a patron use the technology? When will they use it? When will I use it? What other applications might this technology have? And, finally, when will it become obsolete? It is impossible to know precisely, but it is still important to plan for the eventual (and inevitable) obsolescence of any technology (King 2018, 34). The classes and catalogs offered by today's RIS staff surely will not be the same five years from now. Years ago, our libraries offered basic instruction on tablets and smart phones. Classes were packed and waitlisted. Now, basic classes are rarely full and patrons flock to iCloud, 3D printing, and photo storage classes. The adoption of smart phones and tablets, according to a recent Pew Research Center Poll, is at 77 percent and 50 percent, respectively (Pew 2018, paras 2 and 4). Many patrons are exhibiting a declining interest in or perceived need for instruction in basic technology skills. RIS staff in the libraries still offering only the basics should consider expanding or alternating their courses. Staff should ask each other what patrons don't know. What questions are patrons still asking? How do staff ensure that the library continues to offer basic instruction to those who still need it while proffering new classes with limited staff? One option could be to offer one-on-one sessions for those that still need basic instruction and to reserve class time for more advanced topics.

Obsolescence affects not only the devices that patrons own, but the instruction and programs implemented. Given staff limitations, it may not be possible to offer everything, but staff should consider their patrons' needs and what they are asking for most. Keeping a close eye on and continuing to be familiar with technologies will make it easier to implement new offerings when patterns of use shift.

A natural curiosity and a desire to learn new technology also can be applied to attaining a familiarity with library resources like public access systems, databases, computers, and printing services. These technologies often fall under the instructional duties of RIS staff, but the selection, customization, and implementation may be outside of RIS staff's regular duties. Understanding how a search works in a new discovery layer and why particular results are returned is invaluable information for staff as they help patrons navigate. In the decades gone by, librarians expected to do much of this for a patron. In our experience, however, more and more patrons wait to ask for help until they've hit a wall. They bring their phone or tablet with them to the stacks and expect to find an item or a location alone. Staff may be roaming or at a help desk but should always be ready to offer support. The databases we offer and the policies, catalogs, or discovery layers we implement should be easy to explain and to demonstrate. Database vendors and software designers are focusing more on user experience than in years past. This focus is important for staff to understand and to champion as they think of the lone patrons in the stacks trying to find their material. A few searches, a little research, and a conversation or two with the catalogers or IT folks should be enough to help staff attain a working knowledge of the back-end, which will smooth the interview process at the same time.

DIVERSITY IN FOCUS

Natural curiosity and technical proficiency can carry a reference interview a long way. However, our profession recognizes that some barriers exist in 21st-century communities that prevent patrons from feeling fully comfortable. This can, in turn, keep them from seeking assistance. Likewise, staff may not feel at ease if they suspect a patron is treating them differently because of their ethnicity or gender (VanScoy and Bright 2017, 111). In the United States, white women make up the majority of both professional public librarians and public library staff (ALA 2007, para. 2). This has been the case for decades and though the divide has grown and shrunk, and then grown again, it is worth mentioning here as an element in reference and information services in public libraries particularly. While representing the diversity of our communities is a deciding factor in our practices in developing our collections (numerous efforts exist to encourage this, not the least of which is diversebooks.org), this may not always be the case when we staff our libraries. Acknowledging the comfort level of both staff and patrons is equally important to conducting successful reference transactions. No two communities are alike and our profession's employment of diverse staff, like ensuring that we have a diverse collection, increases opportunities for receptivity in the representative communities. Staff should be encouraged to surmount any language or cultural barriers by learning more about them. Speaking or reading a second language should also be considered as an asset in any prospective staff. The American Library Association offers numerous resources to assist in providing services to communities where English is a second language. Yet, these resources cannot replace the acquisition of a second language. Staff should be prepared to greet language learners and immigrants with all the tools at their disposal, not the least of which may be found in their pocket. Translator apps for smart phones can help smooth conversations if staff themselves do not or cannot acquire a second language. Whether RIS staff are learning a new technology, a new program, or new language, they should continue to rely on inclusive behavior to ensure a successful transaction that overcomes barriers.

IDENTIFYING RELIABLE SOURCES

In the new millennium (and most particularly in the last four years), RIS staff and patrons, alike, are challenged when evaluating online resources. These days, no library textbook would be complete without some mention of fake news and propaganda. With the recent reports of bots and fake news stories storming social media outlets like Facebook and Twitter, identifying the real story takes more time and care than ever before. Advances in artificial intelligence and programmed algorithms allow search engines and news feeds to return incredibly relevant results. Unfortunately, those results may not be the most reliable. The old adage, "check your source!" is a necessary routine when reviewing them. It takes more time to track the reliability of an online article than it did to go to the shelf and pick out an encyclopedia. However, when validated, the information staff and patrons discover online is more current than a three-year-old physical publication. IFLA, ALA, and NPR, as well as countless educational institutions and their libraries, have released numerous publications and tactics to help train the reader and researcher to evaluate online articles and websites. Current RIS staff should be familiar with at least one, if not more, of these publications, as well as a few fact-checking sites (acknowledging that these too may have ideological ties) just to be on the safe side. IFLA's "How to Spot Fake News" (available at https://commons.wikimedia.org/wiki/File:How_to_Spot_Fake_News.jpg) is an important starting point for staff in training (International Federation of Library Associations 2018). A free, creative-commons-licensed image, the infographic identifies several steps in evaluating the legitimacy of a resource: checking into the source, following a quote to see if another news site has used the same quote, checking an image, and checking our own biases.

Advances in technology have greatly affected the tools we use to provide reference services in public libraries. Technological obsolescence, language, culture, and fake sources can be barriers to great service, but there are also opportunities for instruction and training in public libraries. Keeping up with technology takes time, but natural curiosity and access to training can help staff stay a step or two ahead of their communities. Patrons and RIS staff have an expectation and a right to receive services from those who empathize with and try to understand them culturally. Finally, the sources staff use to advise patrons must be true and accurate. Especially with the last requirements in mind, staff should be prepared to commit extra time to the reference transaction, both in person and online.

CONCLUSION

Reference and information service in public libraries has changed with the available technologies, while the methods we use to conduct the proverbial reference interview remain largely the same. RIS staff are experts when it comes to customer service and delivering reliable resources. Whether the hats we wear are collection focused, instructional, or programming, or all of the three, a desire to create an exceptional experience for users should continue to be at the core of our mission. Whether the service is delivered online or face to face, customer satisfaction should be our measurement of success in the 21st century. Diverse and varied voices in the profession will be essential to maintaining outstanding service to our varied communities. As technology, and the media we use and circulate, evolves, future RIS staff in the public sector can benefit from their own natural curiosity and the opportunities for continuing education afforded by their management, online technical forums, and library associations. Staff should expect to be flexible and open to investigating and implementing new technologies to remain necessary and trusted in their community. Our communities should be represented behind the desk and on the floor in much the same way the collection represents them. If we expect and embrace these opportunities for learning, our patrons will continue to view RIS staff as experts and will continue to place their trust in us for decades to come.

REFERENCES

American Library Association. 2007. "Diversity Counts." http://www.ala.org/aboutala/offices/diversity/diversitycounts/divcounts.

American Library Association. 2008a. "Definitions of Reference." http://www.ala.org/rusa/guidelines/definitionsreference.

American Library Association. 2008b. "Guidelines for Behavioral Performance of Reference and Information Service Providers." http://www.ala.org/rusa/resources/guidelines/guidelinesbehavioral.

Anythink Libraries. 2009. "Core Competencies for all Anythinkers." https://www.anythinklibraries.org/sites/default/files/imce_uploads/Microsoft%20Word%20-%20Core%20Competencies%20Cover%20Letter.pdf.

Ax-Fultz, Laura, Barbara E. Eshbach, Evonne N. Loomis, and Richard C. Miller. 2016. "Take Five for Customer Service." *Pennsylvania Libraries: Research & Practice* 4 (1): 6–21. https://doi.org/10.5195/palrap.2016.123.

Central Pennsylvania District Library Directors and Head of Adult Services at Altoona Public Library, Blair County. 2018. Interview. August 22.

International Federation of Library Associations. 2015. "IFLA Digital Reference Guidelines." https://www.ifla.org/files/assets/reference-and-information-services/publications/ifla-digital-reference-guidelines-en.pdf.

International Federation of Library Associations. 2018. "How to Spot Fake News." https://www.ifla.org/publications/node/11174.

King, David Lee. 2018. "Current Technology Trends: How to Prepare and When Not to Pursue." In *How to Stay on Top of Emerging Technology Trends for Librarians*, edited by Samantha Imburgia, 30–35. Chicago: ALA TechSource. https://journals.ala.org/index.php/ltr/article/view/6582.

Petek, Marija. 2017. "Stress Among Reference Library Staff in Academic and Public Libraries." *Reference Services Review* 46 (1): 128–145. https://doi.org/10.1108/RSR-01-2017-0002.

Pew Research Center. 2018. "Mobile Fact Sheet." http://www.pewinternet.org/fact-sheet/mobile/.

Selby, Courtney L. 2007. "The Evolution of the Reference Interview." *Legal Reference Services Quarterly* 26, q. 35. https://doi.org/10.1300/J113v26n01_03.

Tyckoson, David. 2017. "A Reference for That: Personal Service in an Impersonal World." *Reference & User Services Quarterly* 56 (3): 177–179. http://dx.doi.org/10.5860/rusq.56n3.177.

VanScoy, Amy, and Kawanna Bright. 2017. "Including the Voices of Librarians of Color in Reference and Information Services Research." *Reference & User Services Quarterly* 57 (2): 104–114. http://dx.doi.org/10.5860/rusq.57.2.6527.

Vincze, Joseph. 2017. "Virtual Reference Librarians (Chatbots)." *Library Hi Tech News* 34 (4): 5–8. https://doi.org/10.1108/LHTN-03-2017-0016.

Weinstein, Art T., and Donovan A. McFarlane. 2016. "How Libraries Can Enhance Customer Service by Implementing a Customer Value Mindset." *International Journal of Nonprofit and Voluntary Sector Marketing* 22 (1): 1–7. https://doi.org/10.1002/nvsm.1571.

Part III

Collections

10

Is the Print Reference Collection Dead? The Future and Value of Print Reference Collections

Melissa Gasparotto and Manuel Ostos

INTRODUCTION

In 1902, the American Library Association published Alice Bertha Kroeger's extensive, yet still very selective, *Guide to the Study and Use of Reference Books*, establishing the importance of these works—encyclopedias and dictionaries, almanacs, concordances, bibliographies, annuals, directories, and the like—in the formation of a well-trained reference librarian. The work was deemed important and useful enough to reissue in updated editions with supplements five times between 1904 and 1923. While reference collections have come a long way since then, much of Kroeger's introduction still feels current. She laments the limited awareness and low usage of reference works that could save library users time. She also notes that the newest edition of a title may not always be different enough from the previous to justify the added expense of these relatively costly items. And finally Kroeger makes a contemporary-sounding plea to librarians and cataloguers to maintain easy access to these materials, even if they don't believe users will consult them frequently. Although it is tempting to see frustration with, and the general decline of, print reference collections solely as a function of the digital age, it would seem that the low-use nature, expense, and limited accessibility of these materials have long been active points of discussion in the profession.

However, trends in reference services over the past 20 years have certainly provided a compelling new motivation for the transition of printed reference works to electronic publication: the shift to online reference materials mirrors the shift to virtual reference modalities well positioned to take advantage of those online reference works. Point-of-need reference service has moved online, and the reference collection has followed. For example, the hard copy "ready reference" collection supporting onsite and telephone reference service of the past has become the digital reference collection supporting online chat reference, comprised primarily of licensed and purchased e-resources such as Gale's *Virtual Reference Library* product.

These same trends have impacted the availability of electronic reference sources for acquisition as well. Although Kroeger was quick to point out how selective her own compilation was when compared to the extraordinary array of reference sources available for library acquisition at the turn of the century, the current electronic reference environment is truly vast.

There is little doubt that immediate access to online resources and current trends in scholarly communications have deemphasized the importance of print reference collections. The size and scope of print reference collections have been affected as libraries continue to transition from a collection-centered model to a more user-centered approach. As a result of these trends, libraries are in many cases privileging seating and collaborative spaces over stacks. In this new environment, what is the current and future role of the print reference collection in libraries? Is print reference dead?

DEFINING THE REFERENCE COLLECTION

Although what we call a reference collection encompasses a wide array of materials and use purposes, it is possible to classify reference sources into two major categories: resources that furnish the information directly to the user and sources that refer the user to other materials for relevant information. While this distinction is in practice frequently blurred, the first category includes sources such as encyclopedias, dictionaries, handbooks, yearbooks, almanacs, directories, and maps. The second broad category includes catalogs, bibliographies, and indexes. While the first category has largely been supplanted as the result of a clear user preference for Wikipedia and other Internet sources, ebooks, and licensed electronic resources, the second category continues to be part of the print collection in most libraries.

The current editions of materials such as those described previously are typically shelved together near the primary reference service point of a library and designated as non-circulating to ensure their reliable availability for quick consultations by librarians and users. This combination of collection scope, location, and access policies constitutes the traditionally defined reference collection. Over the past two decades, the increasing availability of electronic reference sources has expanded this definition to include multiple formats and varied accessibility, but the traditionally maintained printed reference collection is still to be found in most libraries. As reference service models, user expectations, and local space needs change, however, the value of investing in such a traditional collection has come into question.

CURRENT TRENDS IN REFERENCE COLLECTION MANAGEMENT

Multiple studies have documented low and declining usage of print reference collections (Bradford, Costello, and Lenholt 2005; Heintzelman, Moore, and Ward 2008; Hellyer 2009; Kessler 2010, 2013). In addition, there is a general consensus in the literature that this low usage indicates that the size of the typical reference collection is too large (Kessler 2010). In the recently published edition of *The Evaluation of Library Services*, Joseph R. Matthews (2017, 240) goes even further, concluding that "the print reference collection should be evaluated for use and then extensively weeded (or eliminated entirely)."

Despite the consensus on the need for aggressive weeding to help manage their size, the management of print reference collections is complicated by a lack of collection policies specifically related to these materials. For example, Kessler (2010) found that a significant percentage of libraries surveyed across New York State did not have written collection development policies for the reference collection, and an even larger number did not have written weeding policies for the reference collection. In recent years, the impetus to develop new guidelines for the maintenance of reference collections has often come from library renovation plans and a vision of library spaces supporting collaboration between students rather than simply as spaces for quiet consultation of materials in-house. Further, many of the previously print-only reference materials have migrated to online—and sometimes online-only—formats. These digital reference editions provide greater content exposure to library users, particularly as part of an electronic resources discovery service and are frequently seen as a better investment of collections funds than low-use print editions (Johnson, Finley, and Sproles 2015; Johnston, Stauffer, and Cordell 2017; Oliva 2016).

The rise of online and distance education modalities provides a further rationale for the transition from print to electronic reference sources, as colleges and university libraries are asked to support students no matter where they are physically located. Many libraries have adopted collection development practices to support online education, moving from a print-only environment to an ebook-preferred collection strategy to better support the needs of these users and have adopted marketing strategies to increase usage of those electronic resources (Kennedy and LaGuardia 2013). As a result of this transition from print to electronic reference sources, Stielow (2014) argues that libraries should shift to a sustainable model to support online education and users as well as on-campus students. However, this shift from a print-only to an online reference collection is not always achievable. For many small and medium-sized institutions, the cost of electronic resources could be prohibitive and access to and use of reference collections could also be compromised.

PRINT REFERENCE COLLECTIONS IN ACADEMIC LIBRARIES

As noted previously, academic libraries are going through significant transformations from a stand-alone print collection environment to a collections-as-a-service model, where users have access to information via licensed and purchased e-resources such as ebooks, proprietary databases, and open access platforms. Amid these changes in collection development and service models, academic libraries are facing internal and external financial constraints, diminishing collections and operational budgets over time. Most notably, the percentage of a library's overall materials budget dedicated to serials and monographs has shifted dramatically over the past three decades: the increase in serials expenditures at ARL libraries has outpaced monograph expenditure increases by over 400 percent (Association of Research Libraries n.d.). At the same time, library space previously designated for collections is now being repurposed and opened for service areas such as information commons and learning spaces. In short, space for collections is shrinking as the cost for collection management is rising.

Given these overall trends, there is a growing perception within the library community that low-use collections, of which printed reference materials are a primary example, constitute legacy formats. It is likewise assumed that acquisition of these materials will eventually cease entirely. However, there remain considerable disciplinary differences in the availability and usefulness of printed reference materials. While it may be true that current and historical printed reference collections in the hard sciences have decreasing importance and relevance—easy digital access to the most up-to-date factual information is of primary importance to these areas of study—it is worth surveying those areas where a carefully selected printed reference collection remains important.

The Value of Print

The expectation at the turn of the 21st century that ebooks would eventually replace print materials entirely has not yet materialized and, given current print publication trends, will not likely materialize in the near future. While an increasing number of ebooks are published globally each year, current reference materials are not always released in electronic formats. Reference collections typically include a sizable selection of works on global regions of the world, and these materials may still be produced in print-only editions or may be unavailable for acquisition in ebook format by the US library market. The four largest global ebook vendors—Elsevier, Wiley, Springer, and Taylor & Francis—offer primarily English-language materials produced in the global north, and their ebook packages are heavily science focused (Gutiérrez-Palacios 2012; Hodges 2015; Ward, Freeman, and Nixon 2015). The lack of relevant ebooks available for acquisition may therefore prevent the development of a well-rounded electronic reference collection from supporting humanities, social sciences, and foreign-language and area studies research, necessitating the maintenance of printed reference materials. Therefore, many important historical reference sources continue to be available only in print, and several consortial organizations such as HathiTrust and the Center for Research Libraries are gradually digitizing these resources, including reference materials, and making them available online. However, as a result of copyright restrictions, these digital surrogates may not always meet local access needs, preventing a library from confidently deaccessioning a locally held printed copy.

Although there are undeniable benefits to using the digital editions of reference works, librarians are quick to note the particular conveniences offered by printed reference volumes. These materials are visually designed for quick and easy use, with well-indexed contents, user-friendly tables of contents, and clear headings throughout. These works are often highly valued as a starting point for researchers embarking on a new study and help establish facts that make further research easier. The location of the physical reference collection is an additional efficiency: for researchers studying inside a library, the non-circulating nature of the reference collection guarantees that the materials will be ready at hand for the quick lookup. Having these collections located near to the reference desk also facilitates librarians in serving users. Further, the compact nature of the printed reference collection is efficient, requiring less time spent browsing for the right volumes. And finally, librarians frequently note the importance of retaining past editions of printed reference works such as directories, as vendors may provide only the most current edition through their electronic subscription (Hartman and D'Aniello 2006, 225; Lederer 2016, 309–310; Singer 2012, 5–6).

Nonetheless, the same cost and space constraints that have driven the move toward electronic reference collections have also driven trends in collections storage and resource sharing. One notable trend is the exploration of different ways of housing reference collections onsite. For example, libraries are increasingly embarking upon projects to interfile reference collections into the circulating general collections. This trend also emerges from a desire to make reference collections more visible and accessible to users. Several case studies have noted that the interfiling of reference material has positively impacted usage of those items (Epp and Hochheim 2015; Frase and Salit-Mischel 2007), and similar initiatives are therefore likely to continue.

An additional response to the repurposing of library spaces that were previously dedicated to collections storage is the rise of consortial offsite print repositories

(Clement 2012). To increase the pool of users for low-use materials such as reference works and foreign-language resources, and to make print materials accessible to academic communities beyond the home campus, some institutions have established shared print collection collaborations. For example, Columbia University, Princeton University, and The New York Public Library joined efforts to transform the majority of holdings in their shared offsite storage facility into a shared collection seamlessly available to users at each institution (ReCAP 2018). Founded to preserve member library collections and make them accessible to researchers, this consortium, the Research Collections and Preservation Consortium (ReCAP; https://recap.princeton.edu/about), now allows collections shared between the institutions to be discovered and requested locally via each library's catalog. This partnership forms the basis of current collaborative collection development efforts that will minimize duplication of low-use items, helping to manage storage costs for all institutions while continuing to provide access to the same depth of research collections. Although the ReCAP Shared Collection is more extensive in nature than a reference collection, this preservation repository and resource sharing service initiative includes one of the largest collections of printed reference works available to academic libraries in the United States.

The Cost of Digital Reference Collections

While maintaining a print reference collection comprises an investment in materials and facilities, managing an online reference collection also comes at a cost. Publisher-provided licenses to online content vary dramatically, but reference content is typically acquired as part of large packages or databases. As a result, the librarian has less control and flexibility over what specific content is acquired. And although the per-title cost of materials purchased as a package may be lower than each item acquired separately, the total package is often a larger overall expense, containing many items that the library would not have selected individually. Further, these packages, even when purchased outright, frequently incur an annual access fee in addition to the initial expense. For these reasons, the acquisition of reference ebook collections and databases may not always result in cost savings over the print for libraries.

Further, some evidence suggests that electronic publication may have had an unintended negative impact on the overall diversity of reference collections. Current trends favor the acquisition of reference collection packages including the same titles for every institution, and Singer (2010) has noted that the price of annual access for these packages makes the total titles acquired fewer in number than had the same amount of money been used on comparable print resources (261). This may result in a smaller reference collection that duplicates the reference holdings at other academic institutions.

In addition to the cost of licensing electronic materials, librarians must consider other factors when purchasing and licensing reference collection packages, including ebook functionality and user preferences. Not all ebook platforms are created equally. Although there is evidence that users prefer content available through platforms allowing book and chapter download, a print-friendly display, and a hyperlinked table of contents, among other features, reference content from a given publisher may not be available for acquisition on a platform with this level of access and usability. Although users continue to show a clear preference for using electronic reference sources over the printed edition, librarians must weigh this preference against the usability of a given ebook platform.

PRINT REFERENCE COLLECTIONS IN PUBLIC LIBRARIES

In public libraries, like their academic counterparts, the print reference collection has also declined substantially in size over the past 20 years. Although the trends impacting the size and scope of the reference collection in academic and research libraries apply to the public library context as well, there are some differences. As Puacz (2005, 40) notes, public libraries generally serve a broader variety of users than academic libraries and may therefore have a need for a similarly broad reference collection. Emphasizing that the goal of a reference collection should be to authoritatively meet the information needs of a given local user population, she notes that public library patrons increasingly expect that library resources will be available remotely. As in other types of libraries, these user expectations and trends point toward the growth of electronic reference collections and an accompanying decline in holdings of the printed counterparts.

This trend is visible despite the sometimes distinct character of public library print reference collections. For example, core reference titles frequently included in public library reference collections are rarely to be found in academic library collections. One ready example is the car repair guide, such as Chilton's. These types of practical manuals are now available electronically, and the easily accessible format is met with heavy demand. In cases where a popular reference title can be acquired in ebook format without compromising the user experience, elimination of the printed copy is seen as a sensible move by public librarians, whose budgets may not permit duplication.

Genealogical research is another area where public library reference collections may differ significantly from academic library collections. However, the development of major electronic reference sources supporting genealogists, such as Ancestry.com, has reduced the need to consult difficult-to-use printed reference sources previously located in public library collections. Such electronic resources consolidate multiple printed works into one searchable interface, significantly simplifying the research process for the user: a key advantage for a user population consulting such works casually without an academic or professional research background. This trend, too, has supported the reduction of a printed reference collection in libraries.

Although weeding printed reference collections is one response to these trends, public libraries have also eliminated non-circulating stand-alone reference collections entirely by consolidating remaining titles into the general collections. In one case, a large public library system found that interfiling their remaining printed reference collections into the circulating collections increased the visibility of such materials while easing the burden on staff of maintaining two separate collections (Frase and Salit-Mischel 2007). This is similar to efforts underway in academic libraries.

Due to the incredible diversity of public library user types, however, the move toward electronic reference sources has underscored the importance of library instruction in public libraries in a way that is distinct from research libraries. Public libraries may have a heavy user base of long-time patrons who are less comfortable with the replacement of printed sources like directories with an electronic counterpart, given the learning curve associated with the use of a new technology. Additionally, the electronic version of a directory may not always include the historical editions in which a patron may be interested (Hartman and D'Aniello 2006; Lederer 2016; Puacz 2005).

Overall, the public library, although quite distinct from research libraries in terms of user population and collections, has seen a similar trend toward the adoption of electronic reference sources and concomitant reduction in the use and acquisition of printed reference counterparts. The broad expectation from users that library sources will be available from home, combined with the increasing availability of a wide variety of electronic reference vendors and sources previously only available in print, has supported a similar trend in reduction of the printed reference collection footprint. Efforts to right-size reference collections or to interfile them with circulating collections are expected to continue, but will vary depending on local user needs and expectations.

CONCLUSION: IS THE PRINT REFERENCE COLLECTION DEAD?

The accessibility, use, and maintenance of reference materials in libraries have been the subject of debate for over a century, but such conversations have taken on greater urgency in recent years as trends toward collaborative spaces and digital collections put new pressures on the allocation of space dedicated to onsite printed holdings. It is natural that, in this context, librarians are revisiting the utility of the stand-alone print collection of non-circulating, generally low-use reference works, which is perceived by many as a legacy service with diminishing interest from users. Digitally available reference works are often perceived as easier to use by patrons, can be purchased or licensed as a package that may include access to a larger collection than the library holds in print, can easily be incorporated into a library's existing discovery service, and are available to consult from home. Nonetheless, printed reference collections persist, due to factors including a general lack of reference collection management policies and review processes; a sense among library professionals that the utility of printed editions of reference works is higher than that of a digital surrogate; the lack of an acceptable source for electronic versions of similar information, particularly from non-English-speaking regions; and the cost of licensing access to large collections of reference materials. However, libraries may choose to respond to the aforementioned pressures by opting to interfile reference volumes into the general circulating collections. Such a choice acknowledges the enduring usefulness of these materials and may increase their visibility and circulation. Ultimately, the library's decision to maintain a printed collection of reference materials depends on a multitude of factors including preferences of the user base; the strength of academic programs focusing on areas unrepresented by digitally available reference products to support the humanities, social studies, and particularly foreign-language and area studies research; available space for onsite printed collections; the number of locations needing to be served; and the budget for print and electronic collections. While it is likely that the stand-alone print reference collection will continue to decline in size in many libraries, the long-foretold decline of print has proceeded more slowly in certain disciplines than others and will impact library choices around reference works and reference collections well into the future.

REFERENCES

Association of Research Libraries. (n.d.) "Expenditure Trends in ARL Libraries, 1986–2015." *ARL Statistics 2014–15*. Association of Research Libraries, Washington, D.C. https://www.arl.org/storage/documents/expenditure-trends.pdf.

Bradford, Jane T., Barbara Costello, and Robert Lenholt. 2005. "Reference Service in the Digital Age: An Analysis of Sources Used to Answer Reference Questions." *The Journal of Academic Librarianship* 31 (3): 263–272.

Clement, Susanne K. 2012. "From Collaborative Purchasing Towards Collaborative Discarding: The Evolution of the Shared Print Repository." *Collection Management* 37 (3/4): 153–167.

Epp, Carla, and Laura Hochheim. 2015. "Restricted: Increasing Access to the Reference Collection." *Journal of the Canadian Health Libraries Association (JCHLA)* 36 (2): 59–62. https://doi.org/10.5596/c15-015.

Frase, Rose, and Barbara Salit-Mischel. 2007. "Right-Sizing the Reference Collection." *Public Libraries* 46 (1): 40–44.

Gutiérrez-Palacios, Lourdes. 2012. "Gestión de la Colección de Libros Electrónicos en las Bibliotecas Universitarias." [Ebook Collection Development in University Libraries]. Presentation delivered at Bibliotecas Universitarias: Nuevos Tiempos, Nuevas Soluciones. Valladolid, Spain, September 20–21.

Hartman, Donald, and Charles D'Aniello. 2006. "Subscribe to an Online Directory Today, Frustrate a Researcher Tomorrow: Are Print Directories Dead?" *C&RL News* (April): 222–226.

Heintzelman, Nicole, Courtney Moore, and Joyce Ward. 2008. "Are Reference Books Becoming an Endangered Species? Results of a Yearlong Study of Reference Book Usage at the Winter Park Public Library." *Public Libraries* 47 (5): 60–64.

Hellyer, Paul. 2009. "Reference 2.0: The Future of Shrinking Print Reference Collections Seems Destined for the Web." *AALL Spectrum* (March): 24–27.

Hodges, Dracine. 2015. "Developing a Global E-book Collection: An Exploratory Study." In *E-books in Academic Libraries: Stepping Up to the Challenge*, edited by Suzanne Ward, Robert Freeman, and Judith Nixon, 171–191. West Lafayette, IN: Purdue University Press.

Johnson, Anna Marie, Susan Finley, and Claudene Sproles. 2015. "Dismantling the Reference Collection." *Reference Librarian* 56 (3): 161–173.

Johnston, Lindsay, Kristen Stauffer, and Rosanne Cordell. 2017. "Optimizing Library Services: Managing the 21st-Century Reference Collection." *Against the Grain* 264 (4). doi: https://doi.org/10.7771/2380-176X.6921.

Kennedy, Marie R., and Cheryl LaGuardia. 2013. *Marketing Your Library's Electronic Resources*. Chicago: Neil-Schuman.

Kessler, Jane. 2010. *Print Reference Collections in New York State: Report of a Survey. University Libraries Faculty Scholarship*. https://scholarsarchive.library.albany.edu/ulib_fac_scholar/50.

Kessler, Jane. 2013. "Use It Or Lose It! Results of a Use Study of the Print Sources in an Academic Library Reference Collection." *Reference Librarian* 54 (1): 61–72.

Kroeger, Alice Bertha. 1902. *Guide to the Study and Use of Reference Books*. Chicago, American Library Association.

Lederer, Naomi. 2016 "Why Libraries Should Retain a Core Print Reference Collection." *Reference Librarian* 57 (4): 307–322. doi: 10.1080/02763877.2016.1145093.

Matthews, Joseph R. 2017. *The Evaluation of Library Services*. Santa Barbara, CA: Libraries Unlimited.

Oliva, Victor T. 2016. "Deselection of Print Monographs in the Humanities and Social Sciences in the Digital Age." *Collection Building* 35 (2): 37–47.

Puacz, Jeanne Holba. 2005. "Electronic Vs. Print Reference Sources in Public Library Collections." *Reference Librarian* 44 (91): 39–51.

ReCAP (Research Collections and Preservation Consortium). 2018. "Shared Collections." https://recap.princeton.edu/collections-services/shared-collections.

Singer, Carol A. 2010. "Ready Reference Collections: A History." *Reference & User Services Quarterly* 49 (3): 253–264.

Singer, Carol A. 2012. *Fundamentals of Managing Reference Collections*. Chicago: American Library Association.

Stielow, Frederick. 2014. *Reinventing the Library for Online Education*. Chicago: American Library Association Editions.

Ward, Suzanne, Robert Freeman, and Judith Nixon. 2015. "Introduction to Academic E-books." In *E-Books in Academic Libraries: Stepping Up to the Challenge*, edited by Suzanne Ward, Robert Freeman, and Judith Nixon, 1–16. West Lafayette, IN: Purdue University Press.

FURTHER READING

Arendt, Julie, Neil Chenault, and John Glover. 2015. "Bring Out Your Dead: Digging up Print Reference Issues to Recommend What Is Next for a Collection." Poster presented at Virginia Library Association Annual Conference, Richmond, Virginia, October 22. https://scholarscompass.vcu.edu /libraries_present/46/.

Buss, Stephen. 2016. "Do We Still Need Reference Services in the Age of Google and Wikipedia?" *Reference Librarian* 57 (4): 265–271.

Chan, Tina, and Brandon West. 2015. "Where Does It Fit In? The Use of Print Reference in Upper Division Library Instruction." *Internet Reference Services Quarterly* 20 (3–4): 151–162.

Chavez, Lyena. 2016. "Creating a Research Center: Space for Collaborations and Conversations." *Reference Librarian* 57 (3): 213–223.

Chrzastowski, Tina, Jessica Harris, and Sophia Neuhaus. 2015. "Print Reference Collections Never Die, They Just Fade Away: Or Do They?" Poster presented at ACRL 2015, Portland, OR, March 27. http://scholarcommons.scu.edu/library/41.

Hampton, Nancy. 2015. "A Library of Design: Electronic Collections Inspire Modern Research Spaces." *Journal of the Louisiana Chapter of ACRL* 3 (2): 68–78.

Julien, Heidi, Melissa Gross, and Don Latham. 2018. "Survey of Information Literacy Instructional Practices in U.S. Academic Libraries." *College & Research Libraries* 79 (2): 179–199.

King, Nathaniel. 2012. "Nice Vs. Necessary: Reference Collections in ARL Member Libraries." *The Reference Librarian* 53 (2): 138–155.

Lederer, Naomi. 2016. "Why Libraries Should Retain a Core Print Reference Collection." *Reference Librarian* 57 (4): 307–322.

Miller, Eve-Marie. 2016. "Making Room for a Learning Commons Space: Lessons in Weeding a Reference Collection through Collaboration and Planning." *The Serials Librarian* 71 (3–4): 197–201.

Pierard, Cindy, and Sever Bordeianu. 2016. "Learning Commons Reference Collections in ARL Libraries." *Reference Services Review* 44 (3): 411–430.

Scott, Rachel Elizabeth. 2016. "Music Reference Sources: Analog in a Digital World." *Reference Librarian* 57 (4): 272–285.

Terrell, Heather B. 2015. "Reference is Dead, Long Live Reference: Electronic Collections in the Digital Age." *Information Technology and Libraries (Online)* 34 (4): 55–62.

11

Open Access Digital Projects and Their Relationship to Reference

Elizabeth Clarke

INTRODUCTION

Digital primary source collections are a luxury for all libraries, large or small. When locally created, they require time and money to develop, space and money to store, and expert staff to create and maintain. When licensed, the number of primary source collections available for purchase or lease from Readex, ProQuest, Adam Matthews, and more have made these types of collections more accessible but only to those whose library can afford the price. While the universe of accessible, digital rare and special collections available to the remote researcher has grown dramatically, this access is within the financial reach for only a small portion of libraries. Many smaller institutions cannot even dream of having the funds to make this type of content available. As a research librarian at a master's level institution, I faced this exact situation, leading to my creating two LibGuides, "Historical African American Newspapers Available Online" and "Nineteenth Century Periodicals," composed of open access digitized primary sources to supplement Marist's licensed primary source collections. Open access digitization projects represent an opportunity for libraries to expand their digital reference collections without committing to a long-term fiscal relationship with one of the for-profit information providers.

Aggregating links to third-party open access digital collections is not a radical or new idea by any means. A search of Google or the LibGuides Community for primary sources reveals hundreds if not thousands of guides dedicated to primary sources, where libraries have amassed links to primary source collections, both subscription and open access. Linking to these third-party digital projects does provide access to them, but navigating these projects is not intuitive for the uninitiated user. Each project will have its own organization of materials, search interface, and means of browsing materials. Archival terminology and organization can be disorienting. Users may become overwhelmed by the sheer size of a digital project when they are interested in only a small portion of the whole. With these challenges in mind, the LibGuides I developed drilled down a level into multiple digital projects to bring together a subcollection of primary sources that the user could immediately access, rather than being directed to a search page for the entire collection, requiring the user to conduct the same search a second time. Librarians possess the knowledge and skills to create a more tailored and accessible collection of primary sources for their user population. LibGuides and other web guide programs are an excellent means to guide the user to primary sources and make it immediately understandable how to access them.

In order to offer some context to the creation of the two primary source guides discussed in the following sections, a description of the Marist College library is helpful. The college itself is relatively young. Originally established in 1929 to educate Marist Brothers, who then would become teachers, Marist College was opened to lay students in 1960. The library was housed in a number of different locations during the college's development, moving to its current location, the James A. Cannavino Library, in 2000. Because of the many relocations, Marist's physical collection is not extensive. This, as well as limited funding, has led to a focus on building a digital rather than a physical collection. In order to supplement our licensed and purchased collection, Marist librarians have turned to open access resources, which are aggregated to best support the college's curriculum.

HISTORICAL AFRICAN AMERICAN NEWSPAPERS AVAILABLE ONLINE

As with many projects in academic libraries, my creation of this particular primary source guide began with a request from a faculty member. A history faculty member wanted to know what African American newspapers were available in our collection. An investigation proved that we had few to none, and due to our limited budget Marist could not acquire one of the collections offered through ProQuest or Readex. I was tasked with researching what was available in open access projects and with compiling a "Historical African American Newspapers Available Online" LibGuide that faculty members and others could use. Little did we know that this project would have a much wider audience than just our community.

Digitization projects like Chronicling America from the Library of Congress and Google News Archive formed the basis of my list of newspapers, as both these projects contained newspapers from across the United States. Chronicling America, created by the National Digital Newspaper Program, a partnership between the Library of Congress and the National Endowment for the Humanities, brings together over 2,600 newspapers (Chronicling America n.d.). This collection can be searched using a variety of limits, including title, geography, and date, and can be browsed by geography and ethnicity. While this collection's interface is user friendly and it contains many African American newspapers—69 at last count—it is by no means a one-stop-shop for all African American newspapers. Google News Archive yielded a smaller number of papers but provided access to some of the larger, better-known papers, previously available in subscription databases only. But Google News Archive is much more difficult to use. No information about the paper's audience, geography, or date availability is available without opening the paper and scrolling through a lengthy timeline. Users need to come to this database knowing what paper they are looking for to find the content they seek. For my purposes, however, the newspapers from these two projects provided enough material to create the foundation for my own primary source collection.

While these national digitization projects were a logical point from which to start, the next steps in this process were not as obvious. Searching on Google for African American newspapers did not result in full-text resources. Instead, I found lists of titles to pursue from the Arkansas History Commission, now the Arkansas State Archives, and a Department of Commerce Report from 1938 (Arkansas History Commission n.d.; Roper and Austin 1938). Both sites were educational, but searching the Internet for those individual titles yielded nothing. So, as I would suggest to a researcher, I took the search back a level, and instead of searching for African American newspapers I began looking for projects that were digitizing newspapers—all newspapers—at the state or city level. Libraries conveniently listed out many state and university newspaper digitization projects that I could then examine. The Schomburg Library had a list of free online resources covering "Black Culture" (Schomburg n.d.). This list led me to a wide variety of newspaper preservation initiatives, such as the California Digital Newspaper Collection (Center for Bibliographical Studies and Research (CBSR) at the University of California, Riverside), New York State Historic Newspapers (New York State Library), Kentucky Digital Library (hosted by the University of Kentucky), Historic Newspapers (Washington State Library), and more (for a full list, see Appendix). The Black Press Research Collective also provided a list of papers along with newspaper publishing history (Black Press Research Collective 2018).

Now that I had a strategy, and a strategy that worked quite well, I began searching for other state library, university library, and public library newspaper digitization projects. These searches netted me many projects, including Hoosier State Chronicles: Indiana's Digital Historic Newspaper Program (Indiana State Library); Michiana Memory (St. Joseph County (Indiana) Public Library); and more (for a full list see Appendix). In my search, I located a number of individual papers that were not part of a large newspaper digitization project but one-time digitization of items in a library's collection, including *The Reflector* and *Richmond Planet* (Virginia Center for Digital History, University of Virginia), *Muncie Times Newspaper* (Ball State University), *Freedom's Journal* (Wisconsin Historical Society), and *The Louisville Leader* (University of Louisville Libraries). This was a labor-intensive process and not all projects were found in my first round of research, but the results brought a depth and richness to my collection of newspapers. Now that I had a group of projects to work with, I began pulling out papers to place on the guide. Many of these projects did not have African American newspapers, but many had just started digitizing and it was worthwhile to know what projects were out there so they could be reexamined later. Once the guide was published and publicized, a few digital projects reached out and provided additional papers: The University of West Florida sent links to *The Colored Citizen*, *The Florida Sentinel*, and *The Pensacola Courier*, and the Montana Digital Newspaper Project sent information about the inclusion of *The Colored Citizen*, *Montana Plaindealer*, and *The Butte New Age* in Library of Congress's Chronicling America site. Their contact made it clear that what I had provided was helpful to them since it brought attention to their work.

The next step in the process was to figure out how to present and organize these materials. When the history faculty member requested that we create the project, he asked that the paper's publication dates, dates available online, and city of publication be included. This seemed like a logical way to present the papers to the user, making it clear what content was available at the outset. The display of information about these papers varied from project to project, so I did my best to standardize the information about each paper. Using Chronicling America's US Newspaper Directory, 1690 to present, I was able to document the start and end dates for each paper. These links must be updated as more dates become available, but this maintenance is minor and is worth the time, as it maintains the integrity of the project. Organization of the guide was heavily influenced by the various digital projects that I worked with. Each used different software to display and organize the materials—ContentDM, Islandora, Dublin Core, pdfs of pages, and Veridian, for example. No matter what software or organization was employed, one shortcoming was obvious—many of these projects offered only point of access to the content, be it through searching or browsing. In many cases, the user had to know what they wanted before they could begin their research. To correct this shortcoming, I tried to provide as many entry points to these papers as possible. The Chronicling America site also influenced the organization of the guide, as the search limits of date, geography, and title seemed to be the most inclusive of user needs. Papers were alphabetized by title for those in search of a particular paper. They were then organized by date, which was divided up based upon the papers I located and the eras in American history in which they were published rather than by the decade, adding historical context for the user, which enabled them to relate the papers to the larger social and political issues of the era. Geography as an organizing principle posed the greatest challenge. Each state had too few titles to make a state-by-state structure useful, so I decided upon a regional approach with the papers organized into northeast, southeast, Midwest, southwest, and west, based, for the most part, upon a United States Census Map (United States Census Bureau 2015). Organization by region solved my organizational issues and allowed the users to see what papers were nearby that could have had an impact on places beyond their city of publication. This overall organization allowed a reasonable number of points of entry without overwhelming the user.

Once published, this guide garnered a lot of attention from other librarians, who wished to copy or link to it, making it clear that both librarians and archivists found the aggregation of their content into a third-party research tool to be a good method to drive users to their content. For our users at Marist, this guide was used sporadically at first (the faculty member who had inquired about our collection had left by this time). After it came to the attention of several history professors who made it part of their assignments and to our Center for Multicultural Affairs, who advertised it to students on campus as a great way to do inclusive research, its local use jumped dramatically. The impact beyond our campus has been far more impressive. Researchers from around the world reached out to me, looking for additional papers and guidance on how to get started doing their own research, from family genealogy to doctoral research.

In attempting to fulfill a faculty request, I had created an interface not just for African American newspapers but also for researchers seeking help with their own work. I have been able to share my expertise with those who, as a matter of serendipity, came across my guide while trying to conduct their own newspaper searches. This guide fulfilled a need beyond the needs of a single Marist faculty member to include the general public. This guide highlighted items within much larger newspaper digitization projects and made them more visible and accessible to the user, thus drawing greater attention and awareness to the wonderful work done by hundreds of librarians and archivists across the country.

NINETEENTH-CENTURY PERIODICALS

The "Nineteenth Century Periodicals" LibGuide came as a direct result of the success of "Historical African American Newspapers Available Online." Our library simply did not have a collection of 19th-century journals or magazines, and we had many students looking for primary sources from that time period. I spoke with my colleagues, and they agreed that this was a resource that would be widely used, particularly among fashion majors, who often examine images of historical fashion for inspiration. So I set about creating another guide gathering individual periodicals from a host of open access digitization projects to create our own collection of 19th-century journals and magazines. The parameters of this guide were not as clear-cut in scope as the previous LibGuide's, as thousands of magazines and journals were published in this century and were available online. I embraced the vastness of this challenge, aggregating as many periodicals covering as many subject areas and audiences as possible.

Searching for 19th-century periodicals proved to be more straightforward than searching for African American newspapers as three major and inclusive open access digitization projects were underway: JSTOR, Making of America (Cornell University and University of Michigan), and HathiTrust. In 2011, JSTOR made journals published prior to 1923 available freely in what they called "early journal content" (Shieber 2011). These materials had already been integrated into our library's search engine and journal search but, much like the African American newspapers, were buried among a vast number of digital materials within JSTOR and our library's discovery service. Once I extracted the individual titles, JSTOR would give me an excellent base of journals covering the arts, literature, political science, philosophy, and more. Like JSTOR, Making of America journals and books were already integrated into our collection. The University of Michigan and Cornell University collaborated to digitize out-of-copyright items from their collections to "preserve and make accessible through digital technology a significant body of primary sources related to development of the U.S. infrastructure" (Cornell University Library 2018). This project made many significant journals from the nineteenth century available online. The third open access digital project, HathiTrust, did not immediately get examined as, after JSTOR and Making of America, I began looking at our hard copies of *Nineteenth Century Readers' Guide to Periodical Literature, 1890–1899* for another list of major 19th-century periodicals. Unlike my searches for individual African American newspapers, searching for individual journals and magazines brought up several resources, including the University of Pennsylvania's page of online serials (Ockerbloom n.d.). This site led me to the wealth of resources available through HathiTrust. HathiTrust, a project between "the universities of the Committee on Institutional Cooperation (now the Big Ten Academic Alliance) and the University of California system," gave me an interface to search for specific titles I had gathered through my previous searches (HathiTrust, n.d.). HathiTrust clearly laid out what was available for each periodical. I consulted a few other digital projects, focusing on international periodicals, including the University of Villanova's *Joseph McGarrity Newspapers Collection* and the *Internet Library of Early Journals: A Digital Library of 18th and 19th Century Journals* from the Universities of Birmingham, Leeds, Manchester, and Oxford. Between these five digital projects, I had a vast collection from which I could select titles I would include in my own collection.

With so much to choose from, it was hard to decide where to start. Much like any other user of these massive digital collections, I was overwhelmed by the vastness of digitization projects like HathiTrust, and even the list from University of Pennsylvania provided more than I could process. So I began with the lists from JSTOR and Making of America, as this seemed the most manageable way to begin. Once I began examining these journals, it seemed appropriate to use the elements of date, title, and geography to organize them, as I had done with the African American newspaper collection. But, because of the wide variety of topics these resources covered, this organization structure was not ideal for the user. In my newspaper guide, geography had greater meaning for those looking for a paper from a particular town, but journals and magazines are national in coverage and audience so organizing by geography would result in generic lists by country that would not provide much guidance to the user. This was a much larger and more nuanced collection of materials and therefore I created subject and audience categories to solve this issue. Cataloging of materials by subject is yet another librarian skill; a librarian does this anytime they create a subject or course guide or even a library display, which can be employed to make a set of digitized materials more accessible to the user. Many of the subject categories selected reflected the college's majors and programs with a few additions based upon the subject areas that the periodicals covered. Art, fashion, literature, sciences, political science, and social sciences formed the first subject areas, as they reflected Marist majors and programs. As I began to categorize these periodicals, it became clear that some fit solely within one category and others covered multiple categories. For those that did not fit neatly into one or two areas, I assessed the content and placed the title in every appropriate category, providing the user with cross-referencing. This resulted in a well-curated collection that users could access based upon information need rather than guessing at which periodical would have the most on a topic.

By cataloging the periodicals by subject, I not only added context for the guide's user, I also created a new subject package that could appeal to our college's departments and programs. For our history, art history, and fashion design programs, this resulted in an immediate increase in materials available to them. Other programs and courses, including children's literature courses and women's studies, both of which have a smaller number of majors and thus receive a very small portion of our collections budget, were well supported by this collection, with pages designed for children's and women's magazines. With the breadth of journals this guide included, the resulting resource supported many more students and faculty than a single licensed database, while allowing for local customization to accommodate the expectations of the Marist College community.

Beyond improving our collections for individual departments, this guide was almost immediately put to use by several of our courses and faculty members. Students in one first year seminar course on disability were given the task of searching these journals for depictions of disability. Students came to the desk seeking help with this assignment and had positive and productive interactions with primary sources and librarians. These periodicals were also used to assemble lists of required readings for several courses. A course on Hudson Valley art and artists required writings by Hudson River School Painters, including Thomas Cole and Asher B. Durand. Asher B. Durand's "Letters on Landscape Painting. Letters I–IX" were available in *The Crayon* provided by JSTOR's "early journal content." A collection of Thomas Cole's writing had been published and was now out of print and exorbitantly expensive. Using *The Knickerbocker*, *The American Monthly Magazine*, *The Saturday Evening Post*, and a few books from HathiTrust, I was able to construct a list of Cole's writings for this class. The subject categorization produced discrete subject collections, so the art journals from the guide were included on the course guides for Hudson Valley art and 19th-century art. Students could then access criticism and reactions to art of the 19th century. Our fashion design subject guide also includes 19th-century fashion magazines for students to browse. These journals have also been used to locate the original publication of articles, literature, and more for various students and researchers. One psychology faculty member asked for *The American Journal of Insanity*, which was not on the guide initially. Because of the work I had done to assemble the guide, I was able to locate this title and add it to the guide, something I do not think I would have been able to do prior to this project's completion. With the diversity of subjects covered by this guide, we could now respond to requests for specific primary sources and sculpt a collection of materials that not only filled gaps in our collection, but created collections of primary sources unique to our users' needs. Librarians are positioned uniquely to know how their users' access materials as well as what is appropriate for users' research needs. So rather than settling for a preexisting collection of materials from a database provider, which may include materials that are not needed by your users, librarians can develop customized primary source collections that are tailored to users.

CONCLUSION

Open access digitization projects offer access to amazing resources from libraries, museums, and archives. Smaller libraries can take advantage of them to expand options available to their researchers without trying to stretch their budgets to pay for them. In creating LibGuides like these, I went beyond just filling collections gaps to create and design custom collections of primary sources from these projects to better meet our users' needs. We could have purchased databases with access to these newspapers or periodicals, if we had the funds, but many of the materials may not have been of use to our researchers or appropriate for our majors and programs. Our library now has a collection of primary sources that directly correspond to our faculty, students, and majors that seek them.

Improving accessibility to primary sources for the uninitiated user was another outcome of these guides. In pulling out these individual items from larger projects, they were more easily accessed and provided guidance to users who would not necessarily know where to start when confronted with a browse or search option on an unfamiliar website with new terminology and organization schema. These guides also balance faculty's pedagogical concerns regarding course guides with the library's need to make materials more accessible. In working with faculty in developing guides, there is a concern that linking directly to individual sources can have its downsides as it denies students the chance to explore and learn how to search for materials. But as each of these items could then be individually searched or browsed once clicked upon, it allayed faculty fears of "spoon feeding" students sources as they still faced the task of searching these periodicals or newspapers. This proved to be a popular way of providing primary sources to our students and faculty, as it made the process of finding primary sources less intimidating.

One final takeaway from these projects is that it added to my skill set and enriched my interactions with our patrons at the reference desk. As I worked on finding materials to fill these guides, I became comfortable and familiar with what open access digitization projects were available so that I could direct our patrons to them or use them to locate particular materials that they needed. In one recent case, a student sought primary sources on British disdain for the Australian accent and language prior to 1950. Using the citations from a secondary source, we were able to find a number of primary sources supporting her thesis, all of which were included in one of these open access digitization projects.

REFERENCES

Arkansas History Commission. n.d. "African American Newspapers." https://web.archive.org/web /20120506081920/http://www.ark-ives.com/pdfs/AfricanAmericannewspapers.pdf.
Black Press Research Collective. 2018. "Archives and Online Resources." http://blackpressresearchcollec- tive.org/resources/scholarship-archives/.

Chronicling America. n.d. "All Digitized Newspapers." https://chroniclingamerica.loc.gov/newspapers/.

Cornell University Library. 2018. "About the Project." http://collections.library.cornell.edu/moa_new/about.html.

HathiTrust. n.d. "Our Membership." https://www.hathitrust.org/partnership.

Ockerbloom, John Mark, editor. n.d. "The Online Books Page: Serials." http://digital.library.upenn.edu/books/serials.html.

Roper, Daniel C., and William L. Austin. 1938. *Negro Newspapers and Periodicals in the United States: 1937*. Washington, D.C.: Department of Commerce and Census Bureau. http://wbhsi.net/~wendyplotkin/DeedsWeb/NegroNewspapersandPeriodicals.pdf.

Schomburg Center for Research in Black Culture. n.d. "Digital Schomburg Selected Links." https://www.nypl.org/about/locations/schomburg/digital-schomburg/links.

Shieber, Stuart. 2011. "JSTOR Opens Access to Out-of-Copyright Articles." *Occasional Pamphlet* (blog), September 8. https://blogs.harvard.edu/pamphlet/2011/09/08/jstor-opens-access-to-out-of-copyright-articles/.

United States Census Bureau. 2015. "Geography Atlas-Regions." https://www.census.gov/geo/reference/webatlas/regions.html.

APPENDIX: NEWSPAPER DIGITIZATION PROJECTS CONSULTED

The African American Experience in Ohio, The Ohio Historical Society, http://dbs.ohiohistory.org/africanam/html/nwspaper/.

California Digital Newspaper Collection, Center for Bibliographical Studies and Research (CBSR) at the University of California, Riverside https://cdnc.ucr.edu/.

Civil War Newspaper Collection, PennState University Libraries, https://libraries.psu.edu/about/collections/digital-newspapers/pennsylvania-civil-war-era-newspaper-collection.

Colorado Historic Newspapers Collection, Colorado State Library, https://www.coloradohistoricnewspapers.org/.

The Connecticut Digital Newspaper Project, Connecticut State Library, https://ctdigitalnewspaperproject.org/.

DigitalNC, North Carolina Department of Natural and Cultural Resources, UNC-Chapel Hill University Library, and North Carolina Digital Heritage Center, https://www.digitalnc.org/.

Florida Digital Newspaper Library, University of Florida, http://ufdc.ufl.edu/fdnl1.

Fulton History, an independent digitization project, http://fultonhistory.com/.

The Gateway to Oklahoma History, Oklahoma Historical Society, https://gateway.okhistory.org/.

Georgia Historic Newspapers, University of Georgia Libraries, https://gahistoricnewspapers.galileo.usg.edu/.

Historic Newspapers, Washington State Library, https://www.sos.wa.gov/library/newspapers/newspapers.aspx.

Historic Oregon Newspapers, University of Oregon Libraries, https://oregonnews.uoregon.edu/.

Hoosier State Chronicles: Indiana's Digital Historic Newspaper Program, Indiana State Library, https://newspapers.library.in.gov/.

Kentucky Digital Library, hosted by the University of Kentucky, http://kdl.kyvl.org/.

Michiana Memory, St. Joseph County (Indiana) Public Library, http://michianamemory.sjcpl.org/.

Missouri Digital Heritage, Missouri State Library and Missouri State Archives, https://www.sos.mo.gov/mdh/.

New York State Historic Newspapers, New York State Library, http://nyshistoricnewspapers.org/.

The Portal to Texas History, University of North Texas Libraries, https://texashistory.unt.edu/.

Virginia Chronicle, Library of Virginia, https://virginiachronicle.com/.

12

From Print to Online: The Complexity of Licensing E-Reference Resources

Michael R. Oppenheim and Roxanne Peck

INTRODUCTION

As academic libraries approach the fourth decade of providing patrons access to electronic content, licensing of these resources can be in many ways defined as streamlined. Librarians have worked with major publishers and aggregators of online content for more than the last 30-plus years to negotiate license terms which has made access to electronic journals and databases ubiquitous and the standard method of providing access to content for most subject areas. The current availability of online resources belies what has been a dramatic shift over the last 30 years from an entirely print collection to an interim hybrid environment containing both print plus online content and for certain subjects such as STEM and business a near-complete transition to online only for all relevant content. The ease of access to content can easily be mistaken by faculty, students, and local community users as something that takes little effort on behalf of the library to acquire. At home, an individual's ability to consent quickly to online terms and conditions to gain access is not scalable in an academic library environment that licenses for potentially thousands of users at a time. A 2017 survey by Deloitte found that 91 percent of respondents agreed to terms and conditions without reading them (Cakebread 2017). Librarians in charge of negotiating license agreements on behalf of all users must take into consideration states' governing laws, risk management, principles of licensing for campus-wide access, price, and a variety of institutional needs when undertaking the extremely complex endeavor of licensing electronic reference resources.

In a diverse world of scholarly resources, the transition of such formats as journals and books from print to online is now common operating procedure for most academic libraries. The information needs for faculty and students are not stagnant and have recently evolved to include data that was previously, in many cases, not part of the print collection. There are also new forms of computational research analysis, such as text and data mining, that are now part of the scholarly research environment. In addition to these changes, the recent growth of programs that fall outside of the traditional academic environment, such as entrepreneurship programs in business schools, has fueled a need for access to online resources related to entrepreneurial endeavors, private equity, and venture capital.

For academic libraries, these types of research and academic programmatic changes mean librarians are entering a new phase of license negotiations to manage not only what online content is to be used but also how it is used by patrons.

RIGHTS FOR ACCESS IN AN E-REFERENCE ENVIRONMENT

The transition from print to electronic access for content suddenly required libraries and librarians to become experts at negotiating for the same rights patrons have when utilizing print material. In the new online environment, publishers were, as expected, concerned about their financial bottom line, given the possibility of the rapid dissemination of online materials versus their traditional print counterparts. The need for publishers and vendors to protect their financial health meant that they sought restrictions on the use of online content through newly negotiated license agreements with libraries. Rules regarding how print materials are used are covered by copyright law, but it is not the same with electronic resources. Contract law supersedes copyright law, which means libraries may in some instances sign license agreements that tightly curtail use of the electronic version of a resource compared to the use of its print counterpart (Dygert and Barrett 2016, 334). Given these restrictions between the print and the electronic worlds, librarians strive as much as possible to replicate the same rights available to print materials through license agreements for each electronic resource. Some libraries, including the UCLA Library (2012), openly advocate for replicating the same rights and uses of print materials with electronic resources through their E-Book Value Statement posted on the library website.

Academic libraries, particularly those that are part of publicly funded institutions of higher education, must grapple with a multitude of restrictions when licensing electronic resources. Financial and legal constraints for each institution dictate how librarians approach license negotiations with vendors. To assist librarians with the negotiation process, template license agreements, such as the standard license agreement written by the California Digital Library (CDL 2017), can serve as a guide for incorporating the broadest possible uses into a license agreement. While the CDL standard license is an important tool to utilize for negotiations, the body of the license is geared toward use of academic resources. The CDL license sets out the basic criteria and license language that libraries can use when negotiating a license, such as specifying access methods, interlibrary loan permissions, use in course reserves, privacy, vendor performance expectations, and perpetual rights. The license terms, although applicable to commercial types of resources, do not adequately address the challenges of negotiating an agreement between a commercial publisher and an academic library. Business relationships between academic libraries and corporate information providers are still in a nascent period, which means restrictions on use can tightly curtail the normal usage patterns of patrons (Splenda and Barnhart 2017) due to the challenge of finding common acceptable license terms between a profit-driven partner and the research mission of academic libraries. Commercial vendors desire to keep access to a resource tightly controlled, which is the antithesis of how libraries have historically provided access to materials. Libraries seek to find the right balance between protecting the interests of the copyright owner while still fulfilling a library's mission to "provide the highest level of service to all library users through . . . equitable access" (ALA 2008), as has been articulated in the Code of Ethics by the American Library Association.

When libraries license resources outside of the academic research enterprise, upholding the principle for equitable access for all is likely to be one of several challenges that librarians will face when attempting to incorporate the broadest access possible into a license agreement. Academic libraries by their nature are intended to be inclusive places of learning—not places in which librarians implement barriers to learning and education through obstacles such as requiring access only via ID and password to current users affiliated with the academic institution. Academic libraries often serve as resources for their local community users. In the print-only environment, the library was open to all users without impediments, whether part of an academic institution or non-affiliated "walk-in" users. A local user who seeks to gain information from reference resources must be accounted for in a license agreement. As Aagaard and Arguello (2015, 428) noted, walk-in users tend to be frequently excluded by vendors who provided specialized business content, which leaves librarians as the primary advocates working on behalf of their local users to access these new types of reference resources.

The growth of non-academic-oriented business programs such as those focused on entrepreneurship has grown over the last decade. An article in *Forbes* (Ashoka 2014) highlighted the issue of business school curriculums being too focused on theory in the classroom instead of being more aligned with the daily business needs of companies. The Kauffman report (2013, 2) on entrepreneurship articulated the challenges to creating successful entrepreneurship education programs involving building and interacting with communities both "outside as well as inside the university." Facilitating this transformational process involves the creation of an academic program that is vastly different from the well-worn traditional business curriculum. Instead of a static curriculum repeated year after year, entrepreneurship education is dynamic and ever changing depending not only on factors such as the students, faculty, and economic situation but also, as the Kauffman (2013, 4) report highlights, on "the availability and nature of resources from inside and outside the institution." The growth of these types of programs means that librarians will continue to face challenges when attempting to negotiate license agreements in support of local institutional needs.

Providing access to content underpins the mission of every academic library, whether public or private. Just as libraries have transitioned from print to electronic when it pertains to content owned by the library, so too have faculty and course instructors when it comes to managing their individual course syllabi. Course management systems (CMS), such as Moodle, Blackboard, or Canvas, provide a platform for students with online access to course materials. While some academic publishers have updated their license agreements to reflect this change from print course packs to an online CMS, not every license grants this use. Some license agreements may permit a print copy of an article to be scanned and added to the CMS. In other agreements, content may only be accessible via a direct link embedded into the CMS. Librarians most often see variation in permissions for CMS access when negotiating licenses with academic publishers, versus corporate business information providers. Although access restrictions between publishers and vendors can vary for a multitude of reasons, one likely explanation for the difference could be the lack of familiarity with the needs of academic programs at schools.

VENDOR RELATIONS

Access to a vast majority of digital scholarly content is licensed through third-party vendors. Libraries rely on publishers and vendors to provide access to content instead of taking on any local hosting or management of electronic resources. Licensing content to external vendors means that problem resolution is a matter of libraries notifying vendors about specific issues and waiting for them to troubleshoot and restore access. Negotiating a license agreement when access is managed by an external vendor outside of the academic library makes it imperative for librarians to include specific clauses that outline performance expectations. The absence of performance clauses for overall vendor performance and availability of 365/24/7 access would put libraries at risk of not providing needed content and with little recourse for financial restitution.

Historically, libraries have served as pillars of stability by providing access to content, whether housed locally or via interlibrary loan from another institution. Libraries seek to replicate this stability by codifying access and vendor expectations through specific clauses in the license agreement. Acquiring content from non-academic vendors and publishers has proved challenging in some instances. Over the years, as technological options and web interfaces have improved, vendors and publishers have intermittently undertaken platform changes to meet evolving user needs and expectations when interacting with electronic content. Operating systems, servers, and other technological requirements change or become obsolete, necessitating a transition for both vendors and libraries. Such transitions often happen with advance notice and explanation of the potential impact before, during, and after migration to a new platform. Often, these transitions are truly about moving to the next iteration of a platform, and, with some exceptions, they do not impact the library user's ability to access the content.

Although transitions to new platforms often go as planned with minimal impact on users, there are often situations where access is changed with very little notice or time to plan for alternative options. As the content needs of some programs shift the classroom lens away from traditional academic and theoretical models to a business-oriented curriculum, changes in access methods can leave libraries scrambling to shift to a new method of access or find an alternative resource with similar data. Corporate clients for these electronic resources can often manage access by unique ID and password because the number of users within a business can often be small, and access to the resource is deemed critical. At an academic library, these changes in access methods strike at the very heart of the core tenet of libraries, which is to ensure the privacy of the user. The ALA Code of Ethics states that it is incumbent upon libraries to "protect each library user's right to privacy and confidentiality with respect to information sought or received and resources consulted, borrowed, acquired or transmitted" (ALA 2008). Librarians need to be vigilant about changes at the vendor level and cognizant of whether or not a vendor-initiated change will impact patrons' privacy.

In late 2018, a vendor that provides access to proprietary country and industry reports notified business school library customers that access to the platform would change later in the academic year. The access model was shifting from IP authentication to single sign-on by means of individual network passwords. Although access by means of individual ID and password is not unheard of in business libraries, it does represent for most libraries under contract with the vendor a significant change in an existing license agreement. One of the challenges for academic libraries that encounter a sudden shift in the terms of a fully executed license agreement is determining the next course of action. The first inclination, of course, is to seek out a remedy directly with the vendor. When it comes to a business or entrepreneurial database provider whose primary clientele may be corporations that can frequently accommodate changes in access methods, a resolution to allow access for all in a non-corporate setting is likely not feasible. Because academic libraries do not represent the primary customer base for publishers of corporate business resources, there tend to be few options for librarians to seek out partnerships in the hopes of convincing the vendor to revert back to the original access method.

Gathering enough librarians to take collective action with corporate database providers to change their access model can leave librarians feeling like the Greek god Sisyphus, eternally taking on an endless endeavor resulting in little to no change in the situation. Another challenge to changing these barriers in licensing is that academic libraries inevitably all have different institutional structures and priorities that determine how they approach working with the vendor. Given that libraries rely on third-party vendors to provide content, it is difficult to know if a library may have the requisite IT infrastructure to make the requested vendor changes. Institutional priorities vary greatly, and although one institution may consider this access change a violation of previously negotiated license terms and grounds for canceling the contract, another institution may be willing or sufficiently flexible to seek out IT assistance to implement the change to ensure uninterrupted access. Finally, even if a vendor-initiated change in methods of access is unacceptable to the library, do programmatic needs within the business school supersede any principled stand that libraries can take with a vendor?

Besides being experts in their subject areas, librarians must also be able, to some extent, to master the business environment of the vendors who provide resources to their constituents. When libraries license electronic resources, it's not simply a matter of being able to sign on the dotted line and everyone will be satisfied. In addition to needing to monitor usage to determine return on investment for these purchases, librarians need to maintain awareness and insight regarding the publishing world. In an era marked by an ever-increasing output of scholarly content, annual inflationary increases, and flat budgets, libraries by necessity must seek out the lowest possible price for a resource. Typically, the tradeoff for lower rates means that libraries will be locked into a long-term commitment. Although lower price increases are always the right move to manage a budget, the multi-year approach requires that librarians have enough foresight to envision and plan for changes in vendor operations and at least attempt to negotiate a provision for this type of change to be included in the license agreement.

CONCLUSION

Even as the evolution of licensing electronic reference resources has brought about some streamlined practices, license negotiation remains a highly challenging task for librarians. A corpus of scholarship from librarians across all types of libraries and subjects, as well as the emergence of templates or model licenses, helps to guide librarians when negotiating for new content. Despite these areas of progress, some challenging and complex issues remain when licensing new and emerging formats. Utilizing corporate data resources outside of the traditional academic market means that each license agreement will be fairly unique due to specific requirements on the part of both the licensor and the licensee, which often results in time-consuming and nuanced approaches to negotiating for rights historically enjoyed by academic libraries in a print-only environment.

Those resources that today represent challenges in the negotiation process will likely move along the spectrum into a more streamlined part of license negotiations. Transitioning from today's licensing challenges into tomorrow's solutions means that the next, still-to-be-determined new corpus of scholarly output will become the next licensing challenge for academic librarians. Providing access to content is at the core of what librarians do, but it's necessary to stop and pause before rushing to license the next highly desirable business-oriented resource. Librarians need to make sure they ask the vendor to include the clauses and stipulations that are now part of streamlined negotiations, and, in view of their recent experiences with new and evolving resources, they must be sure to ask questions about long-term plans and prospective changes in access.

REFERENCES

Aagaard, Posie, and Natasha Z. Arguello. 2015. "Practical Approaches to Compliance for Entrepreneurial Uses of Licensed Databases in Libraries." *Reference Services Review* 43 (3): 419–438. https://doi.org/10.1108/RSR-03-2015-0016.

American Library Association. 2008. *Code of Ethics*. Chicago: American Library Association. http://www.ala.org/tools/ethics.

Ashoka. 2014. "10 Ways Universities Can Improve Entrepreneurship Education." *Forbes*, September 10. https://www.forbes.com/sites/ashoka/2014/09/10/10-ways-universities-can-improve-education-for-social-entrepreneurship/#199f74ff5625.

Cakebread, Caroline. 2017. "You're Not Alone, No One Reads Terms of Service Agreements." *Business Insider*, November 15. https://www.businessinsider.com/deloitte-study-91-percent-agree-terms-of-service-without-reading-2017-11.

California Digital Library. 2017. "Standard License Agreement," January. https://www.cdlib.org/cdlinfo/2017/01/25/cdl-model-license-revised/.

Dygert, Claire, and Heather Barret. 2016. "Building Your Licensing and Negotiation Skills Toolkit." *The Serials Librarian* 70 (1–4): 333–342. https://www.tandfonline.com/doi/full/10.1080/0361526X.2016.1157008.

Ewing Marion Kauffman Foundation. 2013. *Entrepreneurship Education Comes of Age on Campus: The Challenges and Rewards of Bringing Entrepreneurship to Higher Education*. Kansas City: Ewing Marion Kauffman Foundation. https://www.kauffman.org/-/media/kauffman_org/research-reports-and-covers/2013/08/eshipedcomesofage_report.pdf.

Splenda, Ryan, and Marcella E. Barnhart. 2017. "Venturing Forth: Venture Capital and Private Equity Information in Academic Business Libraries." *Journal of Business & Finance Librarianship* 22 (3–4): 208–221. https://www.tandfonline.com/doi/full/10.1080/08963568.2017.1372013.

UCLA Library. 2012. "E-Book Value Statement," June. https://www.library.ucla.edu/about/collections/collection-development-initiatives/e-book-value-statement.

13

Government Information in the Age of Trump

Christopher C. Brown

INTRODUCTION

The election of Donald J. Trump as 45th president of the United States sent shock waves throughout many communities, the library community being one of them. Questions immediately arose, such as, Will government information begin to disappear? Will climate change data be suppressed? Will sensitive records begin to disappear? These are all very valid concerns, as a brief look at presidential administrations of the recent past will attest.

The Trump administration is not the first one regarding which concerns have been raised about integrity of data, permanence of documents, or take-down of information. The Obama administration swept in with an immediate promise to right the wrongs of the previous George W. Bush administration. In his first week in office, Obama issued executive orders to fix the lack of transparency of the previous administration. Using the now-defunct Google Hangouts, President Obama participated in a fireside hangout on February 14, 2013, and declared his to be the most ethical administration ever (YouTube 2013). Yet even these noble intentions did not alleviate him from accusations of misuse of government information. Secretary of State Hillary Clinton's use of a private e-mail server to circumvent use of authorized official government e-mail is one example among many of information withheld despite good intentions. No administration is immune from temptations to cover up, withhold, withdraw, and suppress information it deems injurious to itself.

The American Library Association's Washington Office published a serial publication titled *Less Access to Less Information by and about the U.S. Government*, covering the years 1988 through 1998 (in 30 volumes), documenting what it considered to be government denying access to information as a direct result of the Paperwork Reduction Act (1980, P.L. 96–511, as amended) and agency budget cuts (American Library Association 1992). Beginning with the final year of the Reagan administration and continuing into the Clinton administration, the chronological topics covered in this serial include census undercounts, the Government Printing Office not distributing materials as it should have, privatization of government-sponsored technical reports, budget concerns over funding of the National Weather Service with the subsequent privatization of data, concern over possible destruction of computer tapes used by the National Security Council and White House staffers in regard to electronic messages sent back and forth, and detrimental effects of serious budget cuts to the Government Printing Office. These publications are interesting reads and a flashback in history as well as a reminder that government information issues—whether concerning secrecy, document issuances, government records, agency data, technical reports, and free public access to information—are issues citizens need to constantly be concerned about no matter which political party happens to be in power.

In September 2000, USA.gov was launched under the name FirstGov.gov (Public Papers of the Presidents 2000). Given that this was a Clinton administration initiative, it was feared that after the election of George W. Bush the site might be taken down. As it turned out, the project continued to flourish under a new Republican administration (Harris and Peckenpaugh 2001). After a name change in 2007, the new USA.gov survives to this day (USA.gov 2018).

As we will see in following passages, threats to information continue into the Trump administration.

NECESSARY DEFINITIONS AND DISTINCTIONS

We cannot discuss the topic of government information intelligently without first making some crucial distinctions in terms and definitions. "Government information" is a term that encompasses items published by the government, records kept by the government, and data. And then there is that new category of communication: social media.

Government Publications

From the founding of the United States, there were print publications. These documents were officially published by the three branches of government. Initially, there were proposals issued to private printers for contractual work, and then later the Government Printing Office took over these responsibilities (U.S. GPO 2016). Tangible documents range from official publications of each branch of government to ephemeral issuances like National Park Service brochures, grant application forms, and notices of regulations to be promulgated by federal agencies. Each of these can be considered publications.

These publications are a crucial part of citizen awareness and access to what the federal government is doing. Under the Government Publishing Office, the Federal Depository Library Program ensures that users have access not only to current publications but also to historic publications of interest to the regions each library serves. This redundant system of libraries holding historic documents across the states ensures permanent, public access to legacy information.

In the present Internet era, most government publications are issued in digital form. In fact, at least 97 percent of the publications cataloged by the Government Publishing Office are issued online (U.S. GPO 2012). Yet I don't think many people expect that government documents will live forever on agency websites. Reaching here for an apt analogy—we don't expect commercial publishers to always have copies for sale of every book they have ever published. These tasks are all jobs for libraries. Granted, not all libraries intend to keep copies in perpetuity. Public libraries like to keep on the shelves only materials that are likely to circulate. But research libraries see it as their mission to preserve culture and history. Regional depository libraries in particular have as part of their mission preserving and providing access to all government information.

Government Records

Government records, on the other hand, are not the same as publications. Records, briefly stated, are all the materials surrounding transactions of public business. These may include physical items like books, photographs, maps, and machine-readable materials like videos or datasets. They are important because they provide evidence of the organization, policies, decisions, and operations of government (NARA 2018a). Unlike publications, which libraries (at least regional depository libraries) like to keep forever, federal records have disposition schedules. The National Archives and Records Administration (NARA) is tasked with curating government records.

Government Data

Government data form the basis of publicly available statistics. Statistical publications are well known and often accessed by researchers and the public. Raw data sets are less known and are more susceptible to quietly disappearing. NARA implements open data policies for the data under its purview. Thirteen agencies are designated "principal statistical agencies" (Federal Committee on Statistical Methodology 2018). But in addition to that, there are over 100 federal agencies engrossed in such tasks (OMB 2018). Because of the importance of data to academic and scientific researchers, Data.gov was launched in 2009 (*The New York Times* 2009).

Data is regularly taken down by agencies for routine reasons. The Census Bureau takes down data, at least in a readily accessible form. During the 2012 redesign of its primary access tool, *American FactFinder*, several datasets were removed, including the 1990 decennial census and the 1997 economic census (U.S. Census Bureau 2012). Although this was annoying to documents librarians, this is not the same as nefarious removal of data.

Social Media

New technologies present challenges. Traditionally, presidential remarks, speeches, and issuances are first recorded in the *Compilation of Presidential Documents* and later published in the *Public Papers of the Presidents*. But with social media, many presidential remarks are not recorded in those traditional sources. Obama's comments mentioned earlier in this chapter about transparency were made in a Google Hangouts session. Google Hangouts no longer exists, although a YouTube recording of the event still exists online and has been adequately captured by the Wayback Machine. But a unified, easily discoverable record of government information released via social media does not yet exist, and this is a threat to permanent public access to government information.

The National Archives and Records Administration published the *White Paper on Best Practices for the Capture of Social Media Records* (NARA 2013). It surveyed the landscape and made recommendations to government agencies for best practices for dealing with these new technologies. It will likely be some time before social media postings become regularized in the stream of permanent and accessible government information.

Evolution of Presidential Information Flows

Technology has been changing so fast that it has impacted the ways in which presidents communicate and shape their messages and images. Stephen J. Farnsworth in his book *Presidential Communication and Character: White House News Management from Clinton and Cable to Trump and Twitter* (2018) shows how different modes of communication were differently used by the 42nd president through to the present 45th president. For Bill Clinton, it was CNN and cable news. George W. Bush could generally rely on positive coverage from the Fox News Network. Barack Obama knew how to use social media generally when running his initial presidential campaign and touting his successes. And Donald Trump uses Twitter to broadcast his thoughts.

For having existed only for a decade, Twitter has completely changed the way political dialog and presidential communication take place. Then senator Barack Obama issued his first tweet when the service was just over a year old (Newkirk II 2016). He continued to successfully use Twitter to bolster his political run. But by 2016, candidate Trump had learned to use it to speak to his political base and this became a significant factor in the election.

TRUMP'S INFORMATION TRANSGRESSIONS

With the distinctions between publications, records, and data clearly in mind, let's look at a sampling of situations that have come up so far during the Trump administration regarding government information. We are not concerned here with policy issues or changes in priorities. Instead, we are focused upon information integrity: keeping information accessible that has already been released and ensuring that the public can access published government information now and for generations to come. While government secrecy is certainly an ongoing issue, that is not the primary focus here. The focus is rather upon government publications (sometimes called government documents), records, and data. In addition, the quickly evolving social media landscape needs to be explored in relation to its effects on publications and records.

There have been many "information incidents" since the Trump administration began on January 20, 2017, which have been of concern to many in the library community. Of course, there would be deep policy differences, reallocations of budgets, and shrinking workforces within certain government agencies. These are the results of elections having consequences. The deeper concern is when documents, records, or data are made to disappear or are kept from public view when they should not have been.

Documents Disappearing

Under President Trump, there have been several accusations of information taken down from the Internet. We are talking about information which was on the Internet one day and removed the next. One such incident occurred with a section of an EPA website devoted to climate change (Sellers et al. 2017). As of November 2019, the URL https://www.epa.gov/sites/production/files/signpost/cc.html resulted in the following message: "We want to help you find what you are looking for. You can view an archived version of this content on the January 19, 2017, snapshot." Many alleged that this information was made to disappear for obvious policy reasons. The link to archived content was likely in response to the public outcry. This was a situation that was highly public. The following question must be asked: how many documents or websites have disappeared or have been altered without anyone noticing?

Much has been made of Trump's personal objections to the prevailing scientific framing of anthropogenic climate change. *The Washington Post* chronicles changes made to the phrase "climate change" on a Centers for Disease Control and Prevention (CDC) website after the election of 2016 but before Inauguration Day (Mooney 2018). These changes sent waves of anger through scientific communities.

Since the early days of the Trump administration, claims have been made that reports and data hosted on the Environmental Protection Agency, Energy Department, and State Department websites have disappeared. It is difficult to know the extent of this issue, since each of these agencies has a massive web presence. Reports exist of over 2,000 pages of climate change having been altered or removed (Rainey 2018; Wright 2018).

The Sunlight Foundation's Web Integrity Project not only monitors web pages or websites that have disappeared but also tracks subtle changes to government sites. As of early December 2018, they had cataloged 14 such changes or removals (Sunlight Foundation 2018).

Presidential Records

The Presidential Records Act of 1978, as amended in 2014 (44 U.S.C. §2201–2209), ensures that presidential records are transferred to the legal custody of the archivist as soon as the president leaves office. These records are then considered publicly owned. This applies equally to print records and electronic records (NARA 2018b).

It's too early to pass judgment on record management issues under the Trump administration, since electronic records would generally need to be passed along to the National Archives and Records Administration toward the end of an administration. Some have noted problems with the Obama administration and their lack of compliance with electronic record submission (Lipscomb 2018). Based on past experiences, we have reason to be concerned about the integrity of presidential records under the Trump administration and need to stay alert when there is a change in the presidency.

Data Removal

The focus so far has been on government publications or documents. But what about data sets? The Sunlight Foundation states, "Despite widespread concern, we do not have evidence that data has been removed from federal websites after a year into the Trump presidency." They note that the one exception to this was the removal of U.S. Department of Agriculture animal welfare datasets that were taken down, and then partially reinstated after public outcry and a lawsuit (Sunlight Foundation 2017). Their Web Integrity Project (https://sunlightfoundation.com/web-integrity-project/) monitors changes to government websites through several initiatives. "Monitoring Federal Websites" tracks changes to federal websites. "Web Governance Policy" develops policy analyses. And "Documenting Dark Data" tracks data removed from federal websites during the Trump administration.

Social Media and the Official Record

President Trump has used Twitter to place his own spin on news events; castigate members of the opposite party, and even his own cabinet, as he deems necessary; issue policy statements on foreign trade; and issue statements that swing the stock market one direction or another (Flynn and Hartnett 2018). Although the tweets themselves cannot be characterized as threats to information, it is unclear how presidential communication via social media will be reflected in official documents of the presidency in the years to come.

FUGITIVE PUBLICATIONS: AN EVEN GREATER THREAT

While many are intently watching agency websites for any sign of document, record, or data disappearance, an even greater threat to government information security is occurring, and very few are noticing. I am talking about "fugitive documents"—government publications created by agencies that go unnoticed. GPO was never notified of their existence and documents libraries were not made aware of them. In time, if never cataloged and archived, they will just disappear.

Having acknowledged that government information is volatile and that it should be assumed that government agencies are eventually going to remove information they consider out of date, it is up to others to preserve this information. As it always has in the past, that preservation task is one that librarians and archivists are undertaking. The present state of preservation is not sufficient, as government information is disappearing daily. We just don't know when it disappears because we never knew it existed in the first place.

James R. Jacobs discusses the issue of how many fugitives existed in the print era and how many exist in the born-digital times (Jacobs 2017). This disparity can be seen in the number of documents cataloged and distributed to depository libraries versus the number of documents existing on government websites. In 2012, notes Jacobs, just over 10,000 items were distributed to Regional and Selective depository libraries. Compare that to the over 32 million URLs retrieved from the 2012 End of Term crawl, the initiative that attempts to capture government information between presidential administrations.

The tangible documents distributed together with the electronic documents identified and cataloged by the GPO are only a small fraction of the documents that actually exist. Throughout the years, library associations have initiated several projects to reign in print fugitive documents. The Documents Expediting Project, initiated in 1946, was an example of this. This project resulted in hundreds of thousands of documents being identified, reported to GPO for inclusion in the Monthly Catalog, and released on microfiche by the Readex Corporation as the non-depository fiche collection (Shaw 1966).

In fact, the NARA *White Paper on Best Practices for the Capture of Social Media Records* (2013), referenced earlier in this chapter, was itself a fugitive document. When I discovered this, I reported it to the GPO, and within two days it was archived and cataloged in the Catalog of Government Publications. This illustrates how easy it is for important government publications to go unnoticed and possibly disappear forever, as well as how easy it is to report them and have them preserved for future generations.

On August 10, 2018, GPO sent a circular letter to "Printing and Printing Officials of the Federal Government" reminding them that "all U.S. Government publications of public interest or educational value, or produced using Federal funds, are to be provided to depository libraries for public use, in print and electronic formats" (U.S. GPO 2018). Not only does this circular discuss the "stick"; it also presents the "carrot" under the heading "How Working with GPO Benefits Your Agency." But it's not clear that any of these approaches will solve the fugitive documents problem.

WHAT SAFEGUARDS ARE IN PLACE?

Government Publishing Office Initiatives

The Government Publishing Office (formerly the Government Printing Office) began creating permanent uniform resource locators (PURLs) in March 1998 (FDLP 2010). The idea behind PURLs is powerful. When an online resource changes its URL, the PURL can be updated to reflect that change. This way, PURLs in individual library catalogs pointing to the online versions do not need to be updated. The problem is that PURLs themselves need to be continually checked and updated. Many times, government information simply disappears for any number of reasons. In recent years, GPO has been archiving government content that is cataloged using PURLs. This content includes monographs, serials, and integrating resources (such as government websites) so that when resources become unavailable through the original link, content can be reinstated by redirection to the archived content. It should be noted that PURLs, in themselves, are not a preservation scheme but merely an access scheme.

A search of the Catalog of Government Publications in December 2018 revealed that there are 189,607 records containing PURLs. This is encouraging but is only a small step toward capturing all the fugitives that are out there. In cases where the GPO catalogs massive government websites or huge datasets, it is not possible to archive these as though they were simply pdf publications. Other measures must be taken.

Digital Repositories

Projects such as HathiTrust (https://www.hathitrust.org/) and the Internet Archive (https://archive.org/) are the go-to places for digital versions of government documents, especially for older documents. HathiTrust often overlaps with Google Books in its coverage of US federal publications. But often the documents in Google Books are not accessible. HathiTrust, on the other hand, carefully curates access to the copyright-free government publications. As of July 2018, the project contained half a million bibliographic records with over 1.2 million digital objects (HathiTrust 2018). The Internet Archive text initiative, although containing not nearly as many government publications, generally has more accessible formats that are completely downloadable.

Digital Web Archiving

Numerous web archiving projects exist to take snapshots in time and capture content of targeted sites. The Internet Archive Wayback Machine (https://archive.org/web/) is a generally reliable way to recover documents that have disappeared from government websites. There have been many times that I, as a documents librarian, have used the Wayback Machine to recover a lost government publication. Typically, the pattern goes something like this: a library user wants a document, but the link to the document in our local library catalog no longer works. I then use the Wayback Machine to see a previous version of the federal website, download the document, and provide it to the user. I then also take the time to report the issue to the GPO. The document is then cataloged and archived, and preservation is assured via the GPO preservation initiatives.

The End of Term Archive

The goal of the End of Term Web Archive (http://eotarchive.cdlib.org/) is related to digital web archiving (discussed earlier) but is done every four years. The idea is to capture government websites as presidential administrations change, even if it will be a second term. Begun in 2008 with the changeover from George W. Bush to Barack Obama, the project has been resurrected at each subsequent four-year interval to capture more sites. The idea is that as new administrations come, the previous content is taken down. The list of collaborators is impressive, including the Internet Archive, the Library of Congress, the Government Publishing Office, California Digital Library, University of North Texas Libraries, Stanford University Libraries, and George Washington University. The project has been increasing in its capacity, having captured 3,305 websites from the 2008 crawl and 53,324 sites from the 2016 crawl.

LOCKSS-USDOCS

A collaborative effort to preserve government documents, LOCKSS-USDOCS (http://lockss-usdocs.stanford.edu) is a part of the larger Lots of Copies Keeps Stuff Safe (LOCKSS) project of Stanford University. This initiative seeks to be a backup to GPO's information portal, govinfo.gov. Its strength is the fact that it redundantly preserves the information hosted on the GPO discover platform; although in itself it is not searchable, it is an important backup to D.C.-based GPO information redundantly backed up in institutions spread across the country.

The Informed Citizen

As consumers of government information, you can be on the lookout for fugitives from government information databases. Get to know who your local government information librarian is by looking them up in the Federal Depository Libraries Directory (https://www.fdlp.gov/about-the-fdlp/federal-depository-libraries). If you suspect that you have discovered a fugitive, report that to the depository librarian. There is no reward, other than the fact that you are doing your duty as an informed citizen. "Be on the lookout" yourself for fugitive publications and data. If you suspect something may not be properly identified and widely known, start by looking up the title in GPO's Catalog of Government Information (https://catalog.gpo.gov/). You don't have to be an official depository librarian to report a fugitive document. You can simply use the "Ask GPO" service (https://www.gpo.gov/askgpo) and give the details. Be sure to select the category, "Federal Depository Libraries → Fugitive publications/Lost Docs."

These safeguards are not enough. In years past, print publications were "deposited" in libraries across the states—a secure way both of distributing information far and wide and of preserving it. Now, however, information is hosted and posted online, on government servers, but is not "deposited." The change of format from print to online has changed the way we think about access and preservation. GPO still deposits tangible materials to depository libraries that desire it but merely provides a link to the content hosted usually on government servers.

CONCLUSION

Information is at risk under the Trump presidency, just as it has been under all previous administrations. We as librarians and citizens need to use all tools at our disposal to be aware of threats to our right to know what our agents are doing and the mechanisms necessary to preserve this information for future ages.

Librarians and citizens need to be advocates for greater open access to government information, preservation of presidential information in all formats, and figuring out what to do with the challenges of new social media as they relate to the shaping of public policy. Future generations need to know in a unified manner what shaped the machinations of the Trump presidency and not have major swaths of information inaccessible to it. Further, we should be concerned about all government information—much of it is disappearing daily—simply because we are unaware of its existence.

REFERENCES

American Library Association, Washington Office. 1992. "Less Access to Less Information by and about the U.S. Government." Washington, D.C. https://archive.org/details/lessaccesstoless8891amerrich/.

Checklist of United States Public Documents 1789–1909: Congressional: To Close of Sixtieth Congress; Departmental: To End of Calendar Year 1909. 1911. 3rd edition, rev. and enl. Washington: Government Printing Office. https://catalog.hathitrust.org/api/volumes/oclc/759306.html.

Farnsworth, Stephen J. 2018. *Presidential Communication and Character: White House News Management from Clinton and Cable to Trump and Twitter*. New York: Routledge.

Federal Committee on Statistical Methodology. 2018. "Federal Statistical Agencies." https://nces.ed.gov/FCSM/agencies.asp.

Federal Depository Library Program. 2010. "Persistent Uniform Resource Locator (PURL): Explanation, Purpose, and Tracking Usage at Your Library." Last updated July 21, 2016. https://www.fdlp.gov/requirements-guidance/instructions/709-purls.

Flynn, Kian A., and Cassandra J. Hartnett. 2018. "Cutting through the Fog: Government Information, Librarians, and the Forty-Fifth Presidency." *Reference & User Services Quarterly* 57 (3): 208–216.

Harris, Shane, and Jason Peckenpaugh. 2001. "FirstGov Web Portal Finds a Home in New Administration." *Government Executive*, February 23. https://www.govexec.com/technology/2001/02/firstgov-web-portal-finds-a-home-in-new-administration/8543/.

HathiTrust. 2018. U.S. Federal Documents Program Update, July. https://www.hathitrust.org/u-s-federal-documents-program-update-july-2018.

Jacobs, James Robertson. 2017. "'Issued for Gratuitous Distribution': The History of Fugitive Documents and the FDLP." *Against the Grain* 29 (6) (December 2017–January 2018). Stanford Digital Repository. https://purl.stanford.edu/yc376vd9668.

Lipscomb, Thomas. 2018. "Crisis at the National Archives." *RealClear Politics*, June 10. https://www.realclearpolitics.com/articles/2018/06/10/crisis_at_the_national_archives_137241.html.

Mooney, Chris. 2018. "The Mysterious Disappearance of the Phrase 'Climate Change' from a CDC Website." *The Washington Post*, July 2. https://www.washingtonpost.com/news/energy-environment/wp/2018/07/02/the-mysterious-disappearance-of-the-phrase-climate-change-from-a-cdc-website.

National Archives and Records Administration. 2013. *White Paper on Best Practices for the Capture of Social Media Records*, May. https://www.archives.gov/files/records-mgmt/resources/socialmedia capture.pdf.

National Archives and Records Administration. 2018a. "Frequently Asked Questions about Federal Records Management." https://www.archives.gov/records-mgmt/faqs/federal.html.

National Archives and Records Administration. 2018b. "Presidential Records Act (PRA) of 1978." https://www.archives.gov/presidential-libraries/laws/1978-act.html.

The New York Times. "Data.gov." 2009. *The New York Times*, Editorial Letters section, May 26, p. A18. https://www.nytimes.com/2009/05/26/opinion/26tue3.html.

Newkirk II, Van R. 2016. "The American Idea in 140 Characters." The Atlantic (online). March 24. Van R. Newkirk II. https://www.theatlantic.com/politics/archive/2016/03/twitter-politics-last-decade/475131/.

Office of Management and Budget. 2018. *Statistical Programs of the United States Government. Fiscal Year 2018*. https://www.whitehouse.gov/wp-content/uploads/2018/05/statistical-programs-2018.pdf.

Public Papers of the Presidents of the United States: William J. Clinton. 2000. "The President's Internet Address." II Pub. Papers 1904–1905 (September 22). https://www.govinfo.gov/content/pkg/PPP-2000-book2/pdf/PPP-2000-book2-doc-pg1904.pdf.

Rainey, James. 2018. "The Trump Administration Scrubs Climate Change Info from Websites. These Two Have Survived." July 17. NBC News. https://www.nbcnews.com/news/us-news/two-government-websites-climate-change-survive-trump-era-n891806.

Sellers, Christopher, Lindsey Dillon, Jennifer Liss Ohayon, Nick Shapiro, Marianne Sullivan, Chris Amoss, Stephen Bocking, et al. 2017. *The EPA Under Siege: Trump's Assault in History and Testimony.* https://envirodatagov.org/publication/the-epa-under-siege.

Shaw, Thomas Shuler. 1966. "Library Associations and Public Documents." *Library Trends* 15 (1): 167–177.

Sunlight Foundation. 2017. "Tracking U.S. Government Data Removed from the Internet During the Trump Administration." https://sunlightfoundation.com/tracking-u-s-government-data-removed-from-the-internet-during-the-trump-administration/.

Sunlight Foundation. 2018. "Monitoring Federal Websites." https://sunlightfoundation.com/web-integrity-project/monitoring-federal-websites/.

U.S. Census Bureau. 2012. "American FactFinder Communications: AFF2 Expansion and Legacy Sunset." [PowerPoint presentation]. January 11. https://web.archive.org/web/20120917002830/http://www.census.gov/newsroom/releases/pdf/2012-01-11_newaff_slides.pdf.

U.S. Government Printing Office. 2012. GPO Strategic Plan: FY 2013–2017. https://www.gpo.gov/docs/default-source/mission-vision-and-goals-pdfs/2013-2017_StrategicPlan.pdf?sfvrsn=2.

U. S. Government Publishing Office. 2016. *Keeping America Informed, the U.S. Government Publishing Office: A Legacy of Service to the Nation, 1861–2016.* Revised edition. Washington, DC: U.S. Government Publishing Office.

U.S. Government Publishing Office. 2018. "Disseminating Information Products to the Public through GPO's Federal Depository Library Program." Circular Letter No. 1012, August 10. https://www.gpo.gov/docs/default-source/circular-letters-pdf-files/2018/cir1012.pdf.

USA.gov. 2018. "About the Website USA.gov." https://www.usa.gov/history-of-website.

Wright, Pam. 2018. "EPA Chief Scott Pruitt Directly Involved in Scrubbing Climate Data from Website, Emails Reveal." January 30. https://weather.com/science/environment/news/2018-01-30-scott-pruitt-epa-climate-data-emails.

YouTube. 2013. "Obama's 2013 Google+ Fireside Hangout—Complete." Begins at 35:48, February 14. https://www.youtube.com/watch?v=-gU09bWifFo.

Part IV

User Populations

14

Environmental Scanning

Karen Sobel

INTRODUCTION

Every day, librarians engage with fresh cultural and technological changes that their users bring with them to the library. Reference and other public services librarians may know about these changes most immediately and authentically, thanks to the time they spend directly with patrons. Staying informed on these changes is highly relevant to public services librarians so that they can relate to their users and assist them in performing research using the ever-changing technologies that their users prefer.

Changes in culture, technology, and other societal factors surrounding a library—that library's environment—have deeper systemic effects as well. *Environmental scanning* refers to the process of gathering information on factors present in or affecting a particular environment. Numerous examples in scholarly and professional literature demonstrate how beneficial environmental scanning can be, both for handling current change and for planning efficiently for future change.

This chapter introduces the concept of environmental scanning, with a focus on uses by public services librarians and library leaders, who oversee units that include public services. It begins by defining environmental scanning, followed by a discussion of major benefits. Subsequent sections detail various processes and sources of information for environmental scans.

DEFINING ENVIRONMENTAL SCANNING

A classic article on environmental scanning, by Kendra S. Albright (2004, 40), explains that "environmental scanning focuses on the identification of emerging issues, situations, and potential pitfalls that may affect an organization's future." As all librarians know, libraries' environments are both highly complex and highly multilayered. They involve both physical and online environments. They involve factors within the library, within their users' cultures, and within the sociopolitical settings in which they operate (for example, the national economy and trends in funding for education). Academic libraries have additional complications added by layers of their universities' funding and political structures.

It's easy to feel overwhelmed by the sheer number of factors involved in a scan, as well as the amount of information a scan gathers. A good scan, however, is designed to prevent that feeling of being overwhelmed. It involves strategically identifying necessary data, sources for that data, strategies for gathering the data, and a plan for analyzing the data and distributing the results. It also involves setting aside time to analyze data and to use it to plan for change in the library. The environmental scanning process is complex, but it makes the process as efficient as possible and sets it up for optimal application.

BENEFITS OF ENVIRONMENTAL SCANNING

Individuals who have conducted environmental scans inside and outside libraries highlight many benefits. The benefits tend to fall into several major categories. These include (a) forecasting changes ahead, (b) optimizing use of data and input on environmental changes, (c) planning and prioritizing, and (d) supporting your institution in a competitive environment. Relevant literature comes from the field of library and information science as well as others. I will interpret ideas from other fields in terms of library and information science.

Forecasting Change

One of the greatest benefits of environmental scanning is its capacity to forecast changes that are likely to affect your organization. It's worth taking a closer look at that statement, too: *changes that are likely to affect your organization.* That means that—amid all the cultural changes that a public service librarian spots day to day and the overwhelming amount of available information on federal, state, local, and institutional economics and politics that may affect your library—you can pick out the trends that are likely to affect your library. Albright interprets this concept as such: "Environmental scanning reduces the chance of being blindsided and results in greater anticipatory management" (Albright 2004, 40). It's interesting to note that, while much of the "business literature" on environmental scanning (such as Kendra S. Albright's article) focuses on advantages to managers, in libraries that conduct environmental scanning, either all employees or strategically selected groups of librarians are invited to work with data gathered through environmental scans. James Castiglione, an academic librarian, works with Intel CEO Andrew S. Grove's (1996) concept of "strategic inflection points": points at which something fundamental that affects an organization is just about to change. He further discusses the fact that these changes will typically require changes in processes or services (Castiglione 2008, 529). This concept of the strategic inflection point is highly relevant to libraries, where keeping services up to date affects large numbers of users. Change may also require training or materials. Having a lead on potential changes supports smoother transitions.

That said, environmental scanning also offers support for handling problems that do sneak up on libraries. Castiglione (2008, 529)—who advocates conducting a continuous environmental scanning process in academic libraries—notes that scanning can also catch "emerging problems; competitive weaknesses; organizational strengths; and new service opportunities in an early stage." In reality, early-stage identification of needs is among the most pragmatic strengths of scanning.

Optimizing Use of Data and Information on Environmental Change

Feelings of being overwhelmed by both formal and informal data and information are common among those planning for change in an institution. Jill R. Hough and Margaret A. White (2004, 783), who study behaviors related to scanning, note that a well-defined, efficient scanning process helps users to avoid the paralysis that can occur when participants are just too overwhelmed by data to know what to do with it. They note that organizations often scan *less* during times when they are undergoing greater change.

Environmental scanning guides librarians to use data efficiently in several ways. A library's environmental scanning process will likely involve reading of some relevant, externally produced scans, such as the Association of College and Research Libraries' (ACRL) environmental scans, published every two years. These scans cover topics relevant to academic libraries in the United States. Many of the topics relate to trends that public service librarians interact with in person, or that inform their work with students, faculty, and learning materials. ACRL's scans match these trends with data and other research. For example, ACRL's *Environmental Scan 2017* succinctly covers trends in high school graduation rates and other aspects of college preparation, as well as current topics of interest such as textbook purchasing (Association of College and Research Libraries 2017, 6). These reports help librarians and administrators to frame their observations and actions in terms of national trends.

The American Library Association also publishes an annual *State of America's Libraries Report*. The report covers trends that affect all types of libraries, including demographics and technologies. In addition to several sections on trends, the report offers separate sections analyzing the trends in the context of academic libraries, public libraries, and school libraries (American Library Association 2018).

A number of scans of public library systems are available free online. Many of these have been created or commissioned by statewide library systems. Simply searching for "public library environmental scan" brings up a collection of the scans. Looking through a selection of scans will suggest the range of scopes and depths that organizations conducting the scans can encompass. It also provides examples of the sources that the librarians, consultants, and others who conducted these scans turned to for data. Much of the data comes from either city government offices or national censuses. Several examples are worth recommending. The "Environmental Scan for Ontario Public Libraries Report" (Clubb 2011) exemplifies a concise report that highlights key data and objectives. "Environment Scan: Current and Future Needs for Library Services in Rhode Island" (ESC New England 2017) and "Georgia Public Library Service 2007 Environmental Scan" (James 2007) both provide considerably more detailed scans, drawing data from numerous publicly available sources.

Thus, environmental scans make efficient use of data from both within and outside an institution or public library system. They help plan for better future processes. They also help investigate impressions through data.

Planning and Prioritizing

In a continually changing educational environment, as well as in a difficult economic climate, prioritization of funds and efforts matter. Information related to trends discussed in the previous sections can help a library with its strategic planning process, with departmental goals, and with identifying other areas in which updated or new initiatives could benefit users.

Several categories of planning and prioritization receive special attention in planning literature across many fields. One involves the shaping of internal processes. We have all seen examples in our libraries where a certain process that we follow lags behind or needs revision—often due to hanging on too long to a procedure that was helpful in the past. Albright highlights awareness of the need for updating these internal processes as a benefit of scanning. Scans that gather patron feedback (discussed later in this chapter) often uncover challenges or areas of discomfort that arise repeatedly in a single library. Alternatively, turning to a national scan such as ACRL's *Environmental Scan 2017* can uncover trends among other libraries that are worth following. Scans create the opportunity for informed change.

Libraries also benefit when they use environmental scanning to plan selection, purchase, and integration of technologies into their work. Sometimes the barrage of new technologies, as well as real or implied pressure to use them to benefit users, feels overwhelming. Char Booth writes compellingly about environmental scans' capacity to turn from "technolust" toward identifying technologies that our patrons really need and want. She reminds us that, at least once (and probably more), most libraries have implemented a technology that is popular in users' social lives but that they do not actually want to use in an academic setting. Her example is "Skype a librarian" services that academic library users largely ignored, despite using Skype heavily in their personal lives (Booth 2009, 1). Scanning regarding the desires of patrons at one's own institution, as well as reading trend sections of national scans, can help focus efforts and funds in ways that are more likely to succeed.

Support in a Competitive Environment

Articles on environmental scanning written in the business world often focus on getting ahead of the competition. This perspective seems irrelevant or even off-putting to some academic librarians. However, the reality is that our libraries compete for funding within our universities, and departments may compete for some funding within a library. Both libraries and departments are of course subject to the reshuffling of funds each fiscal year.

Environmental scanning guides libraries and departments toward gathering both internal and external data that supports proposals and requests. Being able to make one's case for the strongest funding possible gives those who request funding an edge. Castiglione writes about another type of edge as well. He writes about the benefit of having "lead-time": giving oneself as much time as possible to think through the service implications of a desired change. He writes that, not surprisingly, library administrators are often best convinced by requests that have had time for detailed planning put into them (Castiglione 2008, 530). These initiatives effectively have an edge on internal competition for funding. Any who are eligible for grants or other external funding would, by extension, have an edge there as well.

SCANNING ONLINE VERSUS IN-PERSON USERS' ENVIRONMENTS

When a library is considering conducting an environmental scan, one of the first questions is whether the scan focuses on the experiences of users who interact with the library purely online or those who can use both in-person and online services. While there is less separation of experiences and needs than there used to be between these two groups of users, those who *must* interact with the library because of distance or other factors have different requirements than those who can comfortably meet their needs with a combination of in-person and online services. (For simplicity's sake, I will refer to scans exploring the needs of online-only users as "online" and those who can take advantage of both in-person and online environments as "in-person.")

What's the Same?

A great deal of overlapping information appears in both scans of online and in-person environments. Categories of information that will likely appear in both are as follows:

- Demographics or other background on users.
- Statistics on resources or services, possibly broken down by what's available and usage statistics.
- Users' feedback on their needs or desires. This may be broken down by different user groups and comparisons of usage/desires/awareness/outreach.
- Funding or other support available.
- Outside factors that affect users and their needs, such as trends in technology, cultural or societal changes, and more.

It's important to note that the planning performed before the scan should carefully identify what information is needed to meet the library's specific goals. Gathering of extraneous information makes the process longer and less efficient.

What is Different?

As technology becomes a bigger and bigger part of in-person users' library experiences, the differences between scans of in-person versus online users' environments become smaller and smaller. At present, the difference is primarily in ensuring that online users' needs can be met entirely through the services and resources available to them. Scans focusing on the online environment will emphasize technology. Questions over how users connect with librarians and services will focus on online options. (For example, is research assistance available to online users? How does troubleshooting work for these users? Are there multiple modes of communication available to online users, such as IM and telephone-based assistance?) Librarians who design scans of online environments also often emphasize the library's social media presence. They may also ask significant questions about online library instruction that users have received, as well as online teaching tools like tutorials. Ultimately, goals of online and in-person scans are the same: focusing on users and their needs. The differences are primarily in the medium.

Examples of Scans

Many fine examples of environmental scans are available. Char Booth's (2009) work is a book-length version of one academic library's in-person environmental scan, with emphasis on technology. It provides an all-encompassing look at a library's services and environment. Don't get intimidated, though; most scans are smaller in scale!

The University of Arizona Libraries (UAL) perform continual scanning—meaning that they gather their selected data continuously and evaluate the need for change at selected points. The article on UAL's scan focuses on gathering a broad view of the in-person experience despite the weight placed on technology (Huff-Eibl, Miller-Wells, and Begay 2014). While scans conducted over a shorter period of time are considerably more common than continual scans, UAL's structures and techniques apply just as well to shorter scans.

A number of articles profile scans of online environments. Wendy M. Duff, Catherine A. Johnson, and Joan M. Cherry scanned archives across Canada to explore social media practices. Their methods for identifying and contacting users, as well as their questions and study design, provide an excellent example of scanning a specific online environment (Duff, Johnson, and Cherry, 2013, 77–96). Nicola A. Cecchino (2010, 218–227), by contrast, focuses on scanning a single medical library's online environment at a critical point in its development. While the resources were used heavily by medical students studying in person, it was crucial that a full range of support be available during their hospital work as well as their studies. Paulette Rothbauer's (2009, 465–483) scan provides a detailed examination of a grouping of rural public libraries and other organizations in the community that provide related functions. Her work is a strong example of carefully defining one's community.

Scans that focus on in-person and online environments often incorporate information from major national scans produced by professional and other organizations such as ACRL and the Pew Research Center. These will be discussed later in this chapter.

ORGANIZATION-CENTERED CONTENT AND STEPS

Planning both the steps of a scan and the internal content that needs to be gathered are so closely tied together that it makes sense to discuss them together. Castiglione's article on scanning in libraries sets out basic steps in a pragmatic manner. A condensed list of his steps is as follows:

1. Gaining the buy-in of administrators and librarians who will conduct the scan
2. Developing a list of questions or concerns to study
3. Developing a list of information sources regarding the questions or concerns
4. Gathering and analyzing the information
5. Presenting the information, in print or in person as appropriate (Castiglione 2008, 534)

His outline can be modified to inform the range of information needs of a particular study. They can be modified to inform both in-person and online studies.

Albright's (2004, 44) classic article on scanning adds "making informed decisions" as the final step of the process. She thus reminds us that a crucial part of the process is actually using new knowledge to create change.

One of the most important parts of the scan is the second step in Castiglione's list. At first, the idea of scanning the entire environment of a library, or determining how to explore a particular set of questions or concerns in great depth, can feel overwhelming. How does one turn the life of a library into a set of productive questions to explore?

Once the team that will be conducting the scan has selected its questions, the next step involves interpreting them as instruments and processes that can be used to gather the data. It's important to think about how best to connect with the users whose input is most relevant in terms of answering a question. Is there a setting in which it makes the most sense to approach the intended users? Can you actively seek out users, for example, by sharing a survey through an e-mail list or attending a library- or university-sponsored event? Alternatively, would you prefer to create surveys or polls that users will find and choose to complete on their own, perhaps on the home page of your library's website?

Once you have decided on a proposed methodology, you will need to draft instruments. To make the best instruments possible, consider seeking out expertise from a research methods expert or a research center on your campus. As well, be sure to pilot test your instruments.

BUILDING A PICTURE OF THE EXTERNAL ENVIRONMENT

A good scan also includes significant information on the environment surrounding the study, as well as larger societal trends and issues affecting the study. First of all, it is important to set your study up against the environment of the institution or community the library serves. Your study will likely gather demographics on those who responded. It is important to provide comparable data describing relevant campus or community user populations as appropriate. These give your readers a broader sense of how your findings would apply to a larger population—perhaps especially if you are making the point that you hope to get more users to opt into library services. For academic libraries, your institution's Office of Institutional Research or similar can give you statistics on campus populations as a whole. You may also find that colleagues in your library have already gathered some of the data for IPEDS or ACRL annual reporting. It's also worth investigating the kinds of data that both public services and technical services departments in your library gather regarding users. For example, you may be able to find detailed and highly useful statistics on who receives instruction, which groups tend to use various categories of online resources, and more. For public libraries, you will likely draw much of your data from city government offices or reports, or from census data.

One of the most challenging parts of an environmental scan may be choosing the trends that inform the survey. Depending on what you are working on, these may either provide background evidence and support in your survey or help you to generate questions for your survey that explore current library and societal trends.

Albright highlights six major categories of external information that an environmental scan should explore. They are trends in your industry, technology, regulatory changes, economic factors, social or demographic shifts, and political factors or changes (Albright 2004, 41–42). Users should focus on aspects of these trends that relate directly to their organizations.

Sources for Information on Trends

Both the library world and some research-oriented external organizations offer resources that can help to both identify and provide data on relevant trends. The reports can both inspire questions for your own scan and provide information to incorporate into your study. The following sections briefly break sources down by category of information.

Library Trends

For academic libraries, one of the preeminent sources is ACRL's biennial *Environmental Scan*, discussed earlier in this chapter. ACRL's scans provide a wide range of information covering most of Albright's categories. In particular, it covers trends in library services, discussing the nature of the trends and prevalence of various approaches. It also provides great detail on societal factors affecting libraries and the populations they serve. Every two years, ACRL also puts together a brief report "Top Trends in Academic Libraries" (Association of College and Research Libraries 2016). The trends often have a technological or service-oriented focus. The reports point readers toward extensive resources on the topics.

The aforementioned *State of America's Libraries Report*, published by the American Library Association, provides similar information on trends seen across the United States in a broader context. Librarians interested in researching specific additional trends, particularly in terms of either technological or societal factors, may wish to explore the Pew Research Center's reports online.

Higher Education

Several organizations devoted to higher education provide environmental scans that are very relevant to background for academic libraries. This section highlights several, with brief summaries of their contents.

Ithaka S+R is a not-for-profit organization that states that it "provides research and strategic guidance to help the academic and cultural communities serve the public good and navigate economic, technological, and demographic change" (Ithaka S+R 2017). The organization performs environmental scans of academic libraries nationwide every few years (somewhat irregularly), as well as other surveys that can inform libraries, such as scans of academic faculty. Its reports are available free online through Ithaka S+R's website.

EDUCAUSE works to explore and support effective use of technology in higher education. Its library offers numerous reports on prevalence of specific student and faculty needs, as well as best practices for meeting them.

The University of Oxford has begun a series of annual or biennial reports profiling trends in higher education worldwide (International Strategy Office, University of Oxford, 2017). The reports, available free online, follow a number of trends that often have a focus on international enrollments. They often have a somewhat administrative slant. The reports gather data from a representative set of universities around the world.

The National Center for Education Statistics (NCES) provides rich data sets and evidence-based publications on education in the United States. Users can select and download data to meet their needs. They can also collect data on individual institutions of higher education (though this will not be as rich a source as an Office of Institutional Research can provide). For those who want to explore data that NCES has collected, analyzed, and interpreted, its collection of postsecondary surveys, linked on the "Surveys & Programs" page (https://nces.ed.gov/Surveys/), is a useful place to start.

Trends in Society

A perennial librarian favorite, the Pew Research Center conducts environmental scans related to a wide range of societal trends. While Pew has traditionally focused its work on the United States, it now conducts more and more international surveys. It provides both datasets and reports. Technology is a major category of Pew Research, and one especially useful for academic librarians. The technologies covered are remarkably timely, and Pew interviews a representative swath of society, particularly in its surveys in the United States. Its "Internet & Technology" (http://www.pewinternet.org/) section is a major source of information on tech trends in the United States. This provides an opportunity to learn about new trends, as well as to learn how widespread technologies are, and how accessible they are to different income groups. Pew also explores a number of other areas of trends, such as trends in social behaviors, workplaces, life among the US Hispanic populations, and religious beliefs.

The Call to Share

Once a library has created an environmental scan, it should consider the best ways to share its findings. A library has options for doing this. For example, Castiglione asks academic librarians to consider publishing their reports on their libraries' websites (Castiglione 2008, 534). This makes for easy gathering of information for other libraries who want to see examples or gather data for comparison. Public libraries have already taken the lead in this practice. Of course, libraries can also publish in many scholarly and professional publications.

CONCLUSION

Environmental scanning gives libraries the opportunity to explore their users' needs. It allows them to investigate questions regarding their own services and to give them context for understanding. It may also uncover needs or potential approaches that no one in the library has yet considered. Environmental scans are indeed a tremendous tool for academic and public libraries.

REFERENCES

Albright, Kendra S. 2004. "Environmental Scanning: Radar for Success." *Information Management Journal* 38 (3): 38–45.

American Library Association. 2018. "State of America's Libraries Report 2018." Text. http://www.ala.org/news/state-americas-libraries-report-2018.

Association of College and Research Libraries. 2016. *2016 Top Trends in Academic Libraries: A Review of the Trends and Issues Affecting Academic Libraries in Higher Education.* Chicago, IL: Association of College and Research Libraries. https://crln.acrl.org/index.php/crlnews/article/view/9505/10798.

Association of College and Research Libraries. 2017. *Environmental Scan 2017.* Chicago, IL: Association of College and Research Libraries. http://www.ala.org/acrl/sites/ala.org.acrl/files/content/publications/whitepapers/EnvironmentalScan2017.pdf.

Booth, Char. 2009. *Informing Innovation: Tracking Student Interest in Emerging Library Technologies at Ohio University.* Chicago, IL: Association of College and Research Libraries.

Castiglione, James. 2008. "Environmental Scanning: An Essential Tool for Twenty-First Century Librarianship." *Library Review* 57 (7): 528–536. https://doi.org/10.1108/00242530810894040.

Cecchino, Nicola J. 2010. "A Systematic Approach to Developing an Online Medical Library." *Journal of Electronic Resources in Medical Libraries* 7 (3): 218–227. https://doi.org/10.1080/15424065.2010.505509.

Clubb, Barbara. 2011. "Environmental Scan for Ontario Public Libraries Report." Ottawa, ON, Canada: Ottawa Public Library Board. https://biblioottawalibrary.ca/sites/default/files/Board_Docs/111212/Doc%2010%20Environmental%20Scan%20for%20Ontario%20Public%20Libraries.pdf.

Duff, Wendy M., Catherine A. Johnson, and Joan M. Cherry. 2013. "Reaching Out, Reaching In: A Preliminary Investigation into Archives' Use of Social Media in Canada." *Archivaria* 75: 77–96.

EDUCAUSE. n.d. "Library." https://library.educause.edu/.

ESC New England. 2017. "Environment Scan: Current and Future Needs for Library Services in Rhode Island." Providence, RI: Rhode Island Office of Library and Information Services. http://www.olis.ri.gov/about/5yplan/plan2018/environmentalScan.pdf.

Grove, Andrew S. 1996. *Only the Paranoid Survive: How to Exploit the Crisis Points That Challenge Every Company and Career.* New York: Currency Doubleday.

Hough, Jill R., and Margaret A. White. 2004. "Scanning Actions and Environmental Dynamism: Gathering Information for Strategic Decision Making." *Management Decision* 42 (6): 781–793. https://doi.org/10.1108/00251740410542348.

Huff-Eibl, Robyn, John Miller-Wells, and Wendy Begay. 2014. "Understanding the Voice of the Customer: Practical, Data-Driven Planning and Decision Making for Access Services." *Journal of Access Services* 11 (3): 119–134. https://doi.org/10.1080/15367967.2014.916150.

International Strategy Office, University of Oxford. 2017. "International Trends in Higher Education 2016–17." http://www.ox.ac.uk/sites/files/oxford/trends%20in%20globalisation_WEB.pdf.

"Internet & Technology—Pew Research Center." n.d. http://www.pewinternet.org/.

"Ithaka S+R." 2017. http://www.sr.ithaka.org/.

James, Leslie. 2007. "Georgia Public Library Service 2007 Environmental Scan." Atlanta, GA: Georgia Public Library Service. https://www.georgialibraries.org/directorskb/?q=system/files/2007environ_scanGPLS.pdf.

National Center for Education Statistics. n.d. "Education Statistics Surveys and Program Areas at NCES (National Center for Education Statistics)." https://nces.ed.gov/Surveys/.

"National Center for Education Statistics (NCES) Home Page, Part of the U.S. Department of Education." n.d. https://nces.ed.gov/.

"Pew Research Center." n.d. http://www.pewresearch.org/.

Rothbauer, Paulette. 2009. "Exploring the Placelessness of Reading Among Older Teens in a Canadian Rural Municipality." *Library Quarterly* 79 (4): 465–483.

15

The Global Reach of Reference

Lisa Martin

INTRODUCTION

Reference is no longer tied to a desk in the library but, with the rise of new technologies, reaches users around the world. Services for dispersed and diverse users are vital services for a significant number of library users. Public library users in the United States include those who are younger, poorer, older, parenting, or caregiving, and of different ethnic backgrounds, all of whom rely on public libraries to offer services and programs to meet their needs (Horrigan 2016). Academic libraries are seeing student users who are more often first-generation college students, more likely to identify as people of color, and more likely to be nontraditional students than US college students of previous decades (United States Department of Education 2018). This chapter will focus on the ways in which public and academic libraries in the United States and elsewhere have developed new reference services tailored to meet the needs of changing user populations and changing library identities.

Reference services today are significantly different than they were even 10 years ago. After years of transitioning to new service models, some more successful (combined service desks) than others (roving reference), libraries have settled on a stronger understanding of what reference means in the age of the Internet. This has led to services that are more connected to the broader institutional goals and user needs. Reference is no longer confined to a desk on the main floor of the library, but instead takes place online, in community meetings, in residence halls, in transitional housing, in orientation, and yes, still at a desk in the library. That desk now offers services like college student voter registration (Bonnell 2014), on-call social workers for those in need (Milone Hill 2011), writing center walk-up appointments (Andrews, Wright, and Raskin 2016), and help with technology, from ebook readers to smart phones (Cushing 2016). Reference is no longer distinct from instruction but in fact an additional opportunity to reinforce key concepts or illustrate new ones. Reference is also no longer distinct from outreach but is a mechanism to reach out to the community and engage with their information needs. Reference, the provision of either information or the skills to access it, remains integral to the work of public services library staff but in a wholly re-imagined venue with new goals and priorities. Freed from the traditional model of the desk, libraries have developed successful services designed to truly meet the needs of a variety of users from different backgrounds and in distinct locations.

To meet the needs of these users, successful public and academic libraries have more similarities than differences in their approaches. Successful libraries are more externally focused on their users, more engaged with working within their respective communities, and more interested in using data and assessment to determine whether that work is meeting the outcomes and priorities of libraries and parent institutions. Successful libraries are, as the following will detail, focused on the unique needs of users, the places they are venturing to and the technology they are using to communicate, and the diversity of challenges for which they might be seeking help.

THE NEW NEEDS OF USERS

As the number of reference questions declined in many libraries, libraries sought to re-imagine reference in a way that fits in with the evolving and changing needs of their users. The questions that continued to be asked (O'Gorman and Trott 2009) were a mix of directional (the location of the bathroom remains popular), technological (everything from printer jams to complicated questions about software), and intellectual (the more complex reference questions that remained after the simple ones moved to the Internet). The complex reference questions began to look more like instruction opportunities, while the directional and especially technological questions began to look better suited for others to answer (Elmborg 2002). All of these changes in users' questions necessarily dictated a change in the conceptualization of reference.

The reconceptualization of reference happened in a number of ways. Combined circulation and reference desks became popular, meeting the needs of users who wanted to ask their questions without necessarily knowing how a library was organized or being sent from desk to desk. There was a rise in paraprofessional (public libraries) and student (academic libraries) employees answering or at least triaging reference questions to meet the needs of users coming in at all hours (Faix 2014; James, Shamchuck, and Koch 2015). Colleagues with other expertise (technology or writing or social work) were invited to share desk duties to meet the needs of users with complex challenges. Virtual reference—whether via chat, e-mail, Skype, or another tool altogether—allowed library staff to meet the needs of users who did not or could not come to the physical library. The definition, and conceptualization, of reference was broadened to more accurately include all of the reference activities occurring away from the physical desk (Houston 2016). All of these changes were aimed at adapting reference to meet users' needs.

Another way to accommodate user needs is to schedule reference consultations for a time that is more convenient for participants. Users who are working full-time during normal library hours or who are needing more hands-on support can have their in-depth or complex reference questions answered on an appointment basis. Academic libraries, which have many students who are working or which are unavailable during daytime hours, are scheduling reference consultations through software like YouCanBookMe, Calendly, and LibCal from Springshare (Hess 2014). Public libraries have not embraced scheduled reference consultations as widely as academic libraries, but Multnomah Libraries' Book a librarian service was a notable pioneer (LaRue 2017), and other public libraries also have mechanisms for users to schedule appointments with librarians or receive readers' advisory through e-mail. Overall, the possibilities inherent in scheduled reference allow for greater opportunity by the dispersed user population to use these services.

One user need that has become a significant concern in recent years is the provision of reference services in a manner respectful of users' origin and ability. The essential concepts of cultural competence, critical librarianship, universal design, and equity, diversity, and inclusion are important skills for reference librarians as users who avail themselves of library services come from different backgrounds and with different experiences. These four areas are interrelated and represent critically important skills for reference workers who interact with users who are part of the changing demographics of the communities that libraries support.

Cultural competence, a necessary precursor for the other three areas, is the idea that staff should be familiar with the basics of their own and other cultures in order to successfully interact with users who come from different cultural backgrounds (Association of College and Research Libraries 2012). There is no question that people from multiple cultural backgrounds are frequent users of both public and academic libraries. International students, particularly in graduate studies, represent an increasing percentage of students across the United States (Wingfield 2017). Immigrants, particularly those new to the United States, commonly seek information and connections and programs at public libraries (Carlton 2018). It is helpful for library staff to have some knowledge of the demographics and cultural interests and needs of the users of their community. It is even better for library staff to be members of the community who are employed by or volunteering with the library. Reference questions on topics such as options for Muslim prayer services or the location of vegetarian restaurants that do not serve root vegetables benefit from library workers who can navigate beyond their own cultural assumptions and answer with respect and understanding.

Critical librarianship, focused on interrogating power structures and working to remove policies and procedures that privilege specific groups, offers library workers important concepts to bring to reference interactions with users (Garcia 2015). By critiquing the power dynamics of the traditional reference transaction, library workers can understand the ways in which some users may not feel comfortable with the process and put in place methods to improve user comfort and increase participation from historically underrepresented users. Library workers can look at the structure of the reference or combined services desk, for example, to determine the best ways to stop inadvertently signifying a particular power dynamic through the desk. Even bringing users to the same side of the desk as the library worker, with the ability to control the mouse and keyboard, changes the dynamic. Another method, which does not require a physical desk or space, is for library workers to transition from thinking of the "reference interview" to the "reference dialogue" (Adler 2013). The reference dialogue is conversational and equally participatory and assumes that the user also offers knowledge to bring to the discussion. For library workers offering reference services, it is invaluable to consider these services in the context of the privileges and power dynamics of the library and greater organizational landscape and to move toward offering reference that will accommodate users of diverse backgrounds.

Universal design is the third area where libraries offering reference services should invest learning and professional development. Universal design principles suggest that spaces, programs, and services should be created with every user in mind from the beginning of the process (Burgstahler 2017). Rather than shoehorning accessibility in at the end of the process, or designing for "most" users and then being caught by surprise when users who can't access the service come in, universal design asks designers of a service to account for every user. The classic example is curb cuts in a sidewalk, intended for people who use a wheelchair, but also useful for those who are pushing a stroller or using crutches. In libraries, universal design is often considered in academic instruction sessions and public library space redesign conversations, but it can also be useful in reference services in order to reach a diverse array of users. For example, older adults frequent both public libraries and academic libraries—with very different reference questions—but with similar needs for patient understanding and a willingness on the part of library staff to clearly explain concepts that may have changed from the user's previous experiences. This behavior from library workers also benefits users who are English as a Second or Other Language (ESOL) speakers and those who have auditory processing disorders. Users who have post-traumatic stress or other mental health concerns may need special consideration (well-marked exits, private areas for consultations, etc.) in the space designated for reference, which in turn benefits others who use the space. Reference services that consider every user will by design reach users whose needs may not have been considered in other planning.

Finally, knowledgeability and engagement with equity, diversity, and inclusion (three related concepts that are often talked about together) are key for library workers providing reference to today's users (American Library Association 2017). Diversity is the presence of people who represent different identities and perspectives; inclusion is the process of making everyone, and particularly people who represent those different identities and perspectives, feel welcome to participate; and equity is the actions taken to ensure that everyone has access to the same opportunities while recognizing that not everyone starts with the same advantages. Diversity in libraries is most often discussed in the context of recruitment and retention of library workers, but it plays a role in reference services when users from different backgrounds are able to interact with library workers from similar backgrounds to theirs and find common understanding. Inclusion is a critical component of offering reference services that are dialogues rather than monologues and are successful in allowing users to clarify their needs and provide input about the type of information they are searching for. Examples of equity in reference include targeted marketing and outreach to user populations who might lack understanding of what reference is or how it might help them with their needs. Altogether, these three areas represent important considerations when providing reference services for users from diverse backgrounds.

The changing needs of reference users have led to new ways of providing reference services and the development of new skills in order to meet user expectations. In addition to these new needs and updated skills, reference to dispersed and diverse users is also happening in new places and with new technologies.

THE NEW PLACES AND TECHNOLOGIES OF REFERENCE

The rise of the Internet has allowed users to ask a reference question from nearly any location in the world. It has also allowed library workers to take reference services to the community in a deep and meaningful way. New technologies also enable reference services to have an immediacy even when taking place entirely in a virtual environment with each participant hundreds or thousands of miles apart from the other. The dispersed user, completely untethered by the physical library, has access to similar—if perhaps not yet equal—reference services as the on-location user who stops by the desk or consultation space. Where once the reference desk was both beacon and barrier, now the library worker or the service itself serves as a beacon for users to come forward.

One of the most exciting developments in reference services has been the rise of virtual reference, now almost a necessary and ubiquitous service. Virtual reference allows the user to interact with a library staff member while not being physically present in the library. The technologies for virtual reference have expanded significantly as the ability to reliably converse over the Internet through smart phones and other devices has increased. Today, virtual reference takes a number of forms, from text messages in Malawi (Harvey Chaputula and Mutula 2018) to the WeChat app in China (Wei and Yang 2016) and technologies such as Skype, BlackBoard, LibChat, and LibraryH3lp in the United States and Canada (Farrell and Leousis 2017). The opportunities opened up by virtual reference impact the user with disabilities as well. Although these technologies are not perfect and users with disabilities still struggle to have equal access (particularly to third-party databases and apps), virtual reference does allow for greater equality of opportunity for these users (Coonin and Hines 2012). Another user group that benefits from virtual reference is students enrolled in campuses abroad, either through study abroad or through a branch or international campus abroad, who have access to the reference services they need to complete their academic work while living in another country. In public libraries, users who are homebound can access reference services (in addition to the more traditional books by mail readers' advisory services) without needing to make the difficult or impossible trip into the library and without needing to prove that they merit special services. All in all, the varied technologies of virtual reference allow libraries to interact with users at home, at work, in the field, and even in the library itself, effectively taking the reference transaction out of the library space.

Community engagement is another opportunity to broaden the reach of the reference transaction. Community engagement, also called embedded librarianship or outreach, focuses on bringing the library out into the community it serves. Reference, instead of taking place behind a desk at a library, takes place in the community center or government building or the student center or residence hall. Through the work of community engagement, library workers interact with users who they would not otherwise and therefore answer questions that otherwise would not be asked. Public libraries doing community engagement are exploring how to contribute to their civic governments' information needs during a redevelopment project or a natural disaster (LaRue 2017), working with small businesses seeking information about starting up or expanding (Collins 2012), and speaking to people in transitional housing as they try to resolve challenges (Lee 2013). Academic libraries doing embedded librarianship are working to address the needs of students and faculty in residence halls during finals (Strothmann and Antell 2010), in research labs as graduate students learn together in research groups (Fong and Hansen 2012), and in athletics study areas as they juggle practice and research papers (Caniano 2015). Whether it is called community engagement or outreach and engagement, it is clearly a key component of reaching users of all types.

Another approach to community engagement is bringing the community into the library to explore critical information needs through the community inquiry process. Community inquiry is a learning process through which a community comes together to ask, refine, and solve questions that the community possesses (Bruce n.d.). Evansville Vanderburgh Public Library is one of the first libraries in the United States to try this approach (Reineke n.d.), which is still early in the research and application stage. The impetus for this process was change happening in the community; the library chose community inquiry in order to meet needs expressed as part of this change process. In a space called the Inquiry Lab, which offers privacy and confidentiality, separate from the reference desk and the rest of the library, library workers bring together members of the community to engage in inquiry using the Question Formulation Technique about challenges that the community is facing. The activities that occur during this process make it a reference service with a distinct name and distinct role for library workers. The idea behind using community inquiry to help users ask (and ideally solve) vexing questions is to demonstrate impact on the community in a new and potentially quite exciting way.

All of these services allow reference to have a truly global reach, available anywhere an Internet connection is available. In addition to the consideration of place and technology, libraries are also exploring new connections to parent organizations (typically cities or counties for public libraries and universities or colleges for academic libraries), ways to demonstrate impact, and exploring new services to users.

THE NEW SERVICES OF REFERENCE

The story of reference to users who are dispersed and diverse would not be complete without discussing the demand for data-driven services in libraries. There is a strong interest in using outcomes, alignment, and assessment to demonstrate impact and tell the story of the library's value to its users. Reference services are as integral as other areas of the library to this process. Reference statistics, for years focused on hash marks and later on the time and the type of question, have shifted to include details about the underlying needs of the user that enable libraries to better tell their story. In public libraries, Project Outcome at the national level has had a significant impact on the ways that libraries collect data and develop services (Project Outcome 2017). Public libraries are starting to look at their reference statistics to determine how much they've contributed to business growth and workforce development in their community by using metrics such as job creation and small business start-up or expansion. Other areas of interest include contributions back to local government and fulfillment of unique user needs. Academic libraries are looking at the connection between library services such as reference, and key areas of campus concern such as student success, retention and graduation rates, and faculty research grants. There are multiple studies demonstrating the value of academic libraries to their parent institutions in metrics that provosts and presidents recognize (Stoddart and Hendrix 2017). While data and metrics are important, libraries are only in the beginning stages of determining the best ways to use them in order to tell the story of how users benefit from services, particularly reference services, and to determine the most-needed new services for users. It will be exciting to see in the years ahead the ways in which data allows libraries to better meet user needs while simultaneously better communicating library value.

New services in reference are being developed all the time in accordance with user needs revealed through a combination of data and inquiry. As library workers moved off of the reference desk and into the community, services that had been offered at few (or zero) libraries began to be offered at libraries around the United States. Public libraries in particular made it their mission to focus on users in need, including hired social workers to meet the needs of those who were homeless (Milone Hill 2011), those who had suffered intimate partner violence (Westbrook and Gonzalez 2011), and those who were incarcerated (Drabinski and Rabina 2015). They focused on other users as well, business development councils (Galston et al. 2012) and makerspace users (Hartnett 2016) and people needing assistance with technology (Cushing 2016). Academic libraries shifted focus as well, seeking out high school students (Meyers Martin, Garcia, and McPhee 2012) and veterans trying to start businesses (Hoppenfeld et al. 2013) and makerspace users (Welch and Wyatt-Baxter 2018). As reference continued to be expanded from questions behind a desk to work that engages the broader community and responds to the needs of all types of users, reference services began to take on a new shape and reach people who were otherwise not being seen in the library setting. Reference services, in a global world of users of varying backgrounds who are dispersed around the world, will take on new aspects while remaining true to the core idea.

Services to those who are dispersed around the world and those who come from diverse backgrounds require libraries to change how they offer their reference services in order to meet user needs. The ways in which reference occurred changed and the skills necessary to interact with the new dispersed and diverse users have changed with them. Cultural competence, critical librarianship, universal design, and equity, diversity, and inclusion are all critical skills for library workers answering reference questions from anyone but in particular those of diverse backgrounds. The places and technologies of reference have changed as well. Technology permits users of varying backgrounds to interact with library workers on a more equal playing field and ask reference questions without needing to be present in the library. Library workers have also taken the work of the library into the community and brought the community into the library in new ways. As libraries strive to demonstrate their impact, they use data and metrics to tell new stories about the impact of reference services on users and create new services to meet user needs. Overall, reference services for users who are dispersed around the world and diverse in background are changing and evolving but offer users new opportunities and new abilities.

REFERENCES

American Library Association. 2017. "ODLOS Glossary of Terms." Office for Diversity, Literacy, and Outreach Services. http://www.ala.org/aboutala/odlos-glossary-terms.

Adler, Kate. 2013. "Radical Purpose: The Critical Reference Dialogue at a Progressive Urban College." *Urban Library Journal* 19 (1). https://academicworks.cuny.edu/ulj/vol19/iss1/9.

Andrews, Camille, Sara Wright, and Howard Raskin. 2016. "Library Learning Spaces: Investigating Libraries and Investing in Student Feedback." *Journal of Library Administration* 56 (6): 647–672. https://doi.org/10.1080/01930826.2015.1105556.

Association of College and Research Libraries. 2012. "Diversity Standards: Cultural Competency for Academic Libraries (2012)." http://www.ala.org/acrl/standards/diversity.

Bonnell, Angela. 2014. "Voter Registration Services at an Academic Library: A Non-Traditional Reference Service." *The Reference Librarian* 55 (4): 289–297. https://doi.org/10.1080/02763877.2014.928921.

Bruce, Bertram C. n.d. "What Is Community Inquiry?" https://chipbruce.net/resources/community-inquiry-bibliography/what-is-community-inquiry/.

Burgstahler, Sheryl. 2017. "Equal Access: Universal Design of Libraries." DO-IT, University of Washington. https://www.washington.edu/doit/sites/default/files/atoms/files/EA_Libraries.pdf.

Caniano, William T. 2015. "Library Outreach to University Athletic Departments and Student-Athletes." *Journal of Library Innovation* 6 (2): 89–95.

Carlton, Amy. 2018. "Serving Immigrants and Refugees in Public Libraries." *American Libraries Magazine*. https://americanlibrariesmagazine.org/blogs/the-scoop/serving-immigrants-refugees-public-libraries/.

Collins, Bradley. 2012. "How Public Libraries Are a Boon to Small Business." *American Libraries Magazine*. https://americanlibrariesmagazine.org/2012/08/13/how-public-libraries-are-a-boon-to-small-business/.

Coonin, Bryna, and Samantha Hines. 2012. "Reference Services for Distant Students with Disabilities." *Internet Reference Services Quarterly* 17 (1): 7–12. https://doi.org/10.1080/1533290X.2010.503166.

Cushing, Amber. 2016. "'If It Computes, Patrons Have Brought It In': Personal Information Management and Personal Technology Assistance in Public Libraries." *Library and Information Science Research* 38 (1): 81–88. https://doi.org/10.1016/j.lisr.2016.01.005.

Drabinski, Emily, and Debbie Rabina. 2015. "Reference Services to Incarcerated People, Part I." *Reference & User Services Quarterly* 55 (1): 42–48. https://journals.ala.org/index.php/rusq/article/view/5798.

Elmborg, James. 2002. "Teaching At the Reference Desk: Toward a Reference Pedagogy." *portal: Libraries and the Academy* 2 (3): 455–464. http://works.bepress.com/james_elmborg/14/.

Faix, Allison. 2014. "Peer Reference Revisited: Evolution of a Peer-Reference Model." *Reference Services Review* 42 (2): 305–319. https://doi.org/10.1108/RSR-07-2013-0039.

Farrell, Bridget, and Kasia Leousis. 2017. "Integrated Reference a la Carte: Evaluating, Selecting, and Implementing the Best Features for Your Library." *Journal of Library Administration* 57 (5): 548–562. https://doi.org/10.1080/01930826.2017.1326727.

Fong, Bonnie, and Darren Hansen. 2012. "Engaging Research Groups: Rethinking Information Literacy for Graduate Students." *Issues in Science and Technology Librarianship* 71. http://www.istl.org/12-fall/refereed2.html.

Galston, Colbe, Elizabeth Kelsen Huber, Katherine Johnson, and Amy Long. 2012. "Community Reference: Making Libraries Indispensable in a New Way." *American Libraries Magazine* (May/June). https://americanlibrariesmagazine.org/2012/06/13/community-reference-making-libraries-indispensable-in-a-new-way/

Garcia, Kenny. 2015. "Keeping Up With . . . Critical Librarianship." American Library Association. http://www.ala.org/acrl/publications/keeping_up_with/critlib.

Hartnett, Elizabeth. 2016. "Why Make? An Exploration of User-Perceived Benefits of Makerspaces." *Public Libraries Online.* http://publiclibrariesonline.org/2016/11/why-make-an-exploration-of-user-perceived-benefits-of-makerspaces/.

Harvey Chaputula, Aubrey, and Stephen Mutula. 2018. "Provision of Library and Information Services through Mobile Phones in Public University Libraries in Malawi." *Global Knowledge, Memory and Communication* 67 (1–2): 52–69. https://doi.org/10.1108/GKMC-05-2017-0048.

Hess, Amanda Nichols. 2014. "Scheduling Research Consultations with YouCanBook.Me: Low Effort, High Yield." *College & Research Libraries News* 75 (9). https://crln.acrl.org/index.php/crlnews/article/view/9197/10182.

Hoppenfeld, Jared, Trip Wyckoff, Jo Ann J. Henson, Jenna N. Mayotte, and Hal P. Kirkwood Jr. 2013. "Librarians and the Entrepreneurship Bootcamp for Veterans: Helping Disabled Veterans with Business Research." *Journal of Business & Finance Librarianship* 18 (4): 293–308. https://doi.org/10.1080/08963568.2013.825227.

Horrigan, John. 2016. "Libraries 2016." Pew Research Center. http://www.pewinternet.org/2016/09/09/libraries-2016/.

Houston, Anne. 2016. "What's In a Name: Toward a New Definition of Reference." *Reference & User Services Quarterly* 55 (3): 186–188. https://journals.ala.org/index.php/rusq/article/viewFile/5927/7512.

James, Norene, Lisa Shamchuck, and Katherine Koch. 2015. "Changing Roles of Librarians and Library Technicians." *Partnership: the Canadian Journal of Library and Information Science Practice and Research* 10 (2). https://journal.lib.uoguelph.ca/index.php/perj/article/view/3333.

LaRue, James. 2017. "Public Library Reference Work in 2017." *Public Libraries* 56 (2): 15–19.

Lee, Michelle. 2013. "Reference on the Road." *Library Journal* 138 (18):18–20.,

Meyers Martin, Coleen, Eric Garcia, and Marc McPhee. 2012. "Information Literacy Outreach: Building a High School Program at California State University Northridge." *Education Libraries* 35 (1–2): 34–47.

Milone Hill, Nanci. 2011. "Public Libraries and the Homeless." *Public Libraries* (November/December): 13–22. http://publiclibrariesonline.org/wp-content/uploads/2018/01/November-December-2011-Perspectives-on-Serving-Homeless.pdf.

O'Gorman, Jack, and Barry Trott. 2009. "What Will Become of Reference in Academic and Public Libraries?" *Journal of Library Administration* 49 (4): 327–339. https://doi.org/10.1080/01930820902832421.

Project Outcome. 2017. "Project Outcome: Year in Review. 2017 Annual Report." Public Library Association. https://www.projectoutcome.org/ckeditor_assets/attachments/359/pla-project-outcome-2-year-annual-report-final.pdf.

Reineke, Katie. n.d. "Community Inquiry: Limitless Opportunities through Inquiry." Evansville Vanderburgh Public Library. https://www.evpl.org/issues/community-inquiry/.

Stoddart, Rick, and Beth Hendrix. 2017. "Learning at the Reference Desk: A Pilot Project to Align Reference Transactions with University Learning Outcomes." *Journal of Academic Librarianship* 43 (1): 3–7. https://doi.org/10.1016/j.acalib.2016.11.004.

Strothmann, Molly, and Karen Antell. 2010. "The Live-In Librarian: Developing Library Outreach to University Residence Halls." *Reference & User Services Quarterly* 50 (1): 48–58.

United States Department of Education. National Center for Education Statistics. 2018. *Digest of Education Statistics: 2016.* Report number NCES 2017-094. https://nces.ed.gov/programs/digest/d16/ch_3.asp.

Wei, Qunyi, and Yang Yang. 2017. "WeChat Library: A New Mode of Mobile Library Service." *The Electronic Library* 35 (1): 198–208. https://doi.org/10.1108/EL-12-2015-0248.

Welch, Amber, and Krystal Wyatt-Baxter. 2018. "Beyond Metrics: Connecting Academic Library Makerspace Assessment Practices with Organizational Values." *Library Hi Tech* 36 (2): 306–318. https://doi.org/10.1108/LHT-08-2017-0181.

Westbrook, Lynn, and Maria Gonzalez. 2011. "Information Support for Survivors of Intimate Partner Violence: Public Librarianship's Role." *Public Library Quarterly* 30 (2): 132–157. https://doi.org/10.1080/01616846.2011.575709

Wingfield, Nick. 2017. "The Disappearing American Grad Student." *The New York Times*, November 3. https://www.nytimes.com/2017/11/03/education/edlife/american-graduate-student-stem.html.

Part V

Assessment

16

Methods and Approaches for Assessing Reference Services

Elizabeth Namei and Sarah Pickle

INTRODUCTION

As mission-driven organizations, academic libraries are beholden to our users and campus administrators to ensure our services and resources are succeeding in fulfilling these missions. Through the thoughtful assessment and evaluation of library services and resources, you can get a sense of where your organization is succeeding, where it is falling short, and where or how improvements could be made.

In libraries, the word "assessment" is typically used to include any quantitative or qualitative appraisal of performance in meeting the needs of constituents (e.g., did this instruction session help students become more information literate; do the resources in the art history collection adequately support the art history curriculum?).[1] Such appraisals can help you articulate the value your library provides; they can also help you make evidence-based decisions about where and how the library's resources or services may need to adjust in order to better meet its mission.

For the purposes of this chapter, we explore assessments that *directly examine* library reference services. These assessments are aimed at determining both whether your service is meeting the goals you have for it and what, if anything, you might want to change about it. Beyond the scope of this chapter is the collection of data on things other than the service itself or the activities and outputs the service has some influence over. For instance, analyses of student needs or motivations for utilizing your reference service may well be informative, helping you plan and make decisions about aspects of the service you have some control over, but they do not assess your service; that is, they do not tell you how the service itself is doing in meeting its goals. The data collected for these kinds of analyses might influence the way you market your chat reference service or staff the reference desk in order to better meet those needs or tap into those motivations; but only in assessing the marketing or staffing decisions you have made would you be directly assessing your reference service.

This chapter also focuses on *methods* for assessing your reference service, but the authors have elected not to foreground the methods themselves. Too often, library assessment methods are chosen out of convenience or familiarity rather than letting the question being investigated be the determining factor. We have chosen to organize this chapter in a way that we hope will help others avoid this trap and ensure that, above all else, the method used—convenient or not—will be the one best suited to provide insight into what you want to better understand.

FOUR-PART FRAMEWORK FOR PLANNING YOUR ASSESSMENT PROJECT

Although you may be eager to dive into a project to assess your reference service, we encourage you to take some time to plan first so that your project yields the information you need.[2] We recommend using the four-part framework discussed here to help you select the method most appropriate for assessing your reference service.[3]

1. *Goals: What are the overall aims of your reference service?* Start by reflecting on the purpose and intended impact of your reference service. Since it is not an end in itself, articulate the impact you are aiming for with your service. This will help keep your sights on why your service matters and help you focus in on what questions to explore. Working through this will also help you avoid scope creep and ensure that whatever assessment project you undertake is consistent with the purpose of the service.
   Consider the following questions:

   • What is the broader impact you want the reference service to have on your campus and what difference do you hope it makes to your users? For example, your reference service aims to contribute to the improvement of student learning and success.
   • What are the more day-to-day goals tethered to that bigger picture of impact? To extend the example mentioned previously, your service might seek to contribute to the improvement of student learning and success by (1) providing point-of-need support, (2) reaching a diverse range of students, and (3) teaching transferable concepts/skills in addition to answering students' immediate questions.

   Breaking down your larger goals into bite-sized targets will help you tackle more manageable assessment projects. Depending on how these smaller goals relate to one another, you may wish to assess more than one goal in a single project.

2. *Assessment question(s): What do you want to know about the reference service in terms of working toward one or more of these goals?* Use your goals to help you articulate a clear, measurable question that your assessment project will be designed to answer. Be sure that the questions you identify are aligned with the impact your reference service aims to have. For instance, is the time devoted to reference and the distribution of responsibilities around it satisfying the point-of-need support you aim to provide? Are your efforts to connect with a more diverse range of students yielding more appointments? Do seniors who have multiple research appointments with a librarian result in them using more varied and relevant sources in their theses? Any of these questions could lead to projects that would help shed light on how (or if) the reference service is contributing to improvements in student learning and success.
   When coming up with an assessment question, be sure to focus on the aspects of the reference service you can influence. For instance, you do not have control over students' needs or their motivations for using the service; but you can use information about needs and motivations to make adjustments to the resources invested in your service (e.g., staff time) and the activities that form it (e.g., outreach, appointments, the success of the interactions) and then assess whether those changes have contributed to the goals you set for the service.

3. *Evidence: How will you (or those who can help support your service) know whether your reference service is successful in working toward those goals?* Your answer to this question will help you identify what to measure as you aim to answer your assessment question identified as part of the second step discussed here. Do you need output data (e.g., time of day questions are asked or number and demographics of users served) to corroborate anecdotal knowledge of unmet demand late at night? Do you need demonstrable evidence of student learning (e.g., "Students who have had a consultation with a librarian are able to do X")?

   The evidence you need will also depend on the audience for your assessment. That audience could be you and your reference team, library or campus administration, or the greater academic library community. What evidence will be most informative as you seek to better understand how your reference service is doing? Or, if needed, what evidence will be most persuasive in demonstrating the reference service has either achieved its goals for impact or needs adjustments or more support to be able to do so?

4. *Assessment method: How will you gather the evidence that will tell you whether your service is successful in working toward its goals?* The last step is to select an assessment method that is appropriate for both the question you have and the evidence needed to satisfactorily answer that question. For example, if you wish to ensure your reference venues are appropriately staffed, it may suffice to combine an inventory of staff and their skills with simple reference desk statistics: the number of questions asked at a variety of service points, the time those questions came in, their level of difficulty using the READ Scale (Gerlich and Berard 2007).

   If you want to know whether your service has had an impact on information literacy outcomes and need evidence of student learning in specific demographic populations, you may need to look at artifacts (e.g., research papers, sources referenced) produced by students in those populations who have and have not used your reference service and then use rubrics—a scale, categories, and criteria—to rate and compare the extent to which each group demonstrates information literacy skills.

Finally, note that your attempt to plan your project might not pan out the first time. Practical, ethical, or a variety of other considerations (see Additional Considerations for examples) may arise that require you to step back and reconceive your assessment question, the evidence you wish to gather, or the method you choose to adopt. You may find the evidence you need to answer your question is already available to you—you simply need to retrieve it and analyze it and no further project design is necessary. You may also find that the evidence you need is out of reach due to privacy concerns. Or you may realize that the method most useful for addressing your assessment question and providing the evidence you need requires resources or expertise neither you nor your team possess. Complications like these will almost always arise and you will need to be ready to make adjustments to your project design in order to satisfy any concerns while still ensuring you can get the information you need to determine whether your reference service is meeting its goals.

ASSESSMENT METHODS

Before we provide examples of the four-part assessment framework in action, we want to present an overview of some of the most commonly used methods to assess reference services in academic libraries. Even though our framework recommends that the selection of an assessment method be the final step, it is important to understand the methods as well as their advantages and disadvantages to be better informed in selecting the best one to answer your question. The methods are presented in alphabetical order.

Assessment of Student Learning Outcomes

In order to determine if students have learned what is being taught during instructional interactions, learning outcomes are identified ahead of time so that a determination can be made regarding whether the outcomes were actually achieved. This practice is common when developing library instruction sessions but can also be used to determine if learning has occurred during one-on-one reference interactions. Assessing student learning can be direct or indirect. Direct measures of student learning are performance-based, meaning students demonstrate what they have learned. Indirect measures of student learning are surrogates that capture students' perceptions of what they learned rather than a demonstration (Matthews 2014, 48).

- *Examples:* Pre- and post-tests given before and after reference interactions to measure if learning has occurred and if specific learning outcomes were achieved (Donegan, Domas, and Deosdade 1989). A worksheet that students fill out during the session or having the students write a one-minute paper at the end of reference interactions describing what they learned (Swoger and Hoffman 2015, 203).
- *Advantages:* These methods allow you to determine if learning has happened and possibly follow up or clarify if there has been a misunderstanding or if learning outcomes are not achieved. It can also help reinforce what was covered, which can ensure that the information and concepts taught during the reference interactions are retained. Assessing student learning with these methods is also less invasive than using learning analytics (see following text). Pre-tests, in particular, have more success when used in collaboration with a course or program.
- *Disadvantages:* As mentioned previously, learning outcomes must be developed ahead of time. This can be time consuming and often not possible to do without advance notice of students' reference questions. Learning outcomes also vary student to student, information need to information need, and sometimes only become clear during the reference interview. Worksheets and one-minute papers must rely on self-reported learning (Swoger and Hoffman 2015, 211) since reference interactions are not always conducive for demonstrating higher-level skills. These methods also do not capture if learning is retained long(er) term.

Content Analysis

Content analysis is an extension/hybrid of the assessment of student learning outcomes and observations (depending on what evidence is being analyzed). It involves analyzing content of some sort, such as chat transcripts, research project citations/references, or types of interactions (e.g., advanced, basic, and directional), in order to discern patterns or trends.

- *Examples:* Reviewing the quality or appropriateness of sources used in student research assignments, before and after reference interactions (Reinsfelder 2012, 266), the language used by the reference provider or student during reference interactions (Cordell and Fisher 2010), or the types of questions asked during reference interactions (Fan and Welch 2016).
- *Advantages:* This is an authentic and unobtrusive form of assessment. Data is already being captured for online reference services, so easily available for analysis.
- *Disadvantages:* Focusing solely on artifacts or content leaves a lot of unanswered questions. For instance, focusing on sources used does not provide comprehensive evidence of student learning or information literacy skills gained from reference interactions (Sokoloff and Simmons 2015, 170). Developing a rubric for consistently analyzing large numbers of transcripts or research papers requires testing and norming to ensure inter-rater reliability (if using multiple reviewers) and can be very time consuming (Maximiek, Rushton, and Brown 2010, 368; Reinsfelder 2012, 270). Lastly, there may be potential privacy concerns regarding the use of data, especially if users have not opted in to having their information analyzed.

Ethnographic Methods

Ethnographic methods are "qualitative methods that focus on the close observation of social practices and interactions" and the examination of "the context in which activities occur" (Asher and Miller 2011, 3). These methods, derived from anthropological field-work, involve the close examination of cultures with the purpose of learning about the lives and experiences of a specific group, such as undergraduates, commuter students, first-generation students, or nontraditional students (Ramsden 2016, 355). For libraries, ethnographic methods can help us learn "more about the cultures inhabiting our buildings and using our services" (Ramsden 2016, 355).

- *Examples:* Asking students to videotape themselves (Kinsley, Schoonover, and Spitler 2016, 10), create photo diaries, or journal/log their research efforts and then reviewing the results to look for patterns/trends/insights (Watts and Mahfood 2015) related to when, where, and how they use or would use a reference service. Ethnographic interviews are an option that is less time consuming than larger-scale studies and can ask participants to recall experiences in detail and describe their reasoning for using a reference service, by asking open-ended questions (Asher and Miller 2011, 15).
- *Advantages:* Ethnographic methods provide a window into participants' lives, and as such, are a more authentic way of soliciting feedback. With this information, you get a better sense of where and how the reference service might fit into students' research processes. Ethnographic methods can present detailed data and often reveal information that had not originally been sought or anticipated (Ramsden 2016, 367). This wealth of data might reveal needs that a reference service could address or ways to better promote/market reference services. If changes are implemented to a reference service based on the results of an ethnographic study, the updated service could then be re-assessed using different methods to see if the ethnography-informed changes have had the desired impact.
- *Disadvantages:* Meaningful ethnographic studies require researchers to undergo sophisticated training and make a long-term commitment to design the study, code, and analyze the data. They also require extended engagements from students in terms of participation and informa-tion-sharing (Lanclos and Asher 2016). It may be challenging to motivate students to partici-pate outside of a class requirement without some form of incentive (Watts and Mahfood 2015).

Focus Groups

Focus groups are group interviews where a moderator guides participants through a series of planned discussion questions on a given topic (Watts and Mahfood 2015, 76). Focus groups, like interviews, allow for more nuance to be discerned through organic conversations (in contrast to surveys using questionnaires; Halpern et al. 2015).

- *Examples:* Focus groups can include both users and non-users of your reference service. Focus groups can include a homogenous group (e.g., only first-year students) or a heterogeneous group (e.g., all levels of students).
- *Advantages*: Focus groups provide a more in-depth and varied understanding from multiple per-spectives at once. This method "can be a good alternative and complement to surveys because they allow participants to think collectively about a topic and participants can become more inclined to think through their answers with one another" (Watts and Mahfood 2015, 76). Ses-sions can also be observed by several library staff members (or recorded and transcribed), which helps to ensure more consistent interpretations (Kuruppu 2007, 375).
- *Disadvantages:* Some focus group participants may be reluctant to openly share their opinions in front of others, especially if they don't agree or if others in the group dominate the discussion.

Ensuring successful focus groups requires a well-trained facilitator. Focus groups draw conclusions based on a relatively small number of participants, which may limit their generalizability (Novotny 2001, 108).

Interviews

Interviews are usually held one on one and aim at soliciting qualitative feedback (e.g., to get a sense of users' satisfaction with the service) or assessing if learning occurred. Using consistent and structured interview questions allows for the collection of comparable data. Using semi-structured interview questions allows the interviewer to be flexible and responsive to the conversation at hand, potentially yielding unexpected yet useful data and leaving room for clarifications to be made.

- *Examples:* Exit interviews done immediately following or shortly after reference interactions to gauge satisfaction or learning. Interviews can also be held unrelated to specific reference interactions, with a range of users and non-users to garner more general impressions, opinions, or awareness about the reference service (Dougan 2013, 181).
- *Advantages*: Interviews provide incredibly rich and detailed data. They also allow for follow-up questions to be asked (if using semi-structured format), if needed, to clarify or gain more insight into an issue (Vinyard, Mullally, and Colvin 2017, 257).
- *Disadvantages*: It is challenging to write good interview questions that are clear and logical and that don't lead participants into providing certain kinds of responses. Conducting good interviews is a skill that requires training and practice. Exit interviews limit feedback to those who are using the service, so they will not reveal why the service is not being used by some; the scope of the interviewees can be expanded to include non-users as a complement (Vinyard, Mullally, and Colvin 2017, 264).

Learning Analytics

Learning analytics use data from a variety of institutional sources about students to discern connections or correlations in order to "improve learning contexts and help learners succeed" (Oakleaf 2018, 11).

- *Examples:* Learning analytics can be used to connect the use of reference services to user information, especially GPA and retention data, to gauge the impact and value of the service on the academic success of students.
- *Advantages*: Tying the use of reference services to student success can make a strong case for the value and impact of libraries (if a positive correlation is found).
- *Disadvantages:* Usage of reference services provides only part of the picture surrounding a student's academic success. It can be challenging to discern a direct correlation between a student's use of a service and their academic success. It also does not provide qualitative data such as the quality, satisfaction, and success of the reference interactions. Attempting to tie academic success to the use of reference services presumes "that all reference desk visits are equal," which they are not (Krieb 2018). The data needed to do this kind of analysis can also be difficult to get a hold of due to the volume needed in order to draw responsible and valid conclusions; the data itself isn't always already available or may be inconsistent or located in a variety of campus systems. Attempting to connect the use of reference services to student success is viewed by some as infringing on student privacy and confidentiality (Jones and Salo 2017; Fisher 2018). Another issue to consider is "self-selection bias"—the possibility that students who use reference services may differ (academically or otherwise) from those who do not use it (Kot and Jones 2015, 570; Krieb 2018). Related to this is a need to understand what motivates students to use reference

services and if this motivation is connected to academic success rather than their actual use of the service itself (Kot and Jones 2015, 584).

Observations

Observations of reference interactions can be direct (obtrusive) or indirect (unobtrusive). The difference is when a user or reference provider is aware of the observation (direct/obtrusive) compared to when one or both are unaware they are being observed (indirect/unobtrusive).

- *Examples*: Peer observations—akin to teaching observations—involve colleagues sitting in on reference interactions. This is an example of an obtrusive observation. Examples of unobtrusive observations are secret shoppers where proxies pose as regular library users asking scripted questions (Boyce 2015; Ward 2004) and the stationing of observers in locations not visible to those involved in reference interactions (Strickland and Bonnet 2011). In addition, transcript analysis of chat or e-mail reference interactions or recordings of in-person reference interactions are a form of unobtrusive observation (Bravender, Lyon, and Molaro 2011; Cabaniss 2015; Fan and Welch 2016; Maximiek, Rushton, and Brown 2010; Mungin 2017).
- *Advantages:* Unobtrusive observations tend to be more reliable since real and uninhibited behavior is captured (Kuruppu 2007, 373); online proxies can "observe" multiple interactions with multiple librarians in contrast to in-person proxies who can only conduct one observation (Ward 2004, 53). Benefits of in-person proxies are that they can pick up on nonverbal cues and contextual considerations that might influence the service being provided.
- *Disadvantages:* Having a third party present during reference interactions, or even if not present but if the librarian is aware they are being observed, might influence or alter behaviors or create discomfort or anxiety, which can in turn impact the service provided (Kuruppu 2007, 374; Todorinova and Torrence 2014, 42). Secret shoppers/proxies need to be well trained and consistent in their interactions in order for reliable results to be gathered. Unobtrusive observations may require multiple observers to ensure reliable and consistent results. Proxies might be trained to listen for a "correct answer" from the reference provider, whereas real users who come to the reference service might have an idea of the type of answer they seek, but they might expand or change their minds based on the reference exchange (Kuruppu 2007, 373).

Surveys Using Questionnaires

Surveys using questionnaires can be given in paper or online to users of a reference service shortly after interactions to get feedback on their experience, or they can be sent out to users, reference providers, or non-users to gauge summative perceptions, awareness, satisfaction, or opinions about a reference service.

- *Examples:* Like interviews and focus groups, surveys can be given to both users and non-users of your reference service. Surveys are an option for gathering subjective feedback related to user satisfaction with reference interactions (Fournier and Sikora 2015).
- *Advantages*: They can be disseminated in a variety of formats: paper or online, after an in-person interview or given to users in the library; micro-surveys of 1–2 questions can be an easy way to solicit quick and immediate feedback.
- *Disadvantages*: Online surveys tend to have low response rates; responses may be biased as those who feel strongly one way or another tend to be more likely to respond (Todorinova and Torrence 2014, 42; Boyce 2015, 238). Additionally, writing good questionnaires that are clear, logical, and don't lead participants into providing certain kinds of responses is challenging. For instance, how questions are phrased may inadvertently lead respondents toward a particular

answer or compel them to make "forced choices" where none of the options presented makes sense for that respondent but they choose one anyway (Halpern et al. 2015).

Usage Data Analysis

Usage data analysis involves collecting and analyzing quantitative data about reference interactions (e.g., count, time of day, day of week, length, type of question, and user demographics).

- *Examples:* Usage data can provide insight into how and when the service is being used and can contribute to evidence-based decisions regarding adjustments to service offerings (Fournier and Sikora 2015, 254). A cost-benefit analysis can be conducted with basic usage data to assess how much it costs to staff the reference service and provide each interaction (Novotny 2001, 107).
- *Advantages:* Basic data is easily available, especially for online reference services, as many platforms automatically generate logs documenting the activities those platforms support; the data is fairly straightforward to analyze and interpret.
- *Disadvantages:* This method only provides the quantitative part of the picture; it does not provide qualitative data about the quality, satisfaction, or success of the service. For in-person reference services, the accuracy of usage data is dependent on consistent collection practices of reference providers.

Depending on the assessment question(s) you are trying to answer, how ambitious you are, and the time and resources available to you, you might want to consider including more than one method when designing your assessment project. This may allow you to counteract the disadvantages or shortcomings of a single method. One method alone will only tell you part of the picture, which is sometimes sufficient. Oftentimes, combining two or more methods will present a more accurate and holistic understanding of your reference service. Again, depending on what you plan to do with the results of your project (and who your audience is), keep in mind that you can choose as many methods as you need to answer your assessment question(s).

FOUR-PART FRAMEWORK IN ACTION: DETERMINING WHICH ASSESSMENT METHOD TO USE

Table 16.1 presents the schema outlined in "Four-Part Framework for Planning Your Assessment Project" with examples pertinent to assessing a reference service in your academic library. You start by articulating one of the goals of the reference service and then ask possible assessment questions that will help you determine whether your goal is met. After that, you consider what evidence is needed to answer the assessment question. The last step is to evaluate and choose an assessment method. This table is an attempt to present a framework for determining the best method for the question(s) you want to investigate.

When applicable, we provide examples of taxonomies and rubrics that can be used for the analysis of the evidence gathered. When available, we also cite studies that have used a given assessment method. We did make an effort to give examples of every assessment method outlined in "Assessment Methods." The information in this table is not an attempt to be comprehensive or to evaluate or recommend any of the goals, questions, or methods. Rather, it is an effort to provide examples so you can see the four-part framework in action.

Table 16.1 Assessment Framework and Examples

Goals: What are the overall aims of your reference service?	Assessment questions: What do you want to know about the reference service vis-a-vis your goals?	Evidence: How will you know whether your service is successful in working toward those goals?	Methods: How will you gather the evidence that will tell you whether your service is successful in working toward its goals?
To ensure that a wide variety of users know about the reference service and are utilizing it.	Which students are using our reference service and to what extent are they using it?	Usage data (that includes some demographic information) can capture a wide variety of user types (e.g., grade level, majors, and distance users) and backgrounds (e.g., first-generation and international students) in order to see who is utilizing the library's reference service.	Gather and analyze usage data including basic demographic data, which might require reference providers to ask for these details during the exchange (Côté, Kochkina, and Mawhinney 2016).
	What are user perceptions about the reference service (so that we can better understand if or how to promote the service)?	Responses related to attitudes and opinions, both positive and negative, about the reference service. Can be from both users and non-users, touching on aspects of the service that can influence their satisfaction—real or potential—with the service.	Conduct interviews or focus groups would be best so follow-up questions can be asked if needed. Distribute brief post-interaction surveys (Askew 2015). Send targeted surveys to different groups of users as a point of comparison (Faix, MacDonald, and Taxakis 2014).

(Continued)

Table 16.1 (Continued)

| To ensure a knowledgeable reference provider is available, in person or virtually, to provide high-quality research support when users need it. | Do we have the right reference providers answering questions at the right times of day and days of week? (Might be especially important to investigate if students or paraprofessionals are staffing your reference service.) | Usage data to gather time of day and day of week questions are asked. Transcripts that show what questions are asked and the quality, accuracy, or completeness of responses. Inventory of responses provided to determine the level of expertise needed by the reference providers. | Analyze transcripts (e.g., from chat/e-mail reference service) for evidence of the quality of responses (Maximiek, Rushton, and Brown 2010, 366; Mungin 2017).

• Quality can be measured by using the *RUSA Guidelines for Behavioral Performance of Reference and Information Service Providers* (Novotny 2001, 114; Maximiek, Rushton, and Brown 2010, 366; Reference and User Services Association, 2013). Another option for measuring quality is the Wisconsin-Ohio Reference Evaluation Program (WOREP) designed to help researchers separate satisfaction or service evaluation from success ratings. WOREP involves having patrons and reference providers complete separate surveys and then reviewing the survey pairs to get a complete picture of the interactions. A reference interaction is considered successful if the patron indicates that "they found exactly what they wanted, were fully satisfied with the transaction, and do not indicate any reasons for discontent" (Novotny and Rimland 2007, 383).
• Completeness of responses can be measured using *Childers' scale of Correctness* (Ward 2004, 49; McLaughlin 2011, 541).

Categorizing and then analyzing question types can be done using a rubric like the READ Scale (Gerlich and Berard 2007).
Train proxies to ask different levels of questions at different times of day and summarize (or record) responses given by reference providers (Boyce 2015). |

	What types of questions are being asked (e.g., directional, basic, and advanced), and is our reference service being staffed appropriately to field these questions (e.g., students, paraprofessionals, and librarians; Maximiek, Rushton, and Brown 2010 2010)?	Inventory of questions asked: grouped into relevant categories. These categories will depend on what's salient to your situation: are you interested in differentiating between advanced questions that require expertise and other basic or directional questions that well-trained staff/students could answer? Or, do you want to gather evidence about user needs, such as in-house tech support, for which you would want to categorize technical questions only? (Remember that when you have evidence of user needs, you can make adjustments to your staffing that could later be assessed for effectiveness.)	Code reference questions according to the type of inquiry (e.g., general, technical, directional, and advanced). The READ Scale is an option for this (Gerlich and Berard 2007). You can use online reference questions to do this or ask reference providers to log the questions after in-person interactions (Cabaniss 2015).
To provide high-quality reference service.	What areas of improvement are needed for the library reference service and employee training programs (Boyce 2015)?	Transcripts of reference interactions to gauge accuracy and completeness of answers.	Analyze transcripts (e.g., from chat/e-mail reference service) for evidence of quality (e.g., accuracy, completeness, teaching, and satisfaction of user; Maximiek, Rushton, and Brown 2010; Mungin 2017). Conduct obtrusive or unobtrusive observations where observers are asked to take note of areas that might need improvement.
	How helpful do students find the reference interactions?	Student opinions and feedback after reference interactions about how helpful it was in meeting their expectations/needs.	The concept of "helpful" is subjective. Conduct interviews or focus groups in order to ask follow-up questions for clarity and greater depth, or use a survey questionnaire with a Likert scale (though using a scale runs the risk of oversimplifying responses) or open-ended questions.
	How satisfied are the people who use our reference service?	Student opinions and feedback after a reference interaction about how satisfied they are and why (or why not).	Deploy exit surveys (Butler and Byrd 2016). Hold exit interviews (Vinyard, Mullally, and Colvin 2017).

(*Continued*)

Table 16.1 (Continued)

To teach users skills and concepts in order to answer their immediate question and in anticipation of future information needs.	Are students able to apply skills/concepts introduced by the reference provider after reference interactions?	Record of what was taught in reference interactions and students' research artifacts to see if or how what was taught was utilized.	First draft artifacts (Reinsfelder 2012) from before the reference interactions could be compared with final drafts after a reference interaction in order to see what impact the reference service had. Conduct citation analysis on students' artifacts gauging the types of sources used (Reinsfelder 2012; Sokoloff and Simmons 2015).
	What are students learning during reference interactions?	Students' self-assessments of their learning.	Have students write a one-minute paper asking them to explain what they learned (Swoger and Hoffman 2015); examine for evidence of understanding. Distribute exit survey that gauges learning (similar to the one-minute paper).
	How confident are students in conducting research after a reference interaction?	Student opinions and attitudes regarding their confidence levels before and after (or just after) reference interactions.	Conduct pre- and post-interaction surveys using questionnaires asking for feelings or confidence about research skills; analyze for changes in responses (Magi and Mardeusza 2013).
	Does use of our reference service impact students' academic success (GPA and retention)?	Student grades, enrollment, retention aligned with each of those students' use of the reference service. If students learn during a reference interaction. This would require you to have a way to track who uses your reference service.	Undertake a study using learning analytics: compare usage of reference service with students' GPAs and retention (Soria, Fransen and Nackerud 2013; Krieb 2018). Keep in mind what metrics are best suited to your home institution. For instance, a community college might find GPA less important than retention or transfer rates.
The reference provider will be approachable and make an effort to put the user at ease so that the user feels comfortable in a situation that might be intimidating, confusing, or overwhelming.	Is the location of the reference desk accessible and visible enough for the majority of users to find it?	Opinions and experiences of users about finding the location of the desk.	Conduct an ethnographic wayfinding exercise with non-users of the reference service where they use video cameras to show how they attempt to find the reference desk (Kinsley, Schoonover, and Spitler 2016; Everall and Logan 2017).
	What impacts the approachability of our in-person reference service providers? And what might we be able to do to increase approachability?	Since approachability is subjective (and often unconscious), evidence could be hypothetical or simulated such image-rating exercises.	Conduct unobtrusive observations with protocols to capture multiple variables looking for patterns regarding which reference providers are approached (Strickland and Bonnet 2011). Conduct an image rating study where users are presented with a series of varied images of hypothetical librarians and asked to rate those librarians for their approachability (Bonnet and McAlexander 2013).

ADDITIONAL CONSIDERATIONS

As Table 16.1 reveals, a variety of methods can be used to answer your assessment question. Before settling on which method(s) to use for your assessment project, you will want to be sure to take into consideration the following elements. Doing so may require you to iterate on your assessment question, evidence, or method.

- *Ethics: Are you protecting the rights of your subjects?* Although written 40 years ago, the *Belmont Report* (National Commission for the Protection of Human Subjects 1979) remains the set of principles undergirding ethical human subjects research in the United States. They include a *respect for persons* (research subjects must be "treated as autonomous agents" and those "with diminished autonomy are entitled to protection"), a demonstration of *beneficence* (researchers respect the decisions of research subjects, they protect subjects from harm, and they secure subjects' well-being), and commitment to *justice* (both the benefits and burdens of research are distributed fairly). These principles are most often evoked when studies are required to be reviewed by an Institutional Review Board (IRB), but it is good practice to abide by them even when an IRB is not involved.[4]

  In broad strokes, here is what this might look like in practice. Researchers select a study population not out of convenience but because it is the group most likely to benefit from the project. During recruitment, researchers inform potential study subjects of what that study will entail, how it is expected to benefit them, and what risks it poses to them before they are asked to decide whether they would like to participate. The decisions of the potential subjects are respected by researchers. For those who elect to participate in the study, researchers take every reasonable precaution to protect their privacy to whatever extent the participants agreed to before assenting to join the study (by, e.g., securing data generated by the study and not sharing information from the study that directly or indirectly identifies subjects, unless subjects agree to be identified).

- *Capacity: Do you have the training, experience, and time to carry out this project?* Do you and your co-investigators have a deep enough understanding of the assessment method you have selected to enable you to leverage its advantages and mitigate its disadvantages? Do you have the knowledge and skills to write clear questionnaires, conduct interviews or focus groups, identify the best existing datasets for answering your research question, and so forth? Do you have the knowledge and skills to analyze the data gathered and communicate what you have learned? Are you confident you can protect the rights of your participants throughout your study and after? Do those involved in organizing, carrying out, and completing the project have adequate time to dedicate to these activities, and can they do so within a time period that helps ensure the relevance of the study findings?

  Where the answer to any of the above questions is "no," you may wish to modify the study or seek assistance of colleagues inside or outside of the library. Study up. Consult with experts on data analysis. Bring in collaborators who can augment the assessment team's skills and time.

- *Pragmatics: Is this project worth the effort?* Finally, ask whether the approach you have selected is scaled appropriately for your assessment question and whether you believe that approach will yield valuable enough information to make the time you invest in it worthwhile. If your assessment project is intended to help you make decisions about when to staff your reference desk, a project involving in-depth interviews with users may give you the information you need, but it is likely overkill. Likewise, it would be hasty to draw conclusions about student learning outcomes from reference appointments after examining a handful of papers written by students who have used your reference service. In these examples, there is not only a mismatch of project design and assessment needs but also wasted effort. In the latter case, you are unlikely to get conclusive data about student learning from such a small sample size; in the former case, you can probably answer your staffing questions with usage statistics, which are significantly less labor intensive to gather.

CONCLUSION

The future success of your reference service requires regular and ongoing assessment. As we have outlined in this chapter, the process of assessment is iterative, both due to various issues that might arise when studying human interactions and because of the cyclical nature of assessment itself. Assessment results will either show the service is successful or, more likely, reveal where improvements can be made. In the latter case, you will want to make adjustments to your reference service based on what you learned from the assessment project. Then you will want to embark on a new assessment project to determine if the changes you made have improved the service or not.

In this chapter, we have foregrounded a four-part assessment framework to help you select the most appropriate method(s) for the questions you aim to investigate. We did this to emphasize that the first step of assessment is not to choose a method, but rather to articulate what the goals of the service are. The next step is to identify a question you want to answer and outline what evidence will be needed to answer that question. Only once these steps are done should a method be chosen. The choice of a method is not a simple one. It will need to account for the advantages and disadvantages of the approach itself as well as the audience of the assessment, the resources available to those conducting it, and the expertise needed to carry it out.

Assessment is a process that requires constant reflection, critical engagement, and open-mindedness. Results can sometimes challenge or reinforce long-standing paradigms, but this is what allows librarians to innovate and improve what we do in the service of our missions and, ultimately, for our users. When envisioning the future of reference services in academic libraries, it is a future with assessment at its heart.

NOTES

1. In the academic library world, the word "assessment" tends to cover the ground of what, in fields like Education, is more commonly split into two often complementary terms: "assessment" documents, monitors, and measures whether an activity or intervention has made a difference (e.g., whether a pedagogical method advances student learning outcomes) and "evaluation" makes judgments about the value of an activity or intervention based on implicit or explicit criteria (e.g., whether that pedagogical method is successful in advancing student learning outcomes according to pre-set standards of success).
2. The term "project" is used loosely as shorthand to encompass all assessment work, whether it is well defined and time-bound or more ad-hoc and open-ended.
3. The following series of questions for planning your assessment project is derived from two key sources. First, the W.K. Kellogg Logic Model Development Guide (2006), which aims to help program managers, like those in charge of a reference service, articulate "the relationships among the resources you have to operate your program, the activities you plan, and the changes or results you hope to achieve" (1). Second, Ithaka S+R's tools for planning, including the Framework for Post-Grant Sustainability Planning (Maron and Loy 2011) and the Intake Questionnaire for New Digital Projects (Maron and Pickle 2014) that turn the framework into an accessible questionnaire. While the latter two documents are specifically intended to help individuals and support staff determine how to keep digital projects viable for the long term, their considered approach to planning can be easily abstracted and applied to library services.
4. There is an ever-growing literature that proposes more nuanced and robust standards for ethical research with human subjects. See, for instance, *Proposed Revisions to the Common Rule for the Protection of Human Subjects in the Behavioral and Social Sciences* (National Research Council 2014), which, among other topics, contends with new challenges for protecting research data in our networked world.

REFERENCES

Asher, Andrew, and Susan Miller. 2011. "So You Want to Do Anthropology in Your Library? Or a Practical Guide to Ethnographic Research in Academic Libraries." http://www.erialproject.org/wp-content/uploads/2011/03/Toolkit-3.22.11.pdf.

Askew, Consuella. 2015. "A Mixed Methods Approach to Assessing Roaming Reference Services." *Evidence Based Library & Information Practice* 10 (2): 21–33.

Bonnet, Jennifer L., and Benjamin McAlexander. 2013. "First Impressions and the Reference Encounter: The Influence of Affect and Clothing on Librarian Approachability." *The Journal of Academic Librarianship* 39 (4): 335–346. https://doi.org/10.1016/j.acalib.2012.11.025.

Boyce, Crystal M. 2015. "Secret Shopping as User Experience Assessment Tool." *Public Services Quarterly* 11 (4): 237–253. https://doi.org/10.1080/15228959.2015.1084903.

Bravender, Patricia, Colleen Lyon, and Anthony Molaro. 2011. "Should Chat Reference Be Staffed by Librarians? An Assessment of Chat Reference at an Academic Library Using LibStats." *Internet Reference Services Quarterly* 16 (3): 111–127. https://doi.org/10.1080/10875301.2011.595255.

Butler, Kathy, and Jason Byrd. 2016. "Research Consultation Assessment: Perceptions of Students and Librarians." *The Journal of Academic Librarianship* 42 (1): 83–86. https://doi.org/10.1016/j.acalib.2015.10.011.

Cabaniss, Jason. 2015. "An Assessment of the University of Washington's Chat Reference Services." *Public Library Quarterly* 34 (1): 85–96. https://doi.org/10.1080/01616846.2015.1000785.

Cordell, Rosanne M., and Linda F. Fisher. 2010. "Reference Questions as an Authentic Assessment of Information Literacy." *Reference Services Review* 38 (3): 474–481. https://doi.org/10.1108/00907321011070946.

Côté, Maryvon, Svetlana Kochkina, and Tara Mawhinney. 2016. "Do You Want to Chat? Reevaluating Organization of Virtual Reference Service at an Academic Library." *Reference & User Services Quarterly* 56 (1): 36–46.

Donegan, Patricia Morris, Ralph E. Domas, and John R. Deosdade. 1989. "The Comparable Effects of Term Paper Counseling and Group Instruction Sessions." *College & Research Libraries* 50 (2): 195–205.

Dougan, Kirstin. 2013. "Assessing Music Reference Services in an Age of Vanishing Reference Desks." *Fontes Artis Musicae* 60 (3): 173–181.

Everall, Kyla, and Judith Logan. 2017. "A Mixed Methods Approach to Iterative Service Design of an In-Person Reference Service Point." *Evidence Based Library & Information Practice* 12 (4): 178–185.

Faix, Allison, Amanda MacDonald, and Brooke Taxakis. 2014. "Research Consultation Effectiveness for Freshman and Senior Undergraduate Students." *Reference Services Review* 42 (1): 4–15. https://doi.org/10.1108/RSR-05-2013-0024.

Fan, Suhua Caroline, and Jennifer M. Welch. 2016. "Content Analysis of Virtual Reference Data: Reshaping Library Website Design." *Medical Reference Services Quarterly* 35 (3): 294–304. https://doi.org/10.1080/02763869.2016.1189783.

Fisher, Zoe. 2018. "Who Succeeds in Higher Education? Questioning the Connection Between Academic Libraries and Student Success." Paper presented at the California Academic & Research Libraries Conference, San Francisco, California, April. http://conf2018.carl-acrl.org/wp-content/uploads/2018/08/fisher_whosucceedsinhighereducation_15April2018.docx.

Fournier, Karine, and Lindsey Sikora. 2015. "Individualized Research Consultations in Academic Libraries: A Scoping Review of Practice and Evaluation Methods." *Evidence Based Library & Information Practice* 10 (4): 247–267.

Gerlich, Bella Karla, and G. Lynn Berard. 2007. "Introducing the READ Scale: Qualitative Statistics for Academic Reference Services." *Georgia Library Quarterly* 43 (4): 7–13.

Halpern, Rebecca, Christopher Eaker, John Jackson and Daina Bouquin. 2015. "#DitchTheSurvey: Expanding Methodological Diversity in LIS Research." *In the Library with the Lead Pipe.* http://www.inthelibrarywiththeleadpipe.org/2015/ditchthesurvey-expanding-methodological-diversity-in-lis-research/.

Jones, Kyle, and Dorothea Salo. 2018. "Learning Analytics and the Academic Library: Professional Ethics Commitments at a Crossroads." *College & Research Libraries* 79 (3): 304–323. https://doi.org/10.5860/crl.79.3.304.

Kinsley, Kirsten M., Dan Schoonover, and Jasmine Spitler. 2016. "GoPro as an Ethnographic Tool: A Wayfinding Study in an Academic Library." *Journal of Access Services* 13 (1): 7–23. https://doi.org/ 10.1080/15367967.2016.1154465.

Kot, Felly Chiteng, and Jennifer L. Jones. 2015. "The Impact of Library Resource Utilization on Undergraduate Students' Academic Performance: A Propensity Score Matching Design." *College & Research Libraries* 76 (5): 566–586. https://doi.org/10.5860/crl.76.5.566.

Krieb, Dennis. 2018. "Assessing the Impact of Reference Assistance and Library Instruction on Retention and Grades Using Student Tracking Technology." *Evidence Based Library and Information Practice* 13 (2): 2–12. https://doi.org/10.18438/eblip29402.

Kuruppu, Pali U. 2007. "Evaluation of Reference Services—A Review." *The Journal of Academic Librarianship* 33 (3): 368–381. https://doi.org/10.1016/j.acalib.2007.01.013.

Lanclos, Donna, and Andrew D. Asher. 2016. "'Ethnographish': The State of the Ethnography in Libraries." *Weave: Journal of Library User Experience* 1 (5). http://dx.doi.org/10.3998/weave.12535642.0001.503.

Magi, Trina J., and Patricia E. Mardeusz. 2013. "Why Some Students Continue to Value Individual, Face-to-Face Research Consultations in a Technology-Rich World." *College & Research Libraries* 74 (6): 605–618. https://doi.org/10.5860/crl12-363.

Maron, Nancy L., and Matthew Loy. 2011. "Framework for Post-Grant Sustainability Planning." In *Funding for Sustainability: How Funders' Practices Influence the Future of Digital Resources.* http:// sr.ithaka.org/wp-content/uploads/2015/08/Sustainability_Planning_Tool.pdf.

Maron, Nancy L., and Sarah Pickle. 2014. "Intake Questionnaire for New Digital Projects." In *Sustainability Implementation Toolkit: Developing an Institutional Strategy for Supporting Digital Humanities Resources.* http://sr.ithaka.org/wp-content/uploads/2015/08/IntakeQuestionnaire.pdf.

Matthews, Joseph R. 2014. *Library Assessment in Higher Education,* 2nd edition, Santa Barbara, CA: ABC-CLIO.

Maximiek, Sarah, Erin Rushton, and Elizabeth Brown. 2010. "Coding into the Great Unknown: Analyzing Instant Messaging Session Transcripts to Identify User Behaviors and Measure Quality of Service." *College & Research Libraries* 71 (4): 361–374. https://doi.org/10.5860/crl-48r1.

McLaughlin, Jean E. 2011. "Reference Transaction Assessment: Survey of a Multiple Perspectives Approach, 2001 to 2010." *Reference Services Review* 39 (4): 536–550. https://doi.org/10.1108 /00907321111186631.

Mungin, Michael. 2017. "Stats Don't Tell the Whole Story: Using Qualitative Data Analysis of Chat Reference Transcripts to Assess and Improve Services." *Journal of Library & Information Services in Distance Learning* 11 (1–2): 25–36. https://doi.org/10.1080/1533290X.2016.1223965.

National Commission for the Protection of Human Subjects of Biomedical and Behavioral Research. 1979. "The Belmont Report: Ethical Principles and Guidelines for the Protection of Human Subjects of Research." https://www.hhs.gov/ohrp/sites/default/files/the-belmont-report-508c_FINAL.pdf.

National Research Council (U.S.). 2014. *Proposed Revisions to the Common Rule for the Protection of Human Subjects in the Behavioral and Social Sciences.* Washington, D.C.: National Academies Press.

Novotny, Eric. 2001. "Evaluating Electronic Reference Services: Issues, Approaches and Criteria." *The Reference Librarian* 35 (74): 103–120. https://doi.org/10.1300/J120v35n74_08.

Novotny, Eric, and Emily Rimland. 2007. "Using the Wisconsin—Ohio Reference Evaluation Program (WOREP) to Improve Training and Reference Services." *The Journal of Academic Librarianship* 33 (3): 382–392. https://doi.org/10.1016/j.acalib.2007.01.017.

Oakleaf, Megan. 2018. "Library Integration in Institutional Learning Analytics." *Educause.* November 15. https://library.educause.edu/~/media/files/library/2018/11/liila.pdf.

Ramsden, Bryony. 2016. "Ethnographic Methods in Academic Libraries: A Review." *New Review of Academic Librarianship* 22 (4): 355–369. https://doi.org/10.1080/13614533.2016.1231696.

Reference and User Services Association. 2013. "Guidelines for Behavioral Performance of Reference and Information Service Providers." American Library Association. http://www.ala.org/rusa/resources/ guidelines/guidelinesbehavioral.

Reinsfelder, Thomas. 2012. "Citation Analysis as a Tool to Measure the Impact of Individual Research Consultations." *College & Research Libraries* 73 (3): 263–277.

Sokoloff, Jason, and Rebecca Simmons. 2015. "Evaluating Citation Analysis as a Measurement of Business Librarian Consultation Impact." *Journal of Business & Finance Librarianship* 20 (3): 159–171. https://doi.org/10.1080/08963568.2015.1046783.

Soria, Krista M., Jan Fransen, and Shane Nackerud. 2013. "Library Use and Undergraduate Student Outcomes: New Evidence for Students' Retention and Academic Success." *portal: Libraries and the Academy* 13 (2): 147–164. https://doi.org/10.1353/pla.2013.0010.

Strickland, Beth, and Jennifer Bonnet. 2011. "Are All Reference Interactions Created Equal?: How Gender Might Matter to Our Patrons." In *Association of College & Research Libraries Conference Proceedings*, 7–19. Chicago: American Library Association.

Swoger, Bonnie J. M., and Kimberly Davies Hoffman. 2015. "Taking Notes at the Reference Desk: Assessing and Improving Student Learning." *Reference Services Review* 43 (2): 199–214. https://doi.org/10.1108/RSR-11-2014-0054.

Todorinova, Lily, and Matt Torrence. 2014. "Implementing and Assessing Library Reference Training Programs." *The Reference Librarian* 55 (1): 37–48. https://doi.org/10.1080/02763877.2014.853277.

Vinyard, Marc, Colleen Mullally, and Jaimie Beth Colvin. 2017. "Why Do Students Seek Help in an Age of DIY? Using a Qualitative Approach to Look Beyond Statistics." *Reference & User Services Quarterly* 56 (4): 257–267.

Ward, David. 2004. "Measuring the Completeness of Reference Transactions in Online Chats: Results of an Unobtrusive Study." *Reference & User Services Quarterly* 44 (1): 46–56.

Watts, John, and Stephanie Mahfood. 2015. "Collaborating with Faculty to Assess Research Consultations for Graduate Students." *Behavioral & Social Sciences Librarian* 34 (2): 70–87. https://doi.org/10.1080/01639269.2015.1042819.

W.K. Kellogg Foundation. 1998. "Logic Model Development Guide." https://www.wkkf.org/resource-directory/resource/2006/02/wk-kellogg-foundation-logic-model-development-guide.

Data in Context: Reconsidering Reference in an Academic Library

Harriet Lightman, Geoffrey Morse, and Susan Oldenburg

INTRODUCTION

The 21st-century academic library must be nimble in its deployment of resources. Yet while service adjustments and structural changes can be energizing and empowering, they are often difficult to develop, implement, and manage. We can, and do, observe patron needs changing over time, but anecdotal evidence is rarely enough to justify upending a service. Adjusting job responsibilities and service desk staffing hours can be administratively difficult and there are no guarantees of success. Some of the anxiety that accompanies service transformation can be mitigated by anchoring changes in a larger context, and employing data to guide where and how overhauls need to happen. When data is systematically collected, assessed, and viewed in an institution-specific context, it is often the best marker of how well a service is meeting community needs. In this chapter, we discuss how quantitative and qualitative data helped us redefine our local understanding of reference and research assistance, and reshape our library's service model.

We have long used reference statistics to confirm the need for existing staffing models, collections, and space configurations. As we observed changes in patron behaviors, interactions with the collections and physical plant, and engagement with digital materials, we modified the type of information gathered. Our methods were again modified when our re-visioning of reference was placed into a larger context of rethinking information service delivery at our home institution, Northwestern University Libraries (NUL).

FRAMING THE CONVERSATION

Over the years, library and information science professionals have discussed ways patrons gather information and seek research advice. In the rapidly changing world of information provision, research questions and user expectations are rarely predictable. How, then, do librarians determine best practices and position themselves to provide assistance tailored to their constituencies? Stephen Buss (2016), addressing the broader question of the need for reference in the age of Google and Wikipedia, helps frame the conversation by indicating the importance of using locally gathered reference transactions and other data to make decisions, while Martin Garnar (2016), writing about trends and new models for reference, suggests the importance of subjective measures when he notes that librarians at his home institution view in-person desk staffing as one way to stay current with the community's needs. In our experience, decisions about local service provision are predicated on so many factors that deciding on the most efficacious approach is itself a challenge.

Data on reference transactions, research assistance, chat, and other interactions continue to be key elements in service development, training, and staffing decisions; however, the services studied and the methods used within the library community have varied. Institution-specific case studies that share data-gathering techniques and analyses provide especially helpful frameworks for organizing the strands that make up this complex topic. In 2002, Eric Novotny (the compiler of SPEC Kit 268: *Reference Service Statistics & Assessment*) suggested that libraries' dissatisfaction with their own methods of statistics collection would become one driver in efforts to develop data-gathering methods that would more accurately reflect changing reference practice. Subsequently, studies have detailed the processes by which services have been examined. Some recent examples include Lauren Reiter and J.P. Huffman's (2016) work on research consultations. They used data from a study of student interactions to help predict consultation and desk traffic patterns that allowed for proactive staffing of service points. Similarly, Bradley Wade Bishop and Jennifer A. Bartlett (2013) analyzed face-to-face, phone, e-mail, and chat transactions; the location-based questions helped with staff deployment and development of mobile apps. The many studies of chat include Krisellen Maloney and Jan H. Kemp's (2015) analysis of changes in reference question complexity after implementation of a chat service; they discussed the implications of their findings for online reference services. Sarah LeMire, Lorelei Rutledge, and Amy Brunvand (2016) analyzed reference transactions gathered at physical desks as well as via chat and e-mail to determine how patrons were using their library's reference service; they used the data to help draw conclusions about refining service provision and suggest ways to update collection of reference statistics. Deb Raftus and Kathleen Collins (2015), describing an analysis of desk questions, discussed how their data informed staffing changes. Jason Coleman, Melissa N. Mallon, and Leo Lo (2016) undertook a sizable survey to determine the best combination of services, and concluded with tantalizing suggestions for future work. Others have taken a slightly different path, one which implies that the definition of "data" may be broadened to include qualitative measures. Emily Rogers and Howard S. Carrier (2017) provide a good example of this approach in their study of research consultations, which they undertook to determine the efficacy of that service at one institution. In our experience, a combination of quantitative data and qualitative observation provides a strong foundation for service change.

THE LOCAL CONTEXT

Northwestern University is a private research institution with campuses in Evanston and Chicago, Illinois, and Doha, Qatar. The university has graduate and undergraduate programs in humanities, social sciences, and STEM fields and professional programs in a dozen schools and colleges.[1] The NUL system includes three locations in Evanston, one location in Chicago, and a facility in Waukegan, Illinois.[2] In this chapter, we refer to one area: the NUL reference/research assistance desk in the main library building on the

Evanston campus (hereafter referred to as the reference desk). For decades, this desk was the primary point for such assistance. Until 2013, there were several other service desks on the entry level of the library: Information Commons (IC), which provided technical and directional help; circulation; periodicals/newspapers/microforms; interlibrary loan; and government information.[3]

At NUL, we typically thought of "reference" as a series of transactions: questions of varying complexity (though not directional) answered using single or multiple sources in different formats and coming to the librarian through a variety of means (off- and on-desk, chat, e-mail, and phone).[4] We have increasingly distinguished between "reference" and "research assistance" with the latter including the sorts of in-depth consultations that were traditionally done off-desk, via appointment. Recently, "information service" has been distinguished from "reference" and "research assistance" and implies questions that may not require librarian expertise. These distinctions, which were difficult to disentangle, coalesced in response to local patron behavior, both observed and measured via statistics; the seismic changes in academic libraries; new products (e.g., LibGuides and discovery systems); and a desire to match local needs to innovative service delivery. A complete re-visioning of public services was the final spark that transformed our delivery of these services, especially traditional reference.

The reference/research assistance program evolved over decades. The oldest services are by-appointment research consultations, on-desk in-person reference, and phone transactions. As e-mail reference gained firmer footing, phone traffic declined and chat took root. Coincident with these developments, NUL moved from a reference librarian/bibliographer model to a subject specialist/liaison program. Reference librarians and paraprofessionals had traditionally staffed the desk, with reference librarians providing most of the by-appointment consultations. With the shift to a liaison model, more subject experts were available for consultations and desk staffing; referrals to specialists have become increasingly common. Chat is monitored regularly, on- and off-desk by librarians, paraprofessionals, and students. The healthy numbers of e-mails that come in each day are answered by librarians and paraprofessionals.

As mentioned, we viewed "reference" as discrete on-desk transactions that were answered within a short period of time. While the number of these transactions dropped through the early 2000s, the number of research consultation appointment requests grew. As this pattern unfolded, it became clear that statistics gathered over many years supported observed assumptions: by 2012 use of the library's reference collection, physical desk, and onsite research help had declined from the high traffic seen in the late 1990s and before.[5] While the library's reference room remained a popular study spot, there was no longer the demand for many of the print volumes on its shelves.[6]

Adjustments to physical space paralleled service changes. The reference room was inviting but the physical desk was positioned in such a way that it was bypassed by patrons.[7] After several re-positionings, in fall 2017, the reference desk was merged with the IC desk to create one primary service point. Now called the "information" desk, this point is in a direct sight line from the library's main building entrance. Staff provide on-demand and phone assistance, referrals to specialists, and chat. Support for printing, scanning, and media software is offered. Until fall 2019, guest computer passes were distributed from that desk. Some combination of staff including librarians, paraprofessionals, and students provide assistance seven days a week.

WHAT STORY DID THE DATA TELL?

The transformation of NUL's reference service was rooted in years of observed and gathered data. Statistics compiled over the last decade helped chart the path of, and shifts in, patrons' needs. This evidence of changing patterns in user behavior steered us to recommend staffing, service, and physical location changes.

On-desk transactions. In 2008, our data-gathering methods became more efficient when we started using Desk Tracker software, from Compendium Library Services, to record transactions. In gathering data about reference questions, we initially distinguished between "quick" and "complex."[8] Further categorization allowed us to delineate those complex questions that needed in-depth off-desk consultation. In subsequent years, the categories were refined but a three-tiered approach of quick, complex, and needing consultation was maintained. Using these categories, statistics compiled through Desk Tracker confirmed a continued decline of all types of on-desk transactions.

During the 2008/2009 academic year,[9] over 6,200 transactions were labeled "reference questions" in Desk Tracker. Of these, 15 percent were marked as complex or needing consultation. In 2009/2010, the number of recorded transactions dropped more than 40 percent but those defined as complex and needing consultation comprised 24 percent of the total. Over the same two years, the total number of off-desk research consultations increased by more than 10 percent. By the end of the 2010/2011 academic year, the data confirmed significant changes in patron usage of reference services. This trend of declining reference questions and increasing demand for consultations continued and is illustrated in Figure 17.1.

This quantitative evidence came at an auspicious time. We had long been observing changes in patrons' information-seeking behavior and exploring ways to more effectively serve the community. These discussions culminated in a structural reorganization of NUL's public services division and in the subsequent formation of a task force (the Information Services Task Force, or ISTF) that was charged with proposing a new model for information service delivery, including recommendations for consolidating divisional service points.[10] To examine the reference service point, the ISTF used quantitative and qualitative data. During three sample periods in spring and summer 2012, traffic surveys of areas with service points within NUL were conducted. While the surveys were undertaken to better understand how patrons were using individual service points and how reference questions traveled through the NUL system, the results also confirmed that reference traffic and

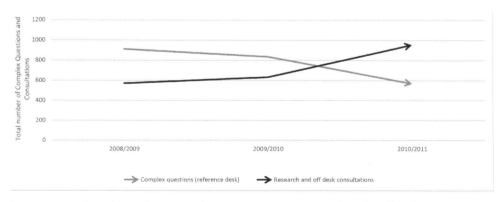

Figure 17.1   Complex Reference Desk Questions versus Research and Off-Desk Consultations, 2008/2009–2010/2011

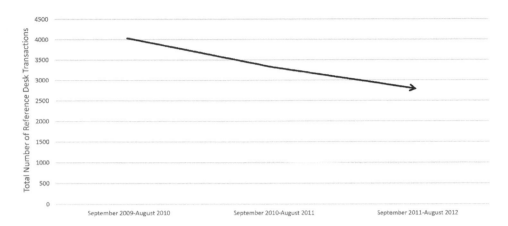

Figure 17.2   Total Reference Desk Transactions

question patterns recorded in earlier years were not aberrations. These overall transactions included any questions or interactions recorded in Desk Tracker, such as simple directionals or queries about hours. Figure 17.2 depicts this decline in overall transactions.

The ISTF's work affirmed that most reference desk activity of all types occurred during weekdays. More support for this trend came from qualitative information gathered from the ISTF's survey of NUL librarians on the libraries' role in research; surveys of outside institutions on their experiences and best practices; and years of anecdotal observations. Based on this evidence, the ISTF recommended merging the reference, government information, and IC desks.[11]

Consolidating service points and finding the best staffing mix was not straightforward. There was support for continuing to staff the reference desk with librarians, partly because some complex questions were still coming to the desk, but also for subjective reasons: the visibility of research staff, and the opportunity to interact spontaneously with the public. There was a further wrinkle. The desk's higher visibility position had a positive impact on the number of overall transactions, at least initially.[12] However, while the number of total transactions rose, the number of actual reference questions, both simple and complex, continued to decline, with many of the interactions being directional queries.[13] Figure 17.3 shows this continued decline relative to the heightened pace of overall transactions during this period.

Refinements. The increase in overall desk transactions was largely positive, but the data showed that the questions being asked were mainly non-research related. During this period, while librarians were partnering with graduate students to staff the desk, it was commonly observed that students, after training, could handle most on-desk questions and provide referrals to subject specialists for in-depth queries. To complicate matters, desk staff observed that patrons were often unclear on the specific functions of each of the library's many service points, in spite of signage, and the data supported the observations that the reference desk was no longer the first place patrons sought research help.[14] By December 2015, when one librarian and one graduate student staffed the desk between the high traffic weekday hours of 10:00 a.m. and 7:00 p.m., a pattern was apparent. The overall number of desk transactions was increasing but the number of research questions was not growing; simultaneously, librarians were, more and more, supporting research and curricular needs off-desk. These observations coupled with the data propelled us to further refine staffing by reducing the amount of time librarians were scheduled to be physically present at the reference desk.

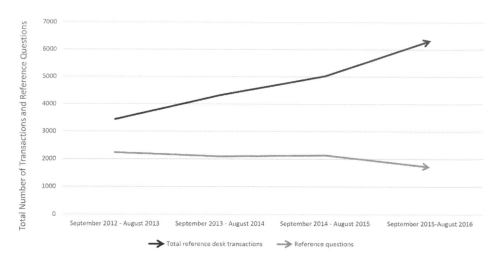

Figure 17.3 Transactions versus Reference Questions

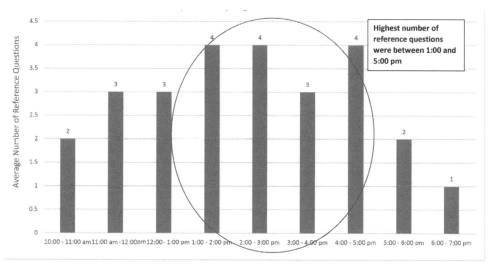

Figure 17.4 Average Number of Reference Questions, Monday-Friday, Fall, Winter, Spring Quarters Fiscal Year 2014

To determine a staffing model that better matched patron behavior and librarians' off-desk work, we returned to past data. An examination of statistics for three fiscal years (September 1, 2014–August 31, 2016) demonstrated that research questions were most likely to be asked between 1:00 p.m. and 5:00 p.m. Figures 17.4, 17.5, and 17.6 illustrate this point.

In Fiscal Year 2015–2016, unlike the preceding two fiscal years, a high number of questions were asked between 6:00 p.m. and 7:00 p.m. However, because the majority of these were not complex questions, we could not justify keeping a librarian on the desk

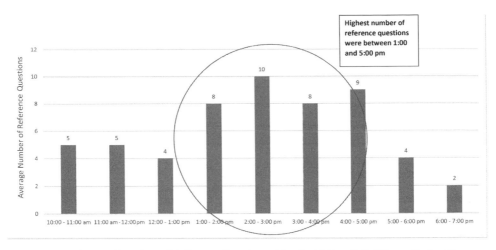

Figure 17.5   Average Number of Reference Questions, Monday-Friday, Fall, Winter, Spring Quarters Fiscal Year 2015

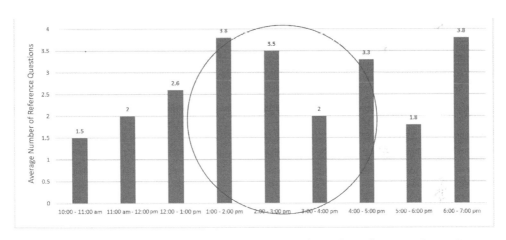

Figure 17.6   Average Number of Reference Questions, Monday-Friday, Fall, Winter, Spring Quarters Fiscal Year 2016

until 7:00 p.m. Figure 17.7 illustrates a general peak of activity between 1:00 p.m. and 5:00 p.m. and an increase in questions between 6:00 p.m. and 7:00 p.m. in Fiscal Year 2015–2016.[15]

Because this newest set of data indicated that librarian expertise was not needed during mornings, staffing was changed accordingly. Monday through Friday, librarians would staff the desk during peak hours of 1:00 p.m. to 5:00 p.m. Graduate students would staff mornings and from 5:00 p.m. to 9:00 p.m. Analysis of weekend activity demonstrated a low number of research questions. While Figure 17.8 illustrates some variation in pattern in the number of questions being asked Saturdays, by hour, most

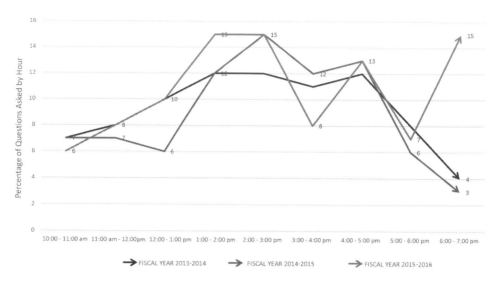

Figure 17.7   Percentage of Questions Asked by Hour, Monday-Friday, Fiscal Year 2014, Fiscal Year 2015, Fiscal Year 2016

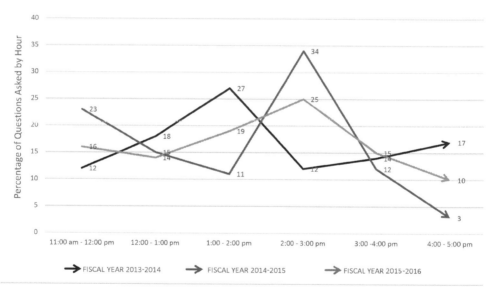

Figure 17.8   Percentage of Questions Asked by Hour, Saturday, Fiscal Year 2014, Fiscal Year 2015, Fiscal Year 2016

activity occurred between 11:00 a.m. and 3:00 p.m. Fiscal Year 2014-2015 saw a sharp drop-off in the number of questions asked between 4:00 p.m. and 5:00 p.m.

These statistics became the basis for shifting librarian desk hours from afternoons (1:00 p.m. to 5:00 p.m.) to midday (11:00 a.m. to 3:00 p.m.). A graduate student was assigned to the desk from 11:00 a.m. to 5:00 p.m. Similarly, Sunday had low numbers of reference transactions. In spring 2016, librarians were staffing the desk Sundays between 1:00 p.m. and 5:00 p.m. An analysis of the number of questions asked for the three years leading up to this time is illustrated in Figure 17.9.

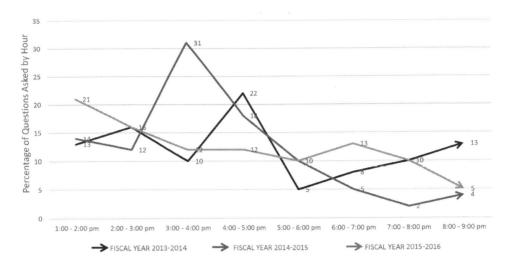

Figure 17.9   Percentage of Questions Asked by Hour, Sunday, Fiscal Year 2014, Fiscal Year 2015, Fiscal Year 2016

Because the data indicated that questions were most likely to be asked in the afternoons on Sundays, librarian desk hours were changed accordingly for fall 2016.

DID DATA TELL THE FULL STORY?

At NUL, we used years of data to change reference services, but we did so within a larger context that matched patron behaviors and librarians' evolving roles. Initial adjustments took into account the changing world of information provision, our local environment and the new ways our constituents were finding and asking for information. While we chiefly defined "data" as the statistics we kept at the reference desk, informal observation, anecdotes, and conversations with librarians helped shape our perspective about what needed to be changed, how often adjustments were warranted, and what statistics should be gathered. Without such evidence, it would have been difficult to deploy resources efficiently, and effectively provide timely service. Our decisions were ultimately based on many factors, but the statistical data was essential and helped us identify some best practices for continual assessment of reference and research services:

- Base staffing recommendations on an examination of trends over at least two to three years. One semester's or quarter's worth of data does not yield an accurate picture, as the local population, courses offered, questions asked, and patron needs change from one academic year to the next. Determine when higher numbers of research questions are asked as opposed to directional and informational questions.
- Do not make predictions that are too specific in terms of when staffing is needed. While data may indicate a trend showing weekday afternoons are busier during the fall semester/quarter, for example, it is unlikely that specific hours of need will be apparent.
- Do not predict desk traffic based on course offerings. Specific class needs, which vary from term-to-term, can be accommodated by subject specialists and research consultations.
- Be ready to recommend frequent staffing adjustments. Present findings to desk staff and solicit input before implementing change. Decisions should mesh with the library's overall mission;

staff input can help keep this on track. Experiment with new models, remembering that models might look promising on paper, but, in reality, prove ineffective.
- Keep statistics-gathering simple. Regularly review the process and questions being asked with desk staff to ensure stakeholders understand why statistics are being gathered. Accumulated data should be relatively simple to export to a spreadsheet and should not require complex analysis.

CONCLUSION

Academic libraries must manage finite resources in a manner that is both efficient and meets the needs of patrons. Service models that were successful in past years may no longer be efficacious. In our experience, services are most effective when they are tailored to a specific local context, based on well-curated data, and are easily modified. The particulars of the data gathered change periodically in conjunction with evolutions in our community's needs and requests. Coupling qualitative observation with quantitative statistics provides valuable frameworks for developing service adjustments. This combination of data was effective for our library in planning and presenting a series of incremental changes to reference staffing in a relatively short period of time. The process described has allowed the Northwestern University Libraries to remain flexible and relevant in a continually evolving environment.

NOTES

1. See Facts. Northwestern, at a glance. https://www.northwestern.edu/about/facts.html. Accessed November 22, 2019.
2. The Pritzker Legal Research Center and the Galter Health Sciences Library, both located on the Chicago campus, and the library in Doha are administered separately from NUL. Additionally, the Styberg Library of Garrett-Evangelical Theological Seminary and Bexley Seabury, located on Northwestern's Evanston campus, is affiliated with NUL, but is not a part of the NUL system.
3. In 2013, the government information reference desk was merged with the main library reference desk. In 2015, the periodicals/newspapers/microform and interlibrary loan desks merged with the circulation desk. Until the end of fall quarter 2019, other separate service points continued to include the discrete area of the libraries' Distinctive Collections: the Herskovits Library of African Studies, the McCormick Library of Special Collections, the Art Library, the Music Library, the Transportation Library, and University Archives. There are also separate service points for the Mitchell Multimedia Center, the Math Library, and the Mudd Library (which serves the northern part of campus, and focuses on STEM fields) as well as the Chicago-based Schaffner Library, which chiefly serves NU's School of Professional Studies. See https://www.library.northwestern.edu/libraries-collections/index.html. Accessed November 22, 2019.
4. This in accordance with the definition provided by the Reference and User Services Association [RUSA]. "Definitions of Reference." American Library Association, 2008. http://www.ala.org/rusa/guidelines/definitionsreference. Accessed November 22, 2019. RUSA defines reference transactions as follows: "**Reference Transactions** are information consultations in which library staff recommend, interpret, evaluate, and/or use information resources to help others to meet particular information needs. Reference transactions do not include formal instruction or exchanges that provide assistance with locations, schedules, equipment, supplies, or policy statements." See also discussion of what is meant by "reference" in Stephen P. Buss, "Do We Still Need Reference Services in the Age of Google and Wikipedia?" *The Reference Librarian* 57, no. 4 (2016): 265–266. Buss also cites RUSA.
5. For instance, during the period from 2001–2002 through 2004–2005, there was a drop from 22,272 interactions at the reference desk in 2001–2002 to 18,663 in 2004–2005. By 2010–2011, this number had dropped to 9,815.

6. By 2012 the reference collection had been reduced by close to 10 percent but still held over 50,000 volumes.

7. See the pictures of the first set of reference desk re-positionings in Harriet Lightman and Qiana Johnson, "Reimagining or Revisioning? How One Library Studied Information Services," *College & Research Libraries News* 75 (8), (Sept. 2014): 446–447.

8. In our local context, a "quick" question is one that requires using a specific resource that will provide the patron with a satisfactory answer while "complex" questions are those that require a level of expertise that is beyond simply pointing the user to a resource. A complex question requires staff consult a resource or resources and assist the patron in using the resources as well as understanding the architecture of the sources and how they will help meet the patron's need. Consultations, as previously suggested, can be done on-desk, but most often require an off-desk meeting that usually involves preparation on the part of a specialist. Like complex questions, consultations require understanding the architecture of the sources and how they will help meet the patron's need. Also note that this distinction between "quick" and "complex" allowed us to exclude other transactions such as directional and technical questions.

9. Northwestern operates on the quarter system, with the academic year typically beginning in late September and ending in June; exact dates vary year-to-year. The fiscal year is September 1–August 31.

10. For more on the process, see Lightman and Johnson, "Reimagining or Revisioning? How One Library Studied Information Services."

11. See note 3 above. This merger took several years to complete.

12. An examination of the statistics from September 2012 (when the desk was in its previous position in the reference room, out of a direct sight line) through August 2015 showed a dramatic increase in the total number of transactions.

13. While the number of research questions asked at the physical government information desk was very low, many non-government information directional/locational questions were asked at that desk. After the desks merged, these questions were directed elsewhere, which may account for some of the increase in such traffic, at least initially, at the main reference desk.

14. The reference desk, for example, received numerous directional and basic information questions that had to be referred to another part of the library because the question was not research-related: printing, approval for hanging a poster in the library, or adding money to a printing account were all referred to the IC desk.

15. In Fiscal Year 2015–2016, the spike may have been at least in part to subjective factors, that is, the closure of buildings across campus, which meant that more classes were held in the main library building.

REFERENCES

Bishop, Bradley Wade, and Jennifer A. Bartlett. 2013. "Where Do We Go from Here? Informing Academic Library Staffing through Reference Transaction Analysis." *College & Research Libraries* 74 (5): 489–500.

Buss, Stephen P. 2016. "Do We Still Need Reference Services in the Age of Google and Wikipedia?" *The Reference Librarian* 57 (4): 265–271.

Coleman, Jason, Melissa N. Mallon, and Leo Lo. 2016. "Recent Changes to Reference Services in Academic Libraries and Their Relationship to Perceived Quality: Results of a National Survey." *Journal of Library Administration* 56 (6): 673–696.

"Definitions of Reference." 2008. American Library Association. http://www.ala.org/rusa/guidelines/definitionsreference.

Garnar, Martin. 2016. "Whither the Reference Desk? 20th Century Values in a 21st Century Service Model." *International Information & Library Review* 48 (3): 211–216.

LeMire, Sarah, Lorelei Rutledge, and Amy Brunvand. 2016. "Taking a Fresh Look: Reviewing and Classifying Reference Statistics for Data-Driven Decision Making." *Reference & User Services Quarterly* 55 (3): 230–238.

Lightman, Harriet, and Qiana Johnson. 2014. "Reimagining or Revisioning? How One Library Studied Information Services." *College & Research Libraries News* 75 (8): 445–448, 462.

Maloney, Krisellen, and Jan H. Kemp. 2015. "Changes in Reference Question Complexity Following the Implementation of a Proactive Chat System: Implications for Practice." *College & Research Libraries* 76 (7): 959–974.

Novotny, E. (Eric C.), Association of Research Libraries. Office of Leadership and Management Services. (2002). *Reference Service Statistics & Assessment: A SPEC Kit.* Washington, D.C.: Association of Research Libraries, Office of Leadership and Management Services.

Raftus, Deb, and Kathleen Collins. 2015. "Does the Reference Desk Still Matter?: Assessing the Desk Paradigm at the University of Washington Libraries." In *Rethinking Reference for Academic Libraries: Innovative Developments and Future Trends*, edited by Carrie Forbes and Jennifer Bowers, 153–166. Lanham, Boulder, New York, London: Rowman & Littlefield.

Reiter, Lauren, and J.P. Huffman. 2016. "Yes Virginia, It Will Scale: Using Data to Personalize High-volume Reference Interactions." *The Journal of Academic Librarianship* 42 (1): 21–26.

Rogers, Emily, and Howard S. Carrier. 2017. "A Qualitative Investigation of Patrons' Experiences with Academic Library Research Consultations." *Reference Services Review* 45 (1): 18–37.

FURTHER READING

Bright, Kawanna, Consuella Askew, and Lori Driver. 2015. "Transforming Reference Services: More than Meets the Eye." In *Rethinking Reference for Academic Libraries: Innovative Developments and Future Trends*, edited by Carrie Forbes and Jennifer Bowers, 117–133. Lanham, Boulder, New York, London: Rowman & Littlefield.

Butler, Kathy, and Jason Byrd. 2016. "Research Consultation Assessment: Perceptions of Students and Librarians." *The Journal of Academic Librarianship* 42 (1): 83–86.

Dinkins, Debbi, and Susan M. Ryan. 2010. "Measuring Referrals: The Use of Paraprofessionals at the Reference Desk." *The Journal of Academic Librarianship* 36 (4): 279–286.

Gerlich, Bella Karr, and Edward Whatley. 2009. "Using the READ Scale for Staffing Strategies: The Georgia College and State University Experience." *Library Leadership & Management* 23 (1): 26–30.

Jacoby, JoAnn, David Ward, Susan Avery, and Emilia Marcyk. 2016. "The Value of Chat Reference Services: A Pilot Study." *portal: Libraries & the Academy* 16 (1): 109–129.

Lenkart, Joseph, Alexandra Krogman, and David Ward. 2017. "Beyond Satisfaction: Investigating Patron Use of Reference Information." *Internet Reference Services Quarterly* 22 (1): 1–24.

Massis, Bruce. 2016. "Data-Driven Decision-Making in the Library." *New Library World* 117 (1/2): 131–134.

McCaslin, David. 2017. "Data-Driven Decision Making." In *Leading in the New Academic Library*, edited by Becky Albitz, Christine Avery, and Diane Zabel, 23–34. Santa Barbara, Denver: Libraries Unlimited.

Peters, Timothy. 2015. "Taking Librarians Off the Desk: One Library Changes Its Reference Staffing Model." *Performance Measurement and Metrics* 16 (1): 18–27.

Poparad, Christa E. 2015. "Staffing an Information Desk for Maximum Responsiveness and Effectiveness in Meeting Research and Computing Needs in an Academic Library." *The Reference Librarian* 56 (2): 83–92.

VanderPol, Diane, and El Shaimaa Sakr. 2017. "Translating Reference Expertise." *Reference Services Review* 45 (4): 575–583.

Ward, David, and JoAnn Jacoby. 2018. "A Rubric and Methodology for Benchmarking Referral Goals." *Reference Services Review* 46 (1): 110–127.

Index

Note: Page numbers for figures are in *italics*, and page numbers for tables are in **bold**

Aagaard, Posie, 113
Adams, Megan M., 10
African American newspapers, 104–6
ALA JobLIST, 10–11, 13, 16–17
Albright, Kendra S., 129, 130, 134, 135
Alexa, 51, 52, 53
Allan, Barbara, 19
Allen, Susan, 52
American Library Association: accredited
    master's degree programs, 3, 4–6; *State of
    America's Libraries Report,* 131, 136
Annotations, 69
Apps, 52
Arguello, Natasha Z., 113
Artificial intelligence (AI), 51
Association of College and Research Libraries
    (ACRL), 131

Bailey, Edgar C., Jr., 3, 5
Bandyopadhyay, Aditi, 38
Bartlett, Jennifer A., 170
Beile, Penny M., 10
Belmont Report, 163
Bielefield, Arlene, 52
Bishop, Bradley Wade, 170
Bodemer, Brett B., 76
Boot camps, 28
Booth, Char, 132, 133
Bowers Sharpe, Krista, 58
Boyd-Byrnes, Mary Kate, 38
Brunvand, Amy, 170
Bush, George W., 117, 118, 120, 124

Business research, 43–49
Buss, Stephen P., 169, 178n4

California Digital Library, 112
California Polytechnic State University San
    Luis Obispo, 76
Calvert, Philip, 51, 52
Cardina, Christen, 8–9
Carrier, Howard S., 170
Castiglione, James, 130, 132, 134, 137
Cecchino, Nicola A., 134
Chat services, 85
Cherry, Joan M., 134
Christopher Newport University, 78
Chronicling America (Library of Congress/
    National Endowment for the Humanities),
    104, 105–6
Chung, Kevin, 57
Clinton, Bill, 117, 118
Clinton, Hillary, 117
Coaching, 25
Colbert-Lewis, Danielle, 24
Coleman, Jason, 170
Collaboration, 33
Collins, Kathleen, 170
Coman, Edwin, 38, 39
Communities of practice, 74–75
Community engagement, 143
Community inquiry, 143–44
Competencies, 24–25
Condic, Kristine, 3, 4
Connolly, David, 10

Cooke, Nicole A., 24
Course management systems (CMS), 113
Critical librarianship, 141
Crowdsourcing, 54
Cultural competence, 141
Customer service, 24–25
Customization, 23

Deliberate practice, 25
DeRue, Scott, 43
Detmering, Robert, 10
Digital reference collections, 97
Diversity, 142
Diversity training, 24
Do-it-yourself reference, 63–64; annotations, 69; images, 68; learning object, 64–67; LibGuides, 67–68; tutorials, 69–70; vendor tutorials, 68–69
Duff, Wendy M., 134
Dworak, Ellie, 79

Ebooks, 96–97
EDUCAUSE, 136
Elmborg, James K., 80
E-mail reference, 85
End of Term Web Archive, 123–24
Engagement Spaces, 76
Environmental Scan (ACRL), 131, 135
Environmental scanning: benefits of, 130–31; definition, 129–30; external environment, 135–37; forecasting change, 130–31; online *vs.* in-person users' environments, 132–34; optimizing use of data and information on, 131; organization-centered content and steps, 134–35; planning and prioritizing, 131–32; support in a competitive environment, 132
E-reference resource licensing, 111–16
Ericsson, K. Anders, 25
Ewing Marion Kauffman Foundation, 113

Fake news, 88
Farnsworth, Stephen J., 120
Figueroa, Miguel, 51
The Five Laws of Library Science (Ranganathan), 37
Fugitive documents, 122

Garnar, Martin, 170
Goffman, Erving, 55, 56

Google News Archive, 104
Government information: definitions, 118–20; fugitive documents, 122; and presidential administrations, 117–18, 124–25; safeguards, 123–24; and Trump, Donald J., 120–22
Government Publishing Office, 118
Governmental changes, 30
Grand Valley State University, 76
Grove, Andrew S., 130
Gruman, Jamie A., 20
Guo, Ya Jun, 52

Harper, Ray, 10, 17
HathiTrust, 107, 123
Hinchliffe, Lisa Janicke, 56
Historical African American Newspapers Available Online LibGuide, 104–6
Hope College, 79
Hough, Jill R., 131
Huffman, J. P., 170

Images, 68
Indiana University Libraries, 78
Information intermediation and instruction, 5
Information service, 171
Intelligent personal assistants, 52–53
Internet Archive, 123
Interviews, 20–21
iSchools (information schools), 4–5
Ithaka S+R, 136

Jacobs, James R., 122
Job postings, 9–18
Johnson, Anna Marie, 3, 5, 59
Johnson, Catherine A., 134
Johnson, Qiana, 179n7
Jordan, Mary Wilkins, 19
JSTOR, 107

Kalin, Sally W., 4
Kani, Justin, 52
Kemp, Jan H., 170
Kennan, Mary Anne, 9
Kessler, Jane, 94
Keyes, Kelsey, 79
Klein, Howard J., 20
Knight, Carley, 9
Kraft, Michelle, 52
Krampe, Ralf T., 25

Kresge Library Services, 43–47, *45*
Kroeger, Alice Bertha, 93
Kuh, George D., 75–76

Laroche, Lionel, 21, 22, 23, 25
Lave, Jean, 74–75
Leadership, 30–31
Learning object, 64–67
Legal issues, 30
LeMire, Sarah, 170
Lessick, Susan, 52
LibGuides, 67–68, 103–4, 109; Historical
    African American Newspapers Available
    Online, 104–6; "Nineteenth Century
    Periodicals," 106–9
Libraries as a useful working space,
    39–40
Library associations, 31
LibRAT (Library Research Assistant
    Technician), 76
Lightman, Harriet, 179n7
Liu, Van Quan, 52
Lo, Leo, 170
Long, Elisabeth, 4
Lots of Copies Keeps Stuff Safe
    (LOCKSS), 124
Lux, Vera, 58–59

Making of America (Cornell University and
    University of Michigan), 107
Mallon, Melissa N., 170
Maloney, Krisellen, 170
Management, 30–31
Marist College, 104
Matteson, Miriam L., 24
Matthews, Joseph R., 94
Michigan State University, 76, 78, 79
Microaggressions, 56–58
Mikitish, Stephanie, 54
Miller, Shelly S., 24
Mitola, Rosan, 76
Mobile services, 52

National Archives and Records Administration
    (NARA), 119
National Center for Education Statistics
    (NCES), 136
Nims, Julia K., 25
"Nineteenth Century Periodicals" LibGuide,
    106–9

Northwestern University Libraries (NUL)
    study, 169–79, *172, 173, 174, 175,*
    176, 177
Norton, Christina, 58
Novotny, Eric, 170

Obama, Barack, 117, 119, 120, 121, 124
O'Connor, Lisa, 3, 4, 6
Onboarding and training, 19–26
Online learning object. *See* Learning object
Open access digitized primary sources,
    103–4, 109; Historical African American
    Newspapers Available Online LibGuide,
    104–6; "Nineteenth Century Periodicals"
    LibGuide, 106–9

Pattni, Emily, 76
Peer-assisted learning (PAL), 73–74
Peer-to-peer reference services in academic
    libraries: best practices, 78–80; peer-assisted
    learning (PAL), 73–74; in practice, 76–78;
    situated learning and communities of
    practice, 74–75; student employment, 75–
    76; theoretical frameworks behind, 73–76
Penn State University, University Park,
    Pattee & Paterno Libraries, 77–78
Permanent uniform resource locators (PURLs),
    123
Pew Research Center, 136
Polin, Beth, 20
Presentation, 32
Presidential Records Act of 1978, 121
Primary sources, 103–4, 109; "Nineteenth
    Century Periodicals" LibGuide, 106–9
Print reference collection, 93–94, 99; in
    academic libraries, 95–97; current trends in,
    94–95; definitions, 94; in public libraries,
    98–99; value of, 96–97
"Professional Competencies for Reference and
    User Services Librarians" (ALA RUSA), 24
Puacz, Jeanne Holba, 98
Public library reference services, 83–84;
    diversity, 87; identifying reliable sources,
    87–88; impact of technology, 86–87; online
    service, 84–86; reference interview, 84
Public speaking, 32
Publishing, 30

Rachlin, David, 24
Raftus, Deb, 170

Ranganathan, S. R., 26, 37, 38, 40–41, 47
Reagan, Ronald, 117
Reference: definition, 171
Reference collection, future of, 41–46
Reference education: current status of, 3–6; at
    iSchools, 4–5; program title variances, 5
Reference librarians, 7–18, *12, 13, 14*;
    continuing education, 27–33; onboarding
    and training, 19–26; research, 13–15;
    service managers and service providers,
    15–16; traditional, 12–13
Reference services: assessment of, 151–64,
    159–62; content analysis during assessment
    of, 154; ethnographic methods during
    assessment of, 155; focus groups during
    assessment of, 155–56; global reach of,
    139–45; interviews during assessment of,
    156; learning analytics during assessment
    of, 156–57; new needs of users, 140–42;
    new places and technologies, 142–44; new
    services, 144–45; Northwestern University
    Libraries (NUL) study, 169–79, *172, 173,
    174, 175, 176, 177*; observations during
    assessment of, 157; student learning
    outcomes during assessment of, 154; surveys
    using questionnaires during assessment
    of, 157–58; usage data analysis during
    assessment of, 158. *See also* Do-it-yourself
    reference; Peer-to-peer reference services in
    academic libraries; Print reference collection;
    Public library reference services; Reference
    collection, future of; Reference education;
    Reference librarians
Reiter, Lauren, 170
Research Collections and Preservation
    Consortium (ReCAP), 97
Rich, Linda, 58–59
Rinto, Erin, 76
Robots, 51
Rogers, Emily, 170
Ross School of Business, University of
    Michigan, 43–46
Rothbauer, Paulette, 134
Roy, Loriene, 4
Rutherford, Don, 21, 22, 23, 25
Rutledge, Lorelei, 170

Safeguards, 123–24
Saks, Alan M., 20
Sarang, Avneet, 52

Saunders, Laura, 3–4, 8
Saving time of the reader, 37–48
Scholarly communication, 31–32
Scholarly identity (SI) support, 51, 54–56
Scholarly Publishing and Academic Resources
    Coalition (SPARC), 31–32
Scott-Branch, Jamillah, 24
Search Bar (Penn State), 77–78
Self-service tools, 37, 41, 48
Singer, Carol A., 97
Siri, 51, 52
Situated learning, 74–75
Smith, Mark, 25
Social justice, 4
Social media and government, 119, 121–22
Social question-and-answer (SQA)
    platforms, 54
Sproles, Claudene, 10
Starr, Joan, 9
State of America's Libraries Report (ALA), 131,
    136
Stevens, Christy R., 79
Stevens, Robert, 25
Stielow, Frederick, 95
Storm, Paula, 25
Student employment, 75–76
Sue, Derald Wing, 56
Sunlight Foundation, 121

Tang, Yingqi, 9
Technology tools, 29–30
Tesch-Römer, Clemens, 25
Todaro, Julie, 25
Todorinova, Lily, 10
Topping, Keith J., 74
Trump, Donald J., 117, 120–22
Tutorials, 69–70

Universal design, 141–42
University of Arizona Libraries, 133
University of Oxford, 136

Vendors, 30
Vendor tutorials, 68–69
Virtual reality (VR), 51–52
Virtual reference service (VRS), 54,
    143
Voice-enabled smart speakers, 52–53
Volunteering, 32
Vygotsky, Lev, 74, 75

Wang, Hanrong, 9
Watts, John, 76
Wayback Machine, 123
Weinzweig, Ari, 46
Wenger, Etienne, 74–75
White, Margaret A., 131
White House Office of Science and Technology
    (OSTP), 30
Wicks, Donald, 8–9
Woodard, Beth S., 22, 25, 26

Woodward, Jeannette, 19
Writing courses, 32

Xu, H., 9–10

Young, Heartsill, 22–23

Zingerman's, 46
Zone of proximal development,
    74, 75

About the Editors and the Contributors

CHRISTOPHER C. BROWN, Professor, is Reference Librarian and Coordinator of Government Documents at the University of Denver, Main Library. For over 20 years, he has overseen the large government information collection and provided reference services to the university community and members of the general public. He is author of *Harnessing the Power of Google: What Every Researcher Should Know* and *Librarian's Guide to Online Searching* (5th edition, with Suzanne S. Bell). Chris has taught as an adjunct professor in the University of Denver Library School for 20 years.

MARIA K. BURCHILL, MLIS, is Head of Adult Services for Schlow Centre Region Library in State College, Pennsylvania, where she facilitates interactions between library staff and patrons, as well as colleagues across departments, and between institutions. With a strong background in cataloging and lending services, Burchill specializes in program development and has experience with encoding bibliographic data, open-source ILS applications, XML, and content management systems. Skills in art history and museum education have also helped her develop a deep understanding of quality digital resources that accurately reflect original format and enhance user experience.

ELIZABETH CLARKE is the Associate Librarian for Research Services at Marist College's James A. Cannavino Library, where she provides reference services, teaches information literacy, and coordinates the library instruction program for first-year students. Elizabeth also enjoys working with Marist's archival collections and serves as the archivist for the Poughkeepsie Regatta Collection, which documents the national collegiate regatta competition held annually on the Hudson River between 1895 and 1949. She holds a BA in history from Vassar College and a MLIS from Long Island University.

HAILLEY FARGO is the Student Engagement Coordinator at Penn State University, University Park campus. In this role, Hailley works to create an aligned approach to support student engagement experiences. Hailley's research interests include the library's role in student engagement, peer-to-peer services, reference services, and undergraduate research. She is also a cofounder of The Librarian Parlor (libparlor.com), a blog dedicated to building community around LIS research. Hailley received her MLIS from the University of Illinois at Urbana-Champaign.

MELISSA GASPAROTTO is Assistant Director of Research Services for The New York Public Library Research Libraries. Her research and recent publications explore changing models of open access publishing and ebook discovery in Latin America and the global information ecology around digital content. She is active in a variety of professional organizations and consortia, including the Seminar on the Acquisition of Latin American Library Materials (SALALM), Latin America Northeast Libraries Consortium, and the Latin American Research Resources Project. She earned an MA in Latin American and Caribbean studies from New York University and an MS in library and information science from Long Island University.

ALIQAE GERACI is the Assistant Director of Cornell University's Catherwood Library, where she leads research support to the Cornell, ILR School, and broader disciplinary communities in employment and labor relations. A former public librarian and union researcher, she is the coauthor of *Grassroots Library Advocacy* (ALA Editions 2012) and serves on the Leadership Team of the Tompkins County Workers' Center. Aliqae holds an MA in labor studies from the CUNY Murphy Institute and an MS in library and information science from Long Island University.

DANIEL HICKEY is the Librarian for Business and Economics at New York University. He did his graduate work at the University of Pittsburgh's School of Information Science and has previously held positions at The Pennsylvania State University and Cornell University. Hickey's public service-focused writing has appeared in *Reference & User Service Quarterly* (RUSQ), *Reference Reborn: Breathing New Life into Public Services Librarianship* (2011), *Assessing Liaison Librarians: Documenting Impact for Positive Change* (2014), *Advances in Library Administration & Organization: Library Staffing for the Future* (2015), and *The Library's Role in Supporting Financial Literacy for Patrons* (2016). Hickey's research focuses on the intersection of information-seeking behavior and needs of business students, with a particular emphasis on career information literacy.

JOHN E. KENNEY has been the Teen Services Librarian at the Hyde Park Branch of the Boston Public Library for more than 10 years. He worked previously in the research library at Copley main branch in the Music and General Reference departments. His first professional positions were at the Boston Conservatory and Boston University Music libraries. John started work at the Boston Conservatory as a graduate assistant, working evenings and weekends, and was eventually offered the full-time day position as Assistant Librarian. He started full-time, even before graduating from both the University of Massachusetts and the Simmons College MS LIS program in 1997, and helped to write two music CD-ROM reviews with a faculty at Simmons. John then sang as a professional at the Saint Paul's Choir School in Cambridge, Massachusetts, for 17 years. While a graduate student in Musicology at UMass Amherst, he was a teaching assistant and could not work in the library at the same time. John's first experience working in libraries was as an undergraduate at Penn State University, next to where he grew up in State College, Pennsylvania. In his senior year, John worked as a library assistant in the music listening room. This was still in the era of linear tracking turntables and CD players. While e-mail was already common via "dumb terminals," much of the work involved retrieving and shelving materials, including scores, for students and faculty. His first library technical service project was helping to accession 78 and 33 rpm discs from a recent gift of Jazz records. John's current work includes a good deal of adult technical and reference help. But his main duties include running the two after school clubs for teens in Hyde Park, Gaming Club, and Anime Club. Gaming Club involves regular sessions on the Guitar Hero and Rock Band titles as well as DJ Hero 2. There are three other consoles normally in use with battle, racing, sports, and adventure games. Anime Club makes use of the multitude of current streaming sites, the new high-speed wireless network, and widescreen projector. Both clubs have established a good core group of teens that stretches over many class years. The new teen culture at the branch has offered something to look forward to, for the kids in the children's room in the years to come.

ANNE LANGLEY is the Dean, University of Connecticut Library. She has been an academic librarian since 1993, and throughout her career she has held a variety of library positions at UConn, Penn State University, Princeton, Duke, NCSU, and the University of Tennessee, Knoxville. She holds a master's degree in library science from the University of Tennessee and a bachelor's degree in creative writing from Georgia State University. She has written books, chapters, and articles on multiple aspects of academic libraries, given many presentations on the same, and has research interests in how academic libraries behave as organizations. She loves to play video games, fronted a band for many years, and loves painting with acrylics and creating papier-mache.

KELLY LAVOICE is the Business Information Librarian for Collections at Vanderbilt University. In her current position, she collaborates with members of the Owen School of Management and Vanderbilt University Library to build and maintain a strong business research collection. She also provides reference services for the business community at Vanderbilt, serving as liaison to Operations, Finance, and Strategy faculty in the Owen School of Management. Kelly previously worked as the Coordinator for Reference & Instruction for the Business & Hospitality Research Team at Cornell University. While at Cornell, she taught a 2-credit Information Retrieval and Research Methods course for the School of Hotel Administration. Kelly holds a BA from The College of New Jersey and an MLS from Rutgers University.

NAOMI LEDERER is Professor, College Liaison Librarian (Reference), and liaison to English, History, Art, Design & Merchandising, and Interdisciplinary Liberal Arts. Through June 2015, she was liaison to Communication Studies and Journalism & Technical Communication (also Ethnic Studies through June 2014). As of November 1, 2015, she is the Government Information Librarian at Colorado State University Libraries, Fort Collins, Colorado, a selective depository collection. She has taught hundreds (over one thousand likely) library instruction sessions that have varied from one-shot to teaching a semester-long course on library research. Her extensive web pages, including "How to Do Library Research" as well as subject-specific pages for her liaison departments, have heavy use and have served as replacements for in-class instruction. She is the author of the book *Ideas for Librarians Who Teach: With Suggestions for Teachers and Business Presenters* (2005) and peer-reviewed and non-peer-reviewed journal articles, book chapters, and newsletter articles. She has given presentations in the United States, Canada, Spain, and Germany, with the most recent (2018) at the Federal Depository Library Conference in Arlington, Virginia.

HARRIET LIGHTMAN is Senior Librarian for Research and Engagement at Northwestern University Libraries. Her many roles at Northwestern have included Head of Research & Learning Services, and Head of Research & Information Services. She has published and presented on topics in both library outreach and collection development. Lightman holds an MLIS from University of Wisconsin-Milwaukee, a PhD and an MA in history from Bryn Mawr College, and a BA in history from Barnard College.

ELIZABETH MAHONEY is the Associate Chair of the Information Culture and Data Stewardship Department (ICDS) in the School of Computing and Information at the University of Pittsburgh. She did her graduate work at SUNY Albany and at the University of Pittsburgh. She was Head of the Information Sciences Library at the University of Pittsburgh for 22 years, providing reference services in-person and virtually to both the school and the university community. She became a full-time lecturer in ICDS in 2011 and has taught reference resources and services, understanding information, knowledge organization, storytelling, and history of children's literature. She supports professional organizations at the local, state, and national levels, having recently served as a mentor in the Commonwealth Libraries, ILEAD Pennsylvania program. She is currently working on a project related to book printing mechanics that have impacted the production of literature for children.

LISA MARTIN is the Coordinator of Outreach & Business Librarian at the University of Houston Libraries. As coordinator, she leads a team focused on liaison engagement to the campus and community; as business librarian, she works closely with faculty and students in her liaison areas. Her research interests include emotional intelligence and leadership, effective outreach efforts, and the post-graduation information skills of business students. Lisa received her MLIS from the University of California at Los Angeles and her BA from the University of Redlands.

GEOFFREY MORSE is Assistant Head of Research Services at the Northwestern University Libraries and is liaison to the departments of Linguistics and Religious Studies. Morse has held various roles at Northwestern, including supervising the research assistance desk, chairing the Resource Discovery Operations Group and, in his role as a public services librarian, configuring the library's discovery system Primo and the library services platform ALMA. Morse is currently Chair of the Emerging Technologies Section of the Reference and User Services Association (ETS/RUSA). Morse holds an MLIS from the University of Wisconsin-Madison and a BA in history from Hampshire College.

ELIZABETH NAMEI is the Director of Research, Teaching, and Learning Services at The Claremont Colleges Library, which serves a consortium of five undergraduate colleges (Claremont McKenna, Harvey Mudd, Pitzer, Pomona, and Scripps) and two graduate institutions (Claremont Graduate University and Keck Graduate Institute) in Claremont, California. She holds an MLIS from Simmons College and an MA in English literature from Hunter College. Before taking on her current role, she worked as a subject liaison and teaching librarian at several different community college and university libraries in Illinois, Louisiana, North Carolina, New York, and California. Her professional interests include user experience, active learning, inclusive pedagogy, assessment, and new models of reference services.

SUSAN OLDENBURG was a GIS and research specialist at Northwestern University Libraries. She enjoyed a variety of roles at the Libraries, including the operational management of the research assistance desk. Oldenburg holds a BA in history from the University of Illinois at Chicago and a GIS certification from Northeastern Illinois University.

MICHAEL R. OPPENHEIM has been Business Research and Collections Librarian in the Rosenfeld Management Library, UCLA Anderson Graduate School of Management, since 1997. Prior to working at UCLA, he was a government information and reference librarian at California State University, Los Angeles, and the federal documents depository librarian at Whittier College. He is active in the American Library Association (ALA) and has held various offices in its Business Reference and Services Section (BRASS) and the Government Documents Roundtable (GODORT), as well as in the California Library Association, the Business & Finance Division of the Special Libraries Association, and California Academic and Research Libraries (CARL). With Eric Forte (OCLC), he co-edited *The Basic Business Library: Core Resources and Services*, 5th edition (2012), and with Wendy Diamond (California State University-Chico) he is coauthor of *Marketing Information: A Strategic Guide for Business and Finance Libraries* (2004). He is the 2013 recipient of the ALA/RUSA/BRASS Award for "Excellence in Business Librarianship."

MANUEL OSTOS is Librarian for Romance Languages and Literatures at Penn State University Libraries. His research areas include foreign-language collection development, cultural studies, and humanities research methods. Manuel has delivered presentations in national and international venues, including the Charleston Conference and the Big Ten Academic Alliance Library Conference, and his work has appeared in *College & Research Libraries* and *The Journal of Academic Librarianship*.

ROXANNE PECK is Program Director, Content Acquisitions and Resource Sharing, at the University of California, San Diego. Prior to this appointment, she was a senior manager at Penn State University Libraries overseeing collections and acquisitions. She has 20 years of experience in acquisitions, scholarly communication, and licensing in addition to cataloging and metadata. For the last six years, she has served on a variety of committees at the consortial level, which gives her a broad view of the issues facing libraries both large and small regarding collection building. At Penn State, she was an active member of both the Big Ten Academic Alliance and the Pennsylvania Academic Library (PALCI) consortia. While at UCLA, she served as a member of three UC committees that helped guide and build the shared collection of the UC library system; the Joint Steering Committee to advise on principles and guidelines for purchase proposals, the Shared Content Leadership Group (interim) for decision making and the ebook DDA Task Force for execution and implementation of decisions. Roxanne is a librarian who seeks out ways of creating and fostering productive work relationships that lead to increased access to content and ultimately provide better services to our users.

SARAH PICKLE is the Director of Planning and Assessment at The Claremont Colleges Library. She came to this role after serving as the CLIR/DLF social science data curation fellow at Penn State Libraries. She began her fellowship in 2014, after working for two years as an analyst at Ithaka S+R; there, her research focused on the sustainability of digital resources and the efforts that academic and cultural heritage institutions have made to support digital scholarship. Prior to joining Ithaka S+R, she completed her PhD in comparative literature at Cornell University.

MARIE L. RADFORD, PhD, is Chair and Professor in the Department of Library and Information Science at Rutgers University, New Jersey. An award-winning author, her latest books are *Familia: Digital and Information Literacy for the Latinx Community* with Stefani Gomez (forthcoming, 2020), *Conducting the Reference Interview*, 3rd edition, with Catherine Sheldrick Ross and Kirsti Nilsen (2019), *Library Conversations: Reclaiming Interpersonal Communication Theory for Understanding Professional Encounters* with Gary Radford (2017) and *Research Methods in Library and Information Science*, 6th edition, with Lynn S. Connaway (2017). Her research areas focus on qualitative research, interpersonal communication within virtual and traditional library contexts, and postmodern approaches to media stereotypes of librarians/libraries. Her current research projects examine scholarly identity work in social networking sites (such as ResearchGate and Academia.edu), information practices surrounding use of smart speakers, and microaggressive behavior in library encounters. She gives frequent keynote speeches and presentations at national and international library conferences and publishes extensively in prestigious LIS journals. She is Co-PI of the "Seeking Synchronicity" (with Lynn Silipigni Connaway) and "Cyber Synergy" (with Lynn Silipigni Connaway and Chirag Shah) grant projects funded by IMLS, Rutgers, and OCLC. She received the 2010 ALA/RUSA Mudge Award for distinguished contributions to reference.

LAUREN REITER is the Business Liaison Librarian at Penn State University. Before joining Penn State in 2012, Lauren earned her bachelor's degree in English from Kenyon College and her master's degree in library and information science from University of Pittsburgh, and worked as a corporate analyst at The Freedonia Group. Her work has appeared in the *Journal of Business & Finance Librarianship*, the *Journal of Academic Librarianship, Reference & User Services Quarterly,* and *College & Research Libraries*. She is an active member of ALA in groups related to reference services (RUSA) and business librarianship (BRASS). In 2016, Lauren was named one of *Library Journal*'s Movers & Shakers and received the Pennsylvania Library Association's New Librarian Honor Award.

COREY SEEMAN is the Director of Kresge Library Services (Ross School of Business at the University of Michigan, Ann Arbor), a position he has held since 2006. Prior to that position, Corey served as Assistant Dean at the University of Toledo, a training consultant at Innovative Interfaces, and a librarian and archivist at historical libraries including the National Baseball Hall of Fame in Cooperstown. Corey has written and presented on customer service and change management within libraries, especially academic ones. He also maintains the Library Writer's Blog (http://librarywriting.blogspot.com/).

LINDA C. SMITH is Professor Emerita and former Executive Associate Dean in the School of Information Sciences at the University of Illinois at Urbana-Champaign, where she joined the faculty in 1977. She worked with graduate students on-campus (MS, CAS, PhD) and online (MS, CAS). She taught courses on Information Organization and Access, Reference and Information Services, and Information Sources & Services in the Sciences. She is a past president of the Association for Library and Information Science Education

(ALISE), Beta Phi Mu, and the Association for Information Science and Technology (ASIS&T). She co-edited five editions of the textbook *Reference and Information Services: An Introduction* (1991, 1995, 2001, 2011, 2016) and received the ALA/RUSA Isadore Gilbert Mudge Award in 2000 for distinguished contributions to reference librarianship.

KAREN SOBEL is an associate professor and teaching and learning librarian for the fine arts and architecture at the University of Colorado Denver. She learned to perform environmental scanning while helping to plan for a major renovation of the university's Auraria Library. She recently completed her Doctor of Education degree where she did research on motivating factors behind students' use of information literacy skills.

DIANE ZABEL is the Benzak Business Librarian and Head of the Schreyer Business Library at Penn State University's University Park campus. She is a past editor of *Reference & User Services Quarterly*. Zabel has edited or co-edited several books, including *Leading in the New Academic Library* (2017), *Rethinking Collection Development and Management* (2014), and *Reference Reborn: Breathing New Life into Public Services Librarianship* (2011). She is an active member of the American Library Association (ALA). Ms. Zabel served as the elected president of the Reference and User Services Association, one of the divisions of ALA, for the period 2005–2006. She was elected to the ALA Council (the governing body of ALA) and served a three-year term as ALA councilor-at-large (2009–2012). In 2011, she was the recipient of the Isadore Gilbert Mudge Award, an ALA award that recognizes distinguished contributions in reference librarianship. She was the 2015 recipient of the President's Award for Engagement with Students, a Penn State award that recognizes a faculty member who encourages student learning.